BLACKBIRD

RISING

Birth of an Aviation Legend

by

Donn A. Byrnes

and

Kenneth D. Hurley

The material in this book has been reviewed by Mr. John Thacker, 645 MATS/CD, Wright–Patterson Air Force Base, Ohio, and found to be unclassified.

Edited by Marsha L. Thole, Don and Mary Stein, and Jack Morris

Cover, graphics, and book design by JDMC Aviation Graphics of Santa Fe, NM

First Edition, 1999.

Library of Congress Cataloging in Publication Data

Byrnes, Donn A.

Hurley, Kenneth D.

    Blackbird Rising: Birth of an Aviation Legend by Donn A. Byrnes and Kenneth D. Hurley

ISBN 0–9673327–0–2

1. SR–71. 2. Military Aviation. 3. Aviation History

99–90757

  CIP

The Air Force Struture of the Blackbird Program
during most of the early days and during most of Category II

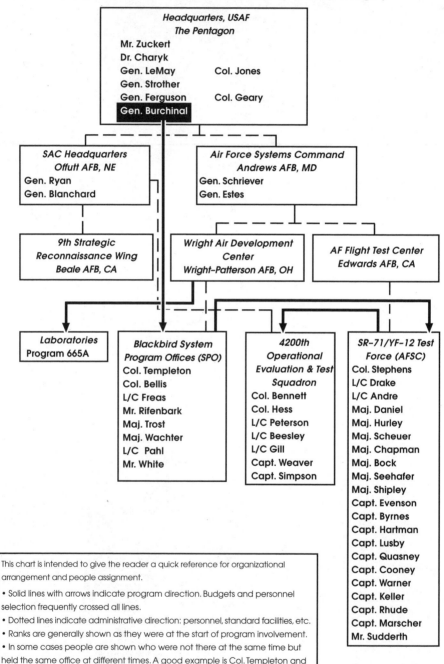

Headquarters, USAF
The Pentagon
Mr. Zuckert
Dr. Charyk
Gen. LeMay   Col. Jones
Gen. Strother
Gen. Ferguson   Col. Geary
Gen. Burchinal

SAC Headquarters
Offutt AFB, NE
Gen. Ryan
Gen. Blanchard

Air Force Systems Command
Andrews AFB, MD
Gen. Schriever
Gen. Estes

9th Strategic
Reconnaissance Wing
Beale AFB, CA

Wright Air Development
Center
Wright-Patterson AFB, OH

AF Flight Test Center
Edwards AFB, CA

Laboratories
Program 665A

Blackbird System
Program Offices (SPO)
Col. Templeton
Col. Bellis
L/C Freas
Mr. Rifenbark
Maj. Trost
Maj. Wachter
L/C Pahl
Mr. White

4200th
Operational
Evaluation & Test
Squadron
Col. Bennett
Col. Hess
L/C Peterson
L/C Beesley
L/C Gill
Capt. Weaver
Capt. Simpson

SR-71/YF-12 Test
Force (AFSC)
Col. Stephens
L/C Drake
L/C Andre
Maj. Daniel
Maj. Hurley
Maj. Scheuer
Maj. Chapman
Maj. Bock
Maj. Seehafer
Maj. Shipley
Capt. Evenson
Capt. Byrnes
Capt. Hartman
Capt. Lusby
Capt. Quasney
Capt. Cooney
Capt. Warner
Capt. Keller
Capt. Rhude
Capt. Marscher
Mr. Sudderth

This chart is intended to give the reader a quick reference for organizational arrangement and people assignment.

• Solid lines with arrows indicate program direction. Budgets and personnel selection frequently crossed all lines.
• Dotted lines indicate administrative direction: personnel, standard facilities, etc.
• Ranks are generally shown as they were at the start of program involvement.
• In some cases people are shown who were not there at the same time but held the same office at different times. A good example is Col. Templeton and Col. Bellis. They were both directors of the Blackbird SPOs at different times.

Events in Blackbird History

Mid 1950s – Early 1960s	MONTECELLO, QUICK CHECK, and 665A programs
July 4, 1956	First U–2 overflight of the Soviet Union
December 24, 1957	First run, J–58 initial design, Hartford, CT
July 25, 1959	U.S. accepts the design for the A–12
January 30, 1960	CIA approves OXCART program
May 1, 1960	Francis Gary Powers shot down
June 1960	Lou Schalk measured for pressure suit, Worcester, MA
Christmas Season 1960	Ken Hurley meets Sid Brewer, Kelly Johnson proposes Mach 3 bomber based on A–12/YF–12
Early 1961	Ken Hurley briefed on OXCART program and given duty assignment to Blackbirds
Early 1961	OXCART briefings at Edwards for Branch and Irwin
Early 1961 – Mid 1962	Study effort, RS–12
April 26, 1962	First flight of A–12, Area 51, Lou Schalk
Mid 1962	Redirection, RS–12 to R–12
June 4, 1962	Mockup review, R–12
Late 1962 – Early 1963	Contracts let for R–12
August 7, 1963	First flight of YF–12, Area 51, Jim Eastham
Early 1964	Donn Byrnes briefed on OXCART learns of 665A importance
February 1964	President Johnson announces YF–12
July 1964	President Johnson announces SR–71
Summer 1964	Test Force begins forming at Edwards. Not officially named SR–71/YF–12 Test Force until mid–1965
December 1964	First flight of SR–71 #950, Bob Gilliland
April 1965	First all–Air Force crew flight: Col. Stephens and Maj. Hurley, #952
May 1965	Nine speed and altitude records set by YF–12
Mid 1965	First Cat II test airplane delivered to Edwards by Col. Stephens and Maj. Hurley, #954
Late 1965	Cat II performance airplane delivered, #953
January 6, 1966	First SR–71 delivered to Beale AFB
April 1968	First operational SR–71 flights

Aircraft Comparison Chart

A-12

Span = 55 ft 7 in, Length = 102 ft, Weight = 120,000 lbs

YF-12A

Span = 55 ft 7 in, Length = 105 ft 2.5 in, Weight = 127,000 lbs

SR-71A

Span = 55 ft 7 in, Length = 107 ft 5 in, Weight = 172,000 lbs

SR-71B

Span = 55 ft 7 in, Length = 107 ft 5 in, Weight = 170,000 lbs

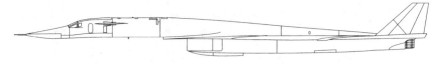

XB-70A

Span = 105 ft, Length = 180 ft, Weight = 542,000 lbs

ALL DRAWINGS ON THIS PAGE TO THE SAME SCALE

Acknowledgements

The support and assistance of many people were necessary to put this story together. The authors are grateful and appreciative of the help, guidance, review, and encouragement provided. So those people will not be nameless, we have listed many of them here along with the support they provided. There is no way any one person could possibly know and be familiar with the variety of materials and situations recorded in this book. We sincerely apologize to anyone we may have missed.

Experts in alphabetical order

Tom Alison — National Air and Space Museum

Bob Banks — Pressure suits, David M. Clark Company

Jack Bassick – Pressure suits, David M. Clark Company

Don Beckerleg — Side looking radar developmental history, 665A flight testing, SR–71 SLR

Tom Bowen — USAF civilian at Beale AFB, personal equipment.

Menko D. Christoph — ANS alignment, progam procedures, and facts. A great story teller.

Charlie Dotson — Side looking radar developmental history, 665A, SR–71 SLR

Norm Drake — Category I and II Test Programs from an early view

Dick Erdman — Backup expert on TEOC history, both test and operational

Dave Harris — Early infrared program history and HRB–Singer program manager

Bruce Hartman — ANS, test range development, and mission planning

Jerry Hogan — Program 665A and HRB–Singer infrared systems

Roger Ingvalson — Vietnam POW consultant

Art Lusby — SR–71 Performance Program Manager and consultant

Jack McDermott — Pratt & Whitney J–58 Program Manager, early engine development history

Dave Nolte — HYCON Camera Company and all–around optics expert and historian

Dean Poeth — Early infrared program history

Fred Rall — Aerodynamicist and engine inlet expert

Don Rhude — ELINT and willing reviewer

Joe Ruseckas — Pressure suits, David M. Clark Company

Tom Smith — Pressure suits, David M. Clark Company

Chuck Woodward — KC–135Q navigator and rendezvous consultant

Scott Willey of the National Air and Space Museum for finding experts in a variety of fields.

Fred Ziegler — HRB people–finder extraordinaire

Finally, thanks to all the Blackbirders who I pestered at reunions for answers and ideas.

Editors

This book and its materials have been edited by a large group of people, and if it hasn't turned out perfectly it's because I forgot to do what they suggested.

Don and Mary K. Stein who did it for their love of Blackbirds and Blackbird people.

Jack Morris of JDMC Aviation Graphics, an aviation historian and a stickler for accuracy.

Marsha L. Thole, a tough retired Air Force Lt.Col. who would not let anything slip by intentionally. Sometimes I did not do what she said.

Unique Critique Inc., Lana Harrigan, Jessie Hickox, Paula Paul, Pat Sutton, Walt Williamson, and Kelly Williams. A group of Albuquerque writers who pushed me toward the finish.

Dedication

Choice: The act of choosing; selecting; a variety from which to choose.

When all facts are present and every what–if can be answered, when collateral areas of impact can be described and identified, the selection of one alternative over another is called a choice.

Decision: The act of deciding; settling a dispute or question by giving a judgement.

There are times when not all impacts are known, some not even imagined, when second and third order results are obscure, when few short and long term results are clear. When technical issues remain hidden under layers of yet to be defined technology, and there is slight information confirming the value of path A over path B, when the science to list pro versus con has not been fleshed out or perhaps even identified, the selection of one alternative over another becomes a decision.

This book is dedicated to the thousands of design, development, and test engineers who craved information to allow choices between alternatives. Instead they found gaps in the data, voids in the existing technology, and only shadows of supporting information. They made decisions. This book is also dedicated to the countless technicians who helped develop and sculpt the ideas and concepts germinated and nurtured by those engineering decisions into the world's fastest operational aircraft. Their long hours, and stubborn pursuit of answers and solutions, put flesh on the concepts and hardware on the hangar floor. They breathed life into the Blackbird aircraft family and sustained these machines and their crews throughout the program.

Foreword

A View From the Distaff Side

—or— "They also serve..."

John Milton

The legend has been planted that the magnificent SR–71 Blackbird sprang, Zeus–like, from the brain of Kelly Johnson and directly to operational status on the ramp at Beale. Not so! How do I know? Because I spent most of the time between those events not knowing. My experience deals only with the SR–71 and not any of the other coterie of Blackbirds.

In late 1958, my husband Ken, whom you will meet later, was assigned to the B–70 Systems Project Office at Wright–Patterson AFB, Ohio. As an automatic controls engineer, navigator and bombardier, he was assigned to the development of the Bomb–Nav system for this super–secret guardian of the skies. This job required a great deal of travel—anywhere from 180–250 days a year. But, I always knew where he was—North American in Los Angeles, IBM in New York, or in the Pentagon. I could always get in touch with him, if necessary.

Early in 1961, this routine changed. The travel did not diminish, but no longer did I know where he was, nor could I reach him personally. I did have two telephone numbers that were supposed to be good for day or night, but I can't vouch for them because I never used them. How's that for faith?! Or luck! I did know whether he was going East or West because I always took him to the airport and I knew the airline schedules—but there's a lot of country both east and west of Dayton, Ohio.

I wasn't the only wife in this situation and we soon found out who we were and started trying to make some sense. Of course, we had no success, but one thing became apparent—they were always home on weekends! This wasn't easy to understand until we realized they all got together and exchanged the papers they had in their ubiquitous briefcases. The second reason was more obvious—they came home to get their laundry done! Anyone who has ever traveled for the government knows there is no way on God's green earth that a person can eat, sleep, get from place to place, and have clean underwear—all on per diem rates.

Ken's travel left a great deal of time for the rest of the family— maybe that was fortunate. At that time our daughter was ten and our son fourteen—lots of opportunity for activities. Those were not the days of "soccer moms," but "car poolers" were in great demand—Girl Scouts, orchestra, tennis, wrestling, chorus, etc. You know the routine.

Evenings, of course, were the worst part of the day, but I did have a standing date with Jack Paar Monday through Friday. I even saw the much discussed "W.C.." routine. Jack left us at 1 AM, a local minister would utter a few words of faith, hope, and charity, and then the national anthem reminded us what this was all about. The announcer told us that "Station WXXX would return to the air at 5:30 AM with the farm and market reports." Now what? Sleep did not come easily, and you can only read so much before everything blurs and the brain fades. But there is always the kitchen floor. I still contend that I was very high on the list for "cleanest kitchen floor" in Montgomery County.

There were the times Ken came home too late to get his briefcase in the office lockup, or he was just too dog–tired to go in and had to hang on to it overnight. Those nights were spent with the case under his side of the bed and my Colt .45 (which he had bought me when he went to Korea back in 1952) at his hand. On one occasion he got home late on a Saturday night too late to go into the office. The next morning was Girl Scout Sunday and there was a ceremony at the local church that

Father had to attend for our daughter. The briefcase went to church and rested under Father's feet during the ceremony. It never left his custody.

One of these days followed another until February 1964, when President Johnson announced the advent of a series of new airplanes—high and fast. So it seems that since January '61 until February '64 hundreds of people had spent countless hours planning, designing and preparing to build this "mistress" we all knew about without knowing about it. It has been declared the best kept secret ever!

Soon after, Ken came home one night with news that "she" would be undergoing testing at the Flight Test Center at Edwards AFB, California, and that "we" – meaning "he," and I, two kids, and a cat – would be going out there to participate in the activity. After six years in Dayton we were ready for a move, but this particular one was a surprise. To give you a feel for this last statement I must go back in time to 1949. Ken had just graduated from college after World War II and returned to active duty with the Air Force. We left Memphis, which was Ken's home, and mine since our marriage, to go to Mather AFB, California. I was apprehensive, but "whither thou goest …" naturally prevails. He swears until this day every mile of highway we covered bears two ruts where I was dragging my feet. One place you might still find those ruts is between Barstow and Mojave in the Mojave Desert. Signs appeared pointing South—to nothing I could see—announcing "Air Force Flight Test Center, Edwards AFB". My immediate reaction was "Who in the world could live in a place like that?!" Please give me credit for being young and naive—it was fifty years ago, but it was the beginning of my learning about "real life." Don't ask a question if you don't want to hear the answer. Now, fifteen years after that trip to Mather, I was going to get my answer.

We arrived at Edwards in mid–July 1964. In the fifteen years since we traveled that path, Wherry and Capehart had convinced Congress that military families deserved a decent place to live, and we were soon settled into our life for the next four years. The cat made his peace with the frequent sonic booms—he bristled and hissed one time and ignored them forever more.

Life at Edwards was little different from other bases—except for the wind, the heat, the wide–open spaces, and a few other meteorological situations. Things settled into a regular routine with golfers golfing, bridge players dealing, and everybody doing a bit for the hospital, the Red Cross, the Thrift Shop, and, of course, the Sunday School, choir or whatever. I discovered the soil we called "granulated granite" could be productive with enough water and fertilizer. So, my rose garden reappeared along with ice plant, California poppies, even a cactus plot.

You notice I haven't mentioned anything about an airplane? That's because we had neither seen nor heard an airplane different from the ones flying when we first went on base. We had heard the word "black" and the name SR–71—meaning nothing at that time to those of us "who only stand and wait."

There came this "big day" (for them, not us) December 23, 1964. Bob Gilliland of Lockheed made the first flight—they told us. Things were still very quiet around the "old ranch" until mid April 1965 when Fox Stephens and Ken Hurley made the first all–Air Force crew flight. Shortly after that Fox and Ken brought the first Category II airplane to Edwards and presented it to the Flight Test Center for the Cat II Test Program. There were great pictures of all the fellows—Fox and Ken in their silver suits with sergeants holding their air conditioning suit cases, all the biggies from the Center grinning from ear to ear. But guess what? Not an airplane in sight—nor would there be for a long time to come! We did hear different noises and the pace of activity increased—but still no airplane that we could see.

In the meantime, we became the owners of 1½ horses—don't ask! It's not really all that complicated. One was a standardbred mare who could match any mule for stubbornness, and the other an honest–to–goodness strawberry roan mustang who had actually grown up on a ranch and worked as a "cowpony." Having the horses was a great hobby. Besides being fun I learned a new set of skills. After all, I was a city girl. Also, there was another side to this hobby! When Ken said "Please, don't have beans or broccoli for dinner tonight—that translated into "I'm flying tomorrow." So, when he left the next morning, I would make my way to the stable, do the chores, and saddle old Babe for a little jaunt in the desert. Generally we would head east to Radar Hill overlooking the runway, but not very closely. "No cameras, no glasses, please. Air Police." Soon the Buicks would start and before long there would be another spectacular takeoff as the Blackbird rose into the fabulous desert sky. Didn't last long, but well worth the effort. And that's as close as I got to the plane for years!

The people in the Test Force were all "Numero Uno" folks, hand picked—every one of them. And as a group, very congenial — engendering friendships that exist to this day. But as the program wound down at Edwards and the birds were deemed ready to do their real job at Beale (remember, we were 7½ years down the road with Kelly Johnson's brain wave), Ken came home one day and said," I just stopped by Personnel and put in my papers."

Military people always talk about "retiring" but when the words come out "for real" it's a surprise. He said, "This is the best job I have ever had and these are the finest people around. I don't want to start over in some 'Mickey Mouse' operation. So let's try something else."

Here we are in the Northwest—sixteen years at Boeing (they are good people, too) and fifteen years on ten acres we share with the deer, coyotes, rabbits, quail, etc., on Whidbey Island. Several months ago we heard a Mach 2 boom—supposedly the last one around, and it brought a lot of emotions to the surface.

We know that Fox, Frenchy, Bill, Walt, and Pete have found the greatest cloud ever above the "wild blue yonder" for their hangar flying. As time goes on Charlie, Merv, Ken, Jim and Noel will find them and the stories will really roll. No, they won't all be *Habu* stories, but without them the *Habus* would not have been able to do the fabulous jobs they accomplished since Kelly's dream appeared on the ramp at Beale.

God bless all Blackbird Flyers—their likes will never be seen again.

Jeanne Hilton Hurley
Whidbey Island Washington
November 11, 1999

P. S.   Thank goodness for museums. I can now say I know what an SR–71 really looks like.

Introduction

To accurately research and describe the sequential events surrounding the birth of the Blackbird is a monumental task. As time continues many facts become merged with myth to form the legend of the SR–71 and its predecessors. This book describes only a portion of the bird's developmental history. A portion that is personally quite familiar to Ken and me.

The story chronicles the airframe and sensor systems development leading to the multi–spectral reconnaissance system of the initial operational fleet of SR–71s. The foundational suite of sensors and their capability represented a major jump in technology. To get tender, delicate, cranky, high–performance equipment to operate and produce meaningful data in one of the most difficult of earth–bound operating environments proved to be a demanding task. The job was there to do, and our drive toward completion was prodded along by the urgent knowledge that the United States needed the information the Blackbird could collect. We did not have all day to get it done.

When the first birds and their crews became operational and started flying against intended targets, they had the very best systems we could support in the field. The engineers, technicians, ground crews, and flight crews all struggled with the challenges in their part of the program. This book chronicles the early beginnings of the Blackbird's story.

Ken explains some of the terms

When we started writing this book we did so without really thinking that it might be accepted and enjoyed by a readership other than people close to the reconnaissance business. In fact, we assumed our readers would probably be familiar not only with reconnaissance but the SR–71 itself. As we talked to people during the two–year gestation period of *Blackbird Rising*, we found a great interest on the part of almost everyone. We also discovered a knowledge gap between some of the "gee whiz" that goes with the SR, and the real purpose of the system and why it existed at all.

Why a Mach 3+ airplane?

The basic role of a reconnaissance airplane is to position a selected set of sensors over a designated area of interest under favorable conditions to obtain critical data needed for national or military purposes. Usually the owners of the territory being surveyed does not want that data collected. They resist by attempting to destroy the intruder. Long before the SR–71 or its predecessor, the A–12, were deployed, the U–2 had been doing an outstanding job of flyover reconnaissance for the United States. In fact, there was a considerable stable of other systems being used, none of which could match the U–2 , and all of which were becoming vulnerable to being destroyed—denying the U.S. needed information to support its national goals.

The U–2 was and still is a high flier, but at subsonic speeds, making it extremely vulnerable to air defense missiles. All this was foreseen at the time of the initial A–12 development. A less vulnerable system was sought, and it was decided that higher and faster were better. The call went out for a new system, and industry responded with proposals. The consensus was that Mach 3+ at altitudes of about 80,000 feet was possible. It was also concluded that meeting these performance numbers would outstrip the known air–to–air missile programs for a significant time period which would permit world–wide operations with almost zero risk of loss due to enemy fire. Increased speed and altitude plus the addition of radar absorbing and radar–defeating technology to the new system

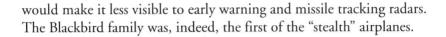

would make it less visible to early warning and missile tracking radars. The Blackbird family was, indeed, the first of the "stealth" airplanes.

How fast is Mach 3+?

An SR–71 cruising at Mach 3.2, the design cruise Mach number, traveled about 3,300 feet per second. The standard infantry rifle of World War II was the Garand M1, carried by millions of U.S. infantrymen. At the muzzle, the M1 bullet is traveling about 2,800 feet per second. That bullet immediately starts to slow down after leaving the muzzle. The SR sped along at 3,300 feet per second for as long as its fuel lasted, well over an hour between refuelings. The speed of 3,300 feet per second equates to about 2,100 miles per hour. The SR–71 was literally "faster than a speeding bullet." If you were one of the defensive gunners, your impossible task was to hit a bullet with a bullet but you had to see it first.

How high is 80,000 feet?

Jet airliners cruise between 35 000 and 40,000 feet altitude. Some aircraft are certified up to 45,000 feet, but seldom fly there. The U–2 can operate in the vicinity of 70,000 feet. Co–author Ken Hurley participated in a test flight to over 89,500 feet in an SR, the highest altitude reached during the Cat II test program.

At 80,000 feet, the SR–71's usual altitude in the target area, only two percent of the earth's atmosphere remained above the aircraft. Not much air up there so you have to keep going fast to stay there. If you slow down you come down.

What else happens at 80,000 feet and Mach 3+?

It gets hot! The stagnation temperature (where air molecules hit the airplane and stop) is about 800 degrees Fahrenheit. Any point on the airplane having a head–on collision with air molecules, like the point of the nose, the temperature is raised to near 800°. The average skin temperature from air friction was about 450° at cruise speed and altitude.

At some locations the temperatures reached 1,100 degrees. Think about it; self cleaning ovens operate between 500 and 800°. We bake cookies at 350. Kelly Johnson once commented that every design decision on the Blackbird was driven by heat. There has never been another airbreather with a design so driven by thermal conditions.

Summary

Remember the purpose of the aircraft was getting sensors over a target, collecting the information, and returning safely. Designing an airplane to go Mach 3+ at 80,000 feet was not aimed at doing a bunch of gee whiz things, however those are the things that seem to get the most attention. If a suite of sensors had not been developed to operate within the Blackbird's flight regime, the whole thing would never have happened. This book treats all facets of the program, including the "gee whiz." But the emphasis of the story is on how it all fits together for the real mission: Learning to use the weapon system, including the airplane, getting the sensor data, refining the product, and providing operational data to the end user.

Donn A. Byrnes

Donn A. Byrnes, the son of a U.S. Army doctor and his wife, was born on 29 May 1931. After many many moves about this country, a short stay in Hawaii and attendance in eighteen different schools, Donn graduated from Edison High School, San Antonio, Texas, in 1949. He enlisted in the U.S. Air Force in 1951, at age nineteen, after after three and a half semesters of Pre–Med at the University of Texas.

Progressing from PFC aircraft mechanic, to Aviation Cadet, and Air Force pilot, he flew F–84s and F–86Ds in the U.S., Japan, and Guam. In 1958 he and his family returned to the U.S. to attend the Air Force Institute of Technology–sponsored program in electrical engineering at the University of Texas, Austin.

Returning to Wright Field in 1962, after more education and with BSEE in hand, he negotiated an assignment to Project 665A (Reconnaissance/ Strike). Unknowingly he had hit upon one of the seed programs for the SR–71 sensors. It was at Wright Field as sensor and systems integration engineer, that Donn met Ken Hurley and was briefed into the SR–71 program in early 1964.

Absorbed by the Blackbird development effort, Captain Byrnes was transferred to Edwards AFB, California, in July 1964, where he was the SR–71 Sensor Test Engineer and Flight Test Engineer. He left Edwards in 1968 to become Base Commander at Ascension Island in the South Atlantic Ocean. Returning to the U.S. in 1969 he was reassigned to the SR–71 Program, and almost immediately transferred to the F–15 Program, where he was Airframe Projects Manager, Deputy Chief Engineer, and finally Director of Projects. In 1975 Donn left the F–15 System Program Office (SPO) and assumed the job of Director of Engineering at the Air Force Contract Management Division, Kirtland AFB, Albuquerque, New Mexico. Colonel Byrnes retired in November 1978 after accumulating more than 3,200 pilot hours, most of which was single engine jet time.

Returning to engineering, he worked for DynCorp, Raytheon, BDM, and other technical services companies until 1987, when he and his oldest daughter, Kathleen, formed an engineering consulting and database management company.

Since 1977 Donn and his wife Sparks have made their home on a small patch of desert mesa near Los Lunas, New Mexico.

Kenneth D. Hurley

Kenneth D. Hurley was born on 9 August 1925 in Bells, Tennessee. His family lived variously in Memphis and Bells during his early years. Ken graduated from South Side High School in Memphis in 1943, where he was commander of his Reserve Officer Training Corps unit. He entered the service soon after graduation, as did most of the young men of the day. He applied for and was accepted by the U.S. Army Aviation Cadet program prior to high school graduation. Ken graduated as a Second Lieutenant Aerial Navigator in December, 1944.

Assigned to B–29s, he flew 25 missions from the island of Guam against the Empire of Japan. Ken's twentieth birthday arrived the day after he completed his 22nd mission. He earned a Distinguished Flying Cross, three Air Medals, and various combat ribbons with battle stars.

After returning from World War II, Ken graduated in 1949 from what is now known as the University of Memphis with a B.E. in mathematics and physics. During college, he married Jeanne Elizabeth Hilton from Nashville and then reentered the Air Force after earning his degree. In 1952, at the USAF Institute of Technology at Wright–Patterson Air Force Base, Ohio, he graduated with an M.S. equivalent in Automatic Controls Engineering. Immediately sent to Korea, he spent a year flying B–26 bombers. Upon return he worked in research and development, including the B–70 System Program Office and SR–71 System Program Office at Wright–Patterson AFB.

When the SR–71 was ready to fly, Ken was sent to Edwards AFB as Chief Systems Engineer, and crewmember. He became Chief Engineer and then Deputy Test Director for the SR–71/YF–12 Test Force. He was the first Air Force Reconnaissance Systems Officer (RSO) in the SR–71 and accumulated approximately 200 hours' test time in the SR–71, earning a second Distinguished Flying Cross, the Legion of Merit, and the Air Force Commendation Medal.

In 1968 Lt.Col. Hurley retired from the Air Force, with an accumulated total of 3,500 combat and non–combat flying hours. He went to work for the Boeing Company, Seattle, Washington, eventually retiring from the job of Chief, Engineering Operations for the 747/767 Programs.

Ken and Jeanne now make their home on Whidbey Island in North Puget Sound, Washington State.

Prologue

Prologue

"If you can't turn the crank, don't come to the party."
Earl Blemmel, Crew Chief, 955, Edwards AFB, 1966

Mercury vapor lamps overhead cast harsh shadows on the ramp below, isolating individuals and pieces of equipment in the predawn chill. Little of this light reflects off of the dusky black fuselage and wings of an SR–71, Blackbird number 955, as she undergoes her final grooming for the day's flight. The smell of jet fuel floats in the still desert air and clings to our clothes.

Start–cart exhausts pop and grumble as the matched pair of V–8s in each cart warm up. The clink of exhaust flappers provides an irregular punctuation to the activities taking place below the wings, where ground crew members wait for a signal to pour the power to the Buicks. Not just converted auto engines, these machines were Buick Wildcat engines fresh from the southern California shop of racing legend Mickey Thompson. Each cart's engine pair drives a single transmission, which, in turn, through an hydraulically extended shaft, reaches up inside the Blackbird's massive J–58 engines and spins them to starting rpm.

Perched on a maintenance stand ten feet above the ground I sit cross–legged level with the aircrew's shoulders. Seated in the pilot's cockpit is Bill Skliar and in the Reconnaissance Systems Officer's (RSO) cockpit is Noel Warner. I see each crew member's lips move as they talk behind the sealed face plates of their helmets. Their voices crackle through my headset. I speak to them and members of the ground crew through an intercom system where the microphones are strapped over our mouths to keep out the surrounding noise. It's not too hard to hear right now, but once the engines start, no conversation is possible without the intercom. Anticipation is strong as all of us work our way through the preflight preparations.

Open in my lap is the all–important checklist. Every single step and action needed to prepare, start, and launch this aircraft are written in this book. These pages also contain special instructions for engineering changes, changes which will be tested on this flight. Everyone on the intercom circuit, air crew, ground crew, including myself is going through the checklist item by item. I read, they respond. I am the flight test engineer for Number Six. Her tail number is 955, but we all call her by the production sequence number. Standing on the ground near the front of the aircraft is Earl, my crew chief, an Air Force tech sergeant. At just five feet nine inches, he was full of guts, determination, and ingenuity, an aircraft mechanical genius. We were both there when this elegant creature was born, and we have been her constant companions ever since. At 6 A.M. the desert is showing only the very first signs of morning light. I am still reading the checklist by overhead light. Earl and I have been here since 3 A.M. patting and smoothing the feathers on this bird. The ground support guys came in at four.

She is full of fuel, liquid oxygen is on board for the aircrew, and fifty gallons of liquid nitrogen for fuel tank explosion suppression is loaded. All the other fluids and parts are ready. The complex and picky cameras are filled with film and installed. Even the infrared system detector has cooled down nicely in its own supply of liquid helium. In each engine nacelle the TEB tanks have been filled with tri–ethylene borate, a hypergolic chemical used to ignite the SK–1 fuel when the engines start. Just one shot for each engine is all it takes. TEB replaces the usual jet engine igniter plugs because the Blackbird's special fuel is much more difficult to light than standard JP–4.

Number Six left the hanger for her outside prelaunch parking space at 4:15 A.M.

The personal equipment technicians and aircrew got here by 4:30 A.M. Now we are working our way through the checklist to the engine start sequence.

Many aircraft maintenance and operations people treat the ground support troops like dirt, but not Earl and me, not in the Blackbird game. We do everything but send these guys flowers. How else could you get four master sergeants to roll out of bed and arrive at work by 4 A.M. when they could have sent us a couple of three stripers? How else could you get a start–cart and crew for each engine at this hour of the morning? Today is a big day for Earl and me, for Number Six, and for Bill and Noel, who are doing the flying. Today is the day we fly the route called Hester.

Hester is an awful name, and this flight route is equally terrible. Four hot legs of nearly eighteen hundred miles each, three refuelings, and about eight hours of flying time. This flight profile consumes everything the bird and crew have. They will return with roughly four thousand feet of exposed film of various widths, empty liquid nitrogen containers, the infrared detector's liquid helium almost gone, the tape recorders out of tape, and the crew exhausted. Because cruising above Mach 3 heats the airframe to very high temperatures, even the inside surface of the pilot's windscreen reaches 275°F. When Number Six parks after the last leg, parts of her will be too hot to touch. This mission was designed to simulate the toughest operational mission we could imagine. If Number Six makes the whole trip successfully today, she will get another red silhouette of a blackbird painted beneath the canopy rails, with a white H, for Hester, stenciled on the silhouette. Earl and I are hopeful, but the batting average for this mission profile is not very high.

Still seated on the maintenance stand, I turn to Bill in the front cockpit and ask, "Ready for engine start?"

His helmet turns to face my way and nods affirmatively.

I look to Noel in the back seat. He nods and I hear, "Ready for engine number one."

Earl does a careful review of the people under the wing and the area behind the engines. "Okay Major, we're ready down here."

I start my chant. "Let's crank number one. Pilot call ten percent. Ground confirm the TEB shot. Call when you see fire in the tailpipe. Pilot confirm rise in exhaust gas temperature."

This is a great job! Where else could a scrawny kid from Texas sit beside the world's fastest aircraft and tell everybody what to do?

What follows the command to start an engine is one of the most gut–wrenching, emotionally haunting sounds ever heard on any flight line anywhere in the world. A wailing song like the sound of a coyote in the moonlit night, the throaty roar, then whine, then the scream of Mickey Thompson's Wildcats straining to spin the J–58 engine, raises goose bumps on my neck every time. You would have to be dead not to get a thrill from that ballad of horsepower audible for twenty miles in the still desert morning. It is a two–part harmony of twin engines singing their way to 6,000 rpm, then popping and backfiring as the operator pulls back the throttles once the bird's engine catches. Now the ground operator pours the coal to the start cart. Everyone listens, no one breathes. We're hanging on each change of pitch, willing everything to go properly. The starter scream is followed by a guttural rumbling roar of the huge jet engine coming to life and tearing away what is left of the morning stillness. I know my wife, along with countless other Blackbird families, will hear the first start. They will stop what they are doing and wait for the second start. Then they will know for sure that Number Six is going to earn her pay today. Engine number two spins and flames to life.

With both engines running we continue down pages of checklist while the ground crew completes the final touches beneath the wings. The area around the bird begins to thin out as the ground crew pulls away the different pieces of support equipment. My stand will be the last thing rolled back before the chocks are pulled, and we all wave good–bye, to what moments ago was a quiet piece of hardware but is now a living, roaring, hungry life form eager to get into the air.

With practiced care and considerable caution, I reach over to pull the safety pins from the gun deployment devices on the pilot's and the

RSO's parachutes. Sticking out of the upper left hand corner of each of their parachute packs is a very short 12–gauge gun barrel. When triggered, these guns fire a heavy slug that hastens parachute deployment by quickly pulling out the pilot chute.

Earl's hard–edged west Texas voice on the intercom stops the process cold. "Hold everything. We have a brake fluid leak on the left main gear."

The safety pins stay in their gun barrels. Bill and Noel look directly at me for more information. I have none. They cannot see what is going on below the wing and about fifty feet behind the cockpit. My view is blocked by the bulk of wheels and tires on the left main gear. Always tense about the possibility of a ground fire, this is a bad time for everybody. I can see into the front cockpit and observe the BRAKE SYS caution light blinking. No one speaks. Every eye is focused on the ground crew huddled around the left main gear. The two huge Air Force fire trucks, present for every test flight launch, inch closer. I watch black smoke belch from their auxiliary pumping diesel engines. Firefighters in silver suits move toward us pulling their hoses. Hands on nozzle cutoffs. Ready. Foam cannons atop the trucks swivel and point directly at us. The aircrew faces have eyes wider than usual.

"Donn, can you see what's going on?" Bill asks.

"There's plenty of people down there working on whatever it is." I am speaking into the mike and both helmets nod. "Enough stripes behind that wheel to fill a zoo," I add.

I turn my back momentarily to look up at the second floor control room windows. They are lined with anxious faces. Lt.Col. Ken Hurley, my boss, is among them. While they cannot hear the intercom conversations, they can talk to the crew over the UHF radio. They are keenly aware of this deviation from normal launch sequence. As I return my attention to the action by the main gear, I see a spurt of fluid soak the front of Earl's coveralls. More fluid covers his face. Both his hands are buried among the wheels. The man beside him reaches over with a red rag and wipes the hot fluid from his face. There is no break in attention to the repairs on Number Six's left foot. I wait. The aircrew waits. The control room faces wait. The firefighters, who can't hear any of the radio or intercom talk, are now straining forward, their faces hidden behind the gold–shaded windows in fireproof hoods.

"We got the leak stopped and tightened a fitting." Earl's voice sounds much calmer now. "Please don't anyone mash on the brakes until we give the okay."

"Roger," I said, with a confidence that somehow didn't seem real to anyone, least of all to me.

I watch, Earl works, and the flight crew listens intently and focuses on their warning lights. Number Six's engines whine and grumble as she waits to be cut loose. I can hear my heartbeat in the headphones. One by one the maintenance guys pull back. Earl is wiping down the strut and brake area with red rags.

Over the intercom comes, "Please apply full left brake." A month–long silence followed. Then the very relieved voice of my crew chief crackles through the earphones, "Anytime you're ready Major, Number Six can roll."

I turn to the faces lining the control room windows above and give a thumbs up signal. I can see the smiles. The fire trucks back away to give the bird room to taxi. Bill and Noel go back to their business in the cockpits; everyone pulls their assigned safety pins; and my stand rolls back out of the way. From now on, the crew chief will direct the actions before departure and the taxi out. We all watch the large in-slanting rudders travel full over as the pilot turns the nose wheel to steer the aircraft out onto the taxiway. Hot engine exhaust washes over us. Earl begins cleaning his tools and putting them back in the box. I close the checklist notebook and begin the climb to the second floor control room. Number Six is already a half mile down the taxiway, exhaust heat waves shimmering in the first rays of the desert sunrise.

Number Six will travel over 8,000 miles before we see her again. Her crew will be very busy with a full test card on this demanding run. Earl and I and the ground crew will bite off all our fingernails while we wait. She will be back shortly after lunch. The Blackbird plan view stencil, a stencil of the letter H, and spray cans of red and white heat–resistant paint wait beside the tidy row of crew toolboxes.

The following story tells how the two authors, the Blackbird, the sensors, the support equipment, and the people, happened to be at Edwards Air Force Base, California. The intent is to present a myriad of diverse factual material to allow the reader to join with the authors in reliving a very exciting period of our nation's history and those early days of the Blackbird program.

Part I

Setting the Scene

Chapter 1

Setting the Scene

"We will bury you!"
Nikita Khrushchev, 1960

"What we really need is some good, clear high resolution photography."
Anonymous photo interpreter, Naval Photo Intelligence Center, 1962

We were living in a paranoid world. Since the end of World War II the Russians aggressively pursued a policy of territorial expansion. We escaped by the skin of our teeth during the resolution of the Berlin Blockade. The USSR was overwhelmingly powerful and ruthless. Spreading their communist doctrine and influence world wide, they mercilessly crushed the Hungarian uprising and were intent on following that course in any other area that struck their fancy. Even our own intelligence services painted the Soviet Union as a larger than life, twenty–foot giant. But it wasn't all pretend and made up. The ratio of free world tanks to Soviet armor waiting to pour through the Fulda Gap and bury us beneath their tank treads was intimidating. The Berlin Crisis in the summer and fall of 1961 maintained the continuing drumbeat of Soviet offensive activity. They beat us into space, they had nuclear weapons, and they had none of the restraint practiced by free nations. In a classic sense they controlled or could influence enough land mass and population to do us in any time they felt like it. The Russian Bear would never hibernate let alone slow down in our lifetime. That behavior shaped our thinking and our actions.

No member of the U.S. military ever forgot Khrushchev's threat, "We will bury you!"

Unarmed American intelligence gathering overflights of the USSR began on 4 July 1956. Earlier the British had tried their hand at this game when they sent a twin–engine Canberra to overfly Kapustin Yar in 1953. The Russians protested the flights from the very beginning. But the free world desperately needed information. The Soviet Union was a closed society, so blatantly set on expansionism, there was no other reliable way to understand their intentions or preparations for the much anticipated World War III. Because of the Russians' reckless behavior, the question was not if, but when. We had to be prepared and forewarned.

On 1 May 1960 Francis Gary Powers and his U–2 reconnaissance aircraft were shot down over Sverdlovsk in Central Russia on a clandestine flight between Incirlik, Turkey, and Bodo, Norway. After the shoot down, we had no window into their internal military preparations or status. The anonymity enjoyed by the U–2 until then and the ability of the U.S. to fly over hostile nations without losses had come to an end. The Soviet Bloc had finally developed an air defense missle that could reach to 70,000 feet. U–2 aircraft were shot down over Eastern China; then, in 1962, flights over Cuba were engaged and damaged by missiles. These happenings were a surprise to most Americans. The country was even more surprised to discover that for many years our government had been engaged in photo reconnaissance flights over the home territories of our most powerful enemy.

What was not common knowledge was Lockheed's and the CIA's growing plans for a new aircraft to assume these overflight chores. The burgeoning missile capabilities of the Russians would sooner or later succeed in killing off the U–2s. To this end, on 30 January, 1960, the CIA approved initial funding for twelve A–12s. Immediately thereafter during February, 1960 the CIA proposed that Lockheed initiate a search for 24 pilots to fly these new machines.

There were, of course, many photo reconnaissance programs ongoing at the time. Perhaps the largest, most successful, and cleverly applied was called BIG SAFARI. In this program airframes of all sizes, shapes, designations, and origins were equipped with cameras of every description. Much like Edgar Allen Poe's *Purloined Letter*, these aircraft were hidden in plain sight. They mingled with countless other utility aircraft being flown throughout the world on their mundane daily duties and methodically collected literally millions of feet of photographic film. Although a very effective concept and a clearly successful program, BIG SAFARI aircraft lacked the ability to fly over hostile territory and return unchallenged with the data. During this same timeframe the SAMOS family of reconnaissance satellites emerged accompanied by their C–119 catchers. The film packets, ejected from the satellites after exposure over intended targets, were snatched from the air over the Pacific. Nothing was easy about any of these efforts. Nothing is ever easy about keeping an eye on your enemies as they build and improve their offensive capabilities.

The Strategic Air Command (SAC) with its RB–47s continually prodded and poked at the border defenses of the Soviet and Chinese bloc, and in some cases, made direct overflights of the arctic regions of Siberia. All around the communist world U.S. aircraft like the RB–57s and souped up F–100s flown from Yokota AB, Japan, were gathering electronic order of battle information as well as long–lens slant photography. They skipped, dodged, and probed the perimeters of our enemy's defenses as opposing fighters rose to confront them. All the while, electronically stuffed B–29s and B–50s loitered off the coasts listening to the enemy's responses to these near–penetrations by our teaser aircraft. The U.S. aircraft were frequently shot at and several were shot down. Brave crew members were lost. Because of our national interests, these instances went unannounced. The people involved and their family members just "sucked it up" and got on with their lives.

The United States desperately needed the ability to go unchallenged anywhere in the world, to collect the intelligence data necessary to pursue our national interests, and to return with the aircraft, the data, and crew intact. The need is even greater today than it was in the 1960s but we seem to have forgotten our history. Satellites are exotic and fashionable but cannot provide the flexibility and quick responses available from piloted, airbreathing airframes doing the hands–on, down and dirty, daily dogwork of going where the action is and sending back or bringing home timely data. In addition, satellites are quite limited in the amount of fuel they can carry to switch orbits to cover the conflict *du jour*. During the 1960s the resolution and coverage capabilities of our photo satellites were extremely crude compared to what could be collected by air breathing photo platforms.

In Washington the bickering and backbiting went unchecked. The military presented modest budgets for shoring up aging inventories. Bright thinkers in both industry and government put forth advanced weapons concepts to bolster our shaky national security in the face of constant Russian and Chinese threats. Defense Secretary Robert McNamara was as much a part of the problem as he was part of the solution. Manufacturing methodologies, research techniques, and procurement doctrine practiced by captains of industry, while sounding attractive to the uninitiated, are not at all applicable to the high risk enterprises of the military environment. An environment where consequences for individuals and the nation far exceed a simple cost–study bottom line.

It was within this environment that arguments for and against the B–70/RS–70 capabilities were hotly debated. Even though our national stakes were high, many programs were clearly on the skids and sinking fast. The Skybolt, an air–launched ballistic missile using the B–52 for its first stage, found itself and its supporters in the same pot of stew. Pentagon planners were still smarting from the fallout associated with the Cuban missile crisis. Chagrined by the lack of military options available to our Command Authority, Pentagon planners struggled to get the ear of any politician who would spend even a few minutes considering spending money on something besides his home district's pork projects. Some things never change.

While the overall outcome of the "Cuban difficulty" was one to our liking, multiple weaknesses remained behind the scenes. Our inability to conduct meaningful all weather reconnaissance over hostile territory was a major hole in U.S. defense armor. This national self–discovery and finger–pointing exercise was compounded by biases within our defense establishment, the ever–present political pork barrel, and a huge military resource sinkhole called Vietnam. Anyone interested in developing and producing an airbreathing strategic strike system or an aircraft–based reconnaissance platform had a political and financial minefield to walk through. This was especially true for next–generation systems needed to answer the challenges of hostilities envisioned by deep and careful thinkers. Challenges simply ignored by our political establishment.

A system to penetrate anticipated air defenses with relative immunity, while carrying multispectral, high performance sensors was the goal. We needed to go beyond the limits of daylight photo reconnaissance. We needed an improved capability. The stakes were very high. The country turned to Kelly Johnson and his Skunk Works at Burbank, California, the people that designed and produced the U–2. Kelly was never bashful about presenting his ideas. Designs began to take shape.

Chapter 2

The RS-12 Story

"Ken, I don't know what you are going to be doing but I have been instructed to have you report immediately to a Col. Horace Templeton down in Building 14."
Brig. Gen. Fred Ascani, Wright Field, 1961

"See, I told you we need this guy."
Lt.Col. Sid Brewer, Wright Field, 1961

L ike the beginnings of so many development programs, the roots of the SR grew from a handful of people chosen for their expertise and talent by individuals seeking to fill gaps in their own knowledge. Before hardware, you must have people with theories, concepts, and ideas. People bring their background skills, expertise, and prejudices. As with any set of circumstances viewed through the all–knowing glass of history, coincidence and individual perceptions play a significant role. One thing that cannot be ignored is the advantages black[1] programs have over normal programs when it comes to acquiring the cream of the crop in people. Sometimes people were selected by chance due to circumstances none could possibly predict or avoid. How they got there, what each person brought, and how they contributed to the overall effort, are deeply imbedded in the birth of an incredibly successful program. How one of the authors, Ken Hurley, arrived on the program is a good example.

---

[1]Black programs are those conducted behind a cloak of secrecy, usually with high governmental priority, and special latitude allowed those who manage and participate in such programs.

Major Ken Hurley, assigned to the B–70 System Program Office (SPO), was a very knowledgeable engineer and an expert in offensive weapons systems. He and his cohorts were managing contracts with IBM, Kerfott, General Electric, and other aerospace firms engaged in building a bombing and navigation system for the B–70. The program director at the time was Brig. Gen. Fred Ascani. General Ascani was affectionately referred to as Uncle Fred by almost everyone, almost everywhere, except to his face. Uncle Fred was a true gentleman. His actions form the backbone of many Air Force research and development stories. In this story he was father confessor, advisor, and mentor to Ken and many of the other officers caught up in the developmental whirlwind that was to become the Blackbird Program.

Finding just the right guy

Approaching the Christmas season of 1960, Ken was asked by a fellow officer, Major Clarence N. (Bud) Chamberlain, if he would be interested in making a liquor run to the east coast. Always in need of flying time and recognizing the opportunity for cheap holiday cheer, Ken agreed. There was more to it than that. Bud's wife was called "Mike" and Mike's family owned the Laird Applejack Company of Fort Monmouth, New Jersey. Every year Bud made a pilgrimage to Laird Applejack to stock up on Christmas cheer.

A few days later Ken met Bud at Patterson Operations to file the flight plan. Another pilot, Lt.Col. Sidney (Sid) Brewer, had also signed up for the flight. The trip to Monmouth went just fine at about 120 mph in an Air Force C–45 Bugsmasher and they collected the booze. On the return trip, however, they ran into bad weather and strong headwinds. Their ground speed was a little less than 30 mph to the west. They decided to land and spend the night at Olmstead AFB, Pennsylvania, because the wind was so strong they would never reach their destination with the fuel on board. In the process of turning back, they were blown to the east of the field and had to fight their way west again to return to land at Olmstead.

Bud had friends at the base, so after they had landed and refueled, they decided to spend the night. Bud went off to visit friends and Ken and Sid spent the evening having dinner and talking. Ken discovered that Sid was some kind of contract weenie working at Wright Air Development Center Headquarters and Ken explained that he was a bombing and navigation and electronics guy assigned to the B–70 SPO. The next day the crew flew uneventfully to Patterson Field, Bud gave each guy some free booze and they shook hands and parted. End of story? Not quite.

You just never know what might happen

Some months later, early in 1961, Ken got a phone call. General Ascani wanted to see him in his office at Ken's earliest convenience. We all know what "earliest convenience" means. Ken had been on and led study groups for Uncle Fred in the past and assumed this would be one of those assignments. The next words Ken heard from Uncle Fred were far from what he had expected.

"Ken, I don't know what you are going to be doing but I have been instructed to have you report immediately to a Col. Horace Templeton down in Building 14. You are to do whatever Col. Templeton asks you to do. My secretary is typing a set of unlimited travel orders for you. Pick those up on your way out. You are to remain assigned to the B–70 office, but until further notice you will report for duty and direction to Col. Templeton."

Ken wasted no time getting to a room in the basement of Building 14. It was large, almost empty, with a few of those awful green–gray government–office partitions and a couple ugly metal desks. He asked for Col. Horace Templeton. The secretary guided him into an office and introduced Ken to Col. Templeton and a Lt.Col. Sidney Brewer. Col. Temp, as he was known, picked up two thick books with plain covers, looked at Ken and said "Come with me." All three went into another partitioned office used as a conference room where the two ushered Ken to one side of the table and they sat on the other facing him. Templeton slid a piece of paper across the table to Ken and instructed him to read and sign it. It was a security oath with a blank space for the code word. The paper contained words making it quite clear how awful one's life would be if any of what was seen or heard, including the code word, were ever disclosed in any manner. Ken asked Temp what the code word was. Temp said he would fill that in after Ken signed the paper. Ken read and signed and Temp filled in the code word. It was

21

OXCART. The paper then became classified TOP SECRET.[2] Ken never saw the paper again, but there was no forgetting the binding nature of the oath he had just signed. It should be noted that, unbeknown to Ken, he had been subjected to an extensive background investigation to confirm his TOP SECRET clearance. Once the paper was signed and Templeton had put away the oath, he unfolded a long piece of paper from one of the books, it was a three–view drawing of an airplane. "Ken, we are building a fighter, have you ever heard anything about this?" Ken had not. Then Temp asked him what he thought about the picture and was there anything he could speculate about the aircraft in the drawing. After thinking for a moment Ken said, "It is a Mach 3 machine and is probably designed by Lockheed."

When asked what led him to that conclusion, Ken allowed as how the wing sweep was about right for Mach 3 and the side view had some of the attributes of the F–104. At this point Sid Brewer spoke for the first time and said, "See, I told you this is the guy we need."

The two then proceeded to brief Ken on the YF–12 that was being built by Lockheed and told him about the A–12 also. Neither of the aircraft had yet flown.

Getting the names and numbers straight

Before continuing it is important to talk about various aircraft, their designations, and how they fit into the early ancestry of the SR–71. This applies to both direct descendents as well as other aircraft being developed at the same time but not by Lockheed.

First there was the A–11. This was a Mach 3 reconnaissance aircraft designed by Lockheed and funded by the CIA as a replacement vehicle for the U–2. The origin of the designation was simple, the first design was the A–1 then the A–2 and so on, finally arriving at the A–11, which was funded for development and production. The A–11 was the aircraft program designated OXCART. The earlier "A"s were designs resulting in intensive study, piles of paper, and some reaching the status of wind tunnel models. None of these early versions ever reached a full

---

[2]These oaths and the code word OXCART have long since been declassified

scale life of their own. These early configurations were either CIA–funded studies or Lockheed–developed refinements proposed to the CIA. The A–11, was eventually called the A–12. There does not appear to be a discrete design refinement or distinct configuration change directly related to the change in designation from A–11 to A–12. Most of the program office people referred to the machine as the A–11 or simply the A–model. This aircraft was developed at the Skunk Works in Burbank. The major pieces were trucked to the "Area" for reassembly. The first "A" was flown at "the Area" (Area 51) on 26 April 1962.

Next came the YF–12. The first flight of the YF–12 at the Area was on 7 August 1963. Intended as the future F–12, it was the interceptor version of this airframe family designed by Kelly Johnson and the Lockheed Skunk Works. Anticipated as the root aircraft for an interceptor series as well as an offensive derivative later designated the RS–12 (RS for Reconnaissance/Strike–12), the YF–12 program, however, never produced more than three aircraft. The YF–12 carried two crew members while the A–12 was a single seat aircraft.

The RS–12 was a paper aircraft. This design resulted from an exhaustive study that involved not only aircraft systems and capabilities but a great debate as to how the Air Force would apply offensive weapons in the future. A Class 1 mockup of this configuration was built.[3]

The R–12 was envisioned to be a full–spectrum strategic reconnaissance aircraft derived from the YF–12 airframe. This design was redesignated the SR–71, as explained later. The R–12 and the SR–71 were the same machine and there were no interruptions in the development cycle after the RS–12 effort was redirected toward the R–12. The design

---

[3]Class I mockups are original concept mockups made from sheet metal or foamcore with "pasties" for instruments. They gave a good idea about layouts, instrument placement, volume considerations and the like. They were easily changed to allow multiple configurations on a single theme to be set up in quick succession.

Class II mockups were the first trials at seriously establishing form and fit. Metal gauges, and true instrument mockups, are installed. Some black boxes were installed if they existed, along with other available hardware.

Class III mockups had the dimensional accuracy of the designed vehicle, tubing and cable runs were established, and interference envelopes for installed equipment were defined. Whether a box could be installed and removed for maintenance, how the seats fit in the cockpits, where control panels went, and a million other things were first tried out in the Class III mockup. This is how it was done in 1962 and 1963. Now it is all done on a computer with greater accuracy, more efficiency, and considerably better results.

and development of this version was funded by the Air Force with money funneled through the CIA. Earnest development of the R–12 began in 1962 with the first mockup review held for the USAF on 4 June of that year. An initial go–ahead for hardware on the R–12 program came 28 December 1962 when Lockheed signed a contract to build the first six R–12 aircraft.

Getting back to the story

Armed with this information let's return to Ken Hurley in 1961, in the basement of Building 14 at W–PAFB. Templeton and Brewer continued to brief Ken. Then Temp handed him the other book. He was instructed to read the book and when finished, he was to tell them what he thought. He was told to give the book and any notes he might make to the secretary when he left the room for any reason, even to go to the bathroom. There were no wastebaskets anywhere in the office except by the secretary's desk, and that was for coffee cups only. Every piece of paper had to be accounted for. No exceptions. Nothing was marked but everything was considered and treated as TOP SECRET.

The book was an unsolicited proposal by Kelly Johnson (Lockheed) to build a bomber version from the A–11/YF–12 airframe family. The initiation of this particular unsolicited proposal was classic Kelly Johnson. Kelly, in his usual no–nonsense manner, just walked into the Undersecretary of the Air Force's office, Dr. Joseph Charyk at the time, and dropped it on his desk. He told Charyk he ought to take a look at Kelly's new idea. The concept was to carry a single mega–megaton nuclear weapon, fly over the target and drop it. Charyk looked it over and then called Temp to Washington to pick up the proposal, take it back to Wright–Patterson, and evaluate it. Temp and Sid Brewer knew about fighters and reconnaissance but were short on bomber knowledge. That is when they recruited Ken.

At this time Col. Templeton's office in the basement of Building 14 was the Air Force's management and liaison focal point for the U–2 program, the A–11 (or A–12 if you prefer) program, and the YF–12 program. The RS–12, the R–12, and the SR–71, none of which existed at the time, were still darkly shrouded in the vapors of the future.

After studying the book for a couple of days, Ken, who had been working on standoff weapons[4] for the B–70, realized that any offensive version of the A/YF airframe would be much more efficient if it used a guided weapon rather than free fall iron bombs. He presented his comments to Temp and was asked how long it would take to put together a counterproposal using standoff weapons. Ken estimated three months for the job and said he would need help. Temp had other resources currently working the YF–12 program and promised sufficient manpower for the task. He told Ken that they were due back to the Undersecretary of the Air Force in ten weeks.

Major Harold Chapman, an expert in flight controls, and aircraft stability and control, arrived at the program office about the same time as Major Hurley. He was short on offensive weapon knowledge but was a tremendous help in developing the counterproposal. A civilian, Ed Rifenbark, who lived and breathed high performance jet engines, entered the picture about this same time. Lt.Col. Ward Protsman, a gutsy, forthright, World War II fighter pilot and West Pointer, arrived with his own brand of drive and insightful thought. Ward was pulled in full–time from Lt.Col. Nye's shop to help with the study. Several other people were assigned to help with the counterproposal. These resources came from both the U–2 office headed by Lt.Col. Wayne Freas. Maj. Don Seehafer worked for Freas and helped with the proposal as well. There was also a YF–12 support office led by Lt.Col. Allen Nye. Nye's shop was maintained separately from Templeton's operation, but in reality Nye was assigned to Temp.

During the next ten weeks this crew sweat bullets. They set about configuring an offensive version of the A–11/YF–12 with a side–looking radar and an adaptation of the GAR–9[5] missile carrying a Polaris A–3 warhead, all integrated through an astro–inertial navigation system and an associated computer processor. The difficulty was that this was no pie

---

[4]Stand-off weapons refers to a type of guided weapon that can be launched at a distance from the intended target. This allows the launch aircraft to avoid many of the target's defenses.

[5]The GAR-9 missile, designed by Hughes, was the armament for the interceptor version of the YF-12 or YF-12A. The GAR-9 later went through additional development and became the AIM-47 Phoenix missile carried by the Navy F-14 Tomcat. The ASG-18 search radar, also a Hughes product in the YF-12A, later evolved into the attack radar for the Air Force F-15 Eagle family.

in the sky exercise. The team had to produce a design that was credible, doable, and based on hardware that existed or was on the very leading edge of existence.

At the end of the assigned ten weeks the team had addressed an unending list of what–ifs. None of their design was made from nonobtanium, or featured a conveniently adaptive metal called baloneyum. They created a very well–documented weapon system for delivering a standoff nuclear weapon from a Mach 3 platform traveling at altitudes above 75,000 feet. They called their baby the RS–12.

What is the next stop?

Temp and Sid and Ken took their counterproposal back to the Undersecretary. Dr. Charyk listened attentively and then told Temp to take it to Burbank and show it to Kelly. Sid and Ken returned to Wright Field. Temp flew directly to Burbank and handed the study/counter proposal to Kelly personally.

A couple of weeks later Temp, Sid, and Ken were summoned to Burbank by Kelly. Ken was told to stay at one of the motels near Los Angeles airport that he frequented on B–70 business, so it would look like he was on B–70 business. Ken was to meet the other two at Hollywood and Vine at a restaurant called Hody's. When Ken walked in wearing his uniform, the other two almost had a stroke. He was told to beat it back to the motel and change to civvies. He never made that mistake again.

When they finally arrived at the Skunk Works to see Kelly, they were ushered up to a place called the hayloft. There were none of the fancy accoutrements of later years. Kelly was sitting behind a desk and there were two books lying on the desktop. A quick glance told the three that one was Kelly's original proposal and the other was the team's RS–12 proposal. Ken was the only "new guy" and was introduced to Kelly by Temp, "This is that young Major I told you about." Kelly came around the desk and acknowledged Ken with a handshake. When Kelly returned to his chair, he opened a bottom desk drawer, threw his original proposal into it and slammed the drawer shut. He looked down at the new RS–12 proposal, then up at the three and said, "Now let's get on with it." From that moment on it was full speed ahead for Temp's review team. The previous ten weeks paled by comparison to the following months.

Big time heartburn and glory

After about a year of exhaustive review, study, and political infighting, the RS–12 effort was canceled in favor of the R–12. That was the fallout of a decision by the Department of Defense that the strike role belonged to the missile force. However, the powers that be did agree there was a role for a high–flying reconnaissance aircraft. This set up a "competition" between the CIA and DoD for the reconnaissance mission and dollars.

The events of this study are worth describing as they give an excellent illustration as to how experts get yanked around by big shooters in the course of birthing new systems. In its brief paper lifetime the RS–12 made a significant contribution to what would eventually become the SR–71. The planning had forced a major review and concept evaluation of high resolution side–looking radar and its application to high speed aircraft in the strike role. One of the essentials of the RS concept was to provide aircrews with in–flight near–real–time correlation of the high–resolution radar data. This type of radar system was the only sensor that could provide all–weather, real–time targeting and reconnaissance imagery, something that had not been done in an operational airplane before.

The RS–12 study also led to definition of the Astro–inertial Navigation System (ANS) necessary for aircraft spatial positioning so the aircrew would know where they were at time of launch and also for the insertion of coordinates into an attack missile to tell it where the target was with respect to the aircraft. Throughout the study period a skilled and expert Air Force team was being assembled at Wright–Patterson AFB in the basement of Building 14.

Ken describes parts of the effort in his own words...

"When we started putting the RS together we knew pretty much what we wanted to do because I had brought the basic concept from the B–70. There were quite a few problems, though. For example, we didn't have a missile. We did have the ASG–18/GAR–9 combination from the YF–12, but neither was readily adaptable to the strike role. We also needed a warhead that would be compatible with the airplane, whatever missile we could get, and the systems we would need. We didn't have a proven concept for designating a target and transferring data to a missile—if we could find a missile.

"We needed a navigation system. The A–11 had a pure inertial system, but we needed something better. At first, we didn't know what that would be. The B–70 had an inertial system that was updated with Doppler and position fixes from the radar. The real problem was that anything from the B–70 was too late for what we knew we would need. Besides, it was way too big.

"We decided that we were going to fly by and launch aft and sideways. That meant we needed a sidelooker and inflight correlation.

"Ward Protsman and I took on the job of finding a navigation system and working out the details of how to transfer data from the parent system to the missile. The missile, we decided, would be based on the GAR–9. We found out that the Polaris A–3 warhead could be fitted to the missile and give it a 225–kiloton punch. We did a lot of work on target hardness, overpressures, CEPs, etc., to be sure the system would be effective.

"While we were doing all this work looking for a system, the GAM–87 got cancelled. Ward and I knew enough about that system to believe we might use some of it. We went out to Nortronics, who had the guidance system for the GAM–87 and took a hard look at it. The GAM–87 had avoided the data transfer problem by putting the inertial system right in the missile. We couldn't do that with internally mounted missiles, so we had to figure out how to transfer data between platforms. The system that GAM–87 had used in the missile was a stellar tracker tied to a platform. To make the story short, that is the system that we put in the RS. It is still in the SR. It also just happened that Nortronics was running flight tests on how to transfer data from one system to another in flight. They had a C–131 for flight test. We picked up that effort and completed the test. There were fourteen systems in the bonded storage room of the GAM–87 program. We grabbed them all.

"We were looking for a small platform that would go in the missile and be good enough to guide the missile in the terminal phase. There were several that would do the job, so we didn't spend too much time on that. About that time we decided that we had better get someone from the Wright Field Laboratories into the act, particularly in the radar area. Russ Borio was briefed and helped us out. Mostly he pointed us in the right directions for surveying the industry. Real in–flight correlation was still just experimental, especially in anything like real time. I went out to Goodyear to look at the program they had. That was when they took me into a darkroom and introduced me to a little guy named Charlie Dotson. They showed me a scrap of film they had generated in flight using their correlator. The real problem was that they had just flown the last authorized flight with the C–97 and the program was over. I listened and finally told them to continue flying and that I would cover them somehow. They did, and got some extremely valuable data.

"About this time Col. Leo Geary told Temp that the CIA had a side–looking radar development going that no one knew about and that we had better take a look. Westinghouse in Baltimore was building it. I went down and took a look. They were doing a good job and had a couple of innovative concepts but their radar was for reconnaissance only and had no correlator. This would come up later.

"Meanwhile, we brought Hughes into the act and they and Lockheed's Advanced Development Projects (ADP) built a mockup of the chines, the missile installation, the radar nose, and rear cockpit. There were a lot of pieces still missing, but nothing that we thought threatened feasibility. As the configuration firmed up we started briefing a lot of generals who had been briefed on the program. I counted 33 stars in a two week time. You count generals like you count buck deer, just add up the points on one side.

"Keep in mind that during a large part of this time, Ward Protsman and I were assigned to support Dave Jones and his *ad hoc* group in the Pentagon, appointed by LeMay to sell the B–70. We would work for Jones in the morning and Leo Geary in the afternoon. This arrangement finally got so hot that Ward and I had to get Jones briefed on the RS–12 before he went to LeMay and got us both fired. When we would disappear for the afternoon Dave would be looking for us and couldn't find us. That didn't make him too happy, as you can well imagine. He thought we were there to support him exclusively.

In fact, we were but we couldn't ignore the RS–12 activity, so we played both sides of the street. Dangerous!"

Red eyes and dirty laundry

During October and November 1962 the Wright Field experts were frequently in Washington and briefed everyone from the President's Scientific Advisory Council at the White House to the Joint Chiefs of Staff in the Joint Chiefs' room. Pretty heady stuff for a mere major and one lieutenant colonel. The purpose of this round of briefings was to introduce the powers that be to the Recce/Strike concept and convince them that it was real. The RS mission was always couched in terms of the RS–70 during these briefings and the RS–12 was not discussed at this level.

Behind the scenes were continual shuffling and maneuvering by the military services and politicians as well as governmental bureaucrats to consolidate positions and discover just exactly where the great white charger was stabled. That way, at the end of the fray, they would come out riding the right horse. All this positioning took place in anticipation of the Hearings on Military Posture before the House Armed Services Committee, scheduled for late January and throughout February, 1963. The icing on the cake was the fact that RS–12 knowledge was privy to very few folks, a knowledge closely held within the executive branch and the military. At the same time the B–70 program was out in the open and was thought by many to be the great white charger of choice to ride off into the next gathering of glory for their careers. In almost every briefing conducted for the B–70/RS–70 there was someone who knew about the ongoing study and planning effort for the RS–12. During the closely held RS–12 briefings everyone knew about the B–70 and its derivations.

North American was lobbying hard and fast. In the blue smoke and black magic world of promises and arm waving, it is tough to beat a paper airplane. The capabilities and virtues of the B–70 design were presented and plastered everywhere. In fact the campaign gave rise to an inside joke.

"A recent divorcee (third divorce) was going to counseling because of terrible emotional problems. During one of the sessions she explained to her therapist that her first husband had been a skirt–chaser of the first order so she dumped him. Her second husband turned out to be a homosexual, so she ran him off.

" 'So what was the story with your third husband?' asked the counselor.

"The woman replied, 'He was an engineer from North American and never would do anything. He just sat on the edge of the bed telling me how good it was going to be when we got around to it.' "

The original B–70 configuration was to be a conventional bomber (if you can call Mach 3 conventional) using gravity weapons. As the system developed it became a missile launcher, and eventually evolved the "six–shooter" concept carrying eighteen air–launched missiles in its internal bays. All the B–70's weapon family were intended to be nuclear. Free–falling bombs were not considered seriously because of the significant difficulty associated with separating "dumb" unpropelled munitions from the bomb bay of an aircraft screaming along at Mach 3 and 70,000 feet or better. Assisted separation was a must. And the anticipated distances between launch and target dictated some form of terminal guidance. The B–70 design was eventually redesignated the RS–70 and equipped with standoff weapons — weapons that could be launched from farther away than would be possible from a direct overhead pass. It added to the survivability of the B/RS–70 offensive profile without making it such a suicide mission to attack targets deep inside the Soviet Union. A "pretend–like RS–70 system" was the foundation for the developmental tasking taken on by the Recce–Strike program called 665A.

The plot thickened when Col. David Jones, one of General Le May's former aides and later destined to become Air Force Chief of Staff and Chairman of the Joint Chiefs, was assigned the job of running an *ad hoc* effort and review panel to sell the B–70 program and its operational concept. Jones called Ken Hurley and Ward Protsman from Wright Field to the Pentagon for a briefing tour on the RS/B–70. These two "experts" from Wright Field were the hired guns to answer technical questions and handle any what–ifs originating during the presentations. They went from general's office to general's office while Jones did the lion's share of the briefings. Ken and Ward answered technical questions in their areas of expertise. Jones was a very quick study, and after a couple of these question and answer sessions he was able to hold his own on almost all the issues. In some of the offices, the two Wright Fielders had been there earlier briefing the RS–12. While the generals acknowledged the two, they did not mention anything about those previous encounters. This apparent familiarity between his Wright Field backup weenies and some of the generals was noted by David Jones (he was the consummate, politically astute, staff officer) and he seemed puzzled and troubled by it. But he never asked the pair about their relationships with the senior staff.

On one particular trip Ken and Ward had been asked to come in for a couple of days so they had brought underwear for three. They were there for two weeks. They worked day and night on briefings both to the black side of the house as well as the open side. They slept on conference tables, went to the barber shop in the Pentagon basement to get shaves and, in general, got pretty grungy. General Ascani found out that the two were there working for Jones and came to Washington, D.C. to see how things were going. This was near the end of their two week stint and Uncle Fred told them he was pleased with the way they were handling the situation. One morning, while General Ascani was still there, David Jones stuck his head into their briefing room hangout. The two had spent the night in this room putting another set of briefing charts together and then, as usual, caught a couple of winks while stretched out on the conference table. It was about 9 A.M.

Jones said, "Mr. Zuckert wants to see you in his office as soon as you can get there."

Ken's reaction was one of complete wonder. "What on earth could the Secretary of the Air Force possibly want to see me about?"

Jones replied, "I have no idea but you had best get it in gear and get up there." Grimy, unshaven, rumpled from another night on the conference table and no shower in 36 hours, Ken hustled up to the Secretary's office. Here is exactly what happened.

I'm here, Sir!

Ken marched into the Office of the Secretary of the Air Force and announced to Zuckert's secretary who he was.

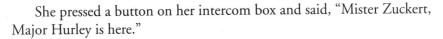

She pressed a button on her intercom box and said, "Mister Zuckert, Major Hurley is here."

Ken could see Zuckert through the open door and as soon as the announcement came he stood up and met Ken, shook his hand and said, "Hello Major Hurley, I understand that you are God in radar."

What do you say to that? "Glad to meet you Sir."

Zuckert motioned Ken to a chair in front of the desk and announced, "As you know, we have been working this RS–70 thing assuming that the Goodyear radar is the best available. I just today found out about this other system up in Baltimore." (The Westinghouse side looker being built to go into the A–11/12.) At this point in the conversation General LeMay walked into the office through a back door and took a chair without a word to either of the other occupants. He just sat there and listened.

Zuckert continued, "Curt LeMay and I don't necessarily agree on this thing, but I want to discuss this situation with you a bit."

At that point the intercom interrupted as his secretary's voice announced, "Mr. Zuckert, you are due to speak to a luncheon downtown in fifteen minutes and you need to leave now."

Zuckert replied, "Major Hurley is to have anything he needs for the next hour to do what I have asked him to do." Then he turned to Ken and said, "I want you to write down a comparison of the two radars (Goodyear and Westinghouse) and then tell me which one I should be pursuing for the RS–70." LeMay got up and left, having never said anything. Ken was sure his career was over as he had just been told to take a position on "something Curt and I don't necessarily agree on," and he had no clue to which radar either of the two men favored.

Walking to the secretary's desk in the outer office, Ken asked for writing materials, an office, and a phone. The lady picked up her phone, punched in a number, and after a moment said "General, Mister Zuckert will be needing your office for the next couple of hours; why don't you go to lunch now, and take your time." Ken saw a brigadier general get up from behind some partitions and head for the hall. She handed Ken pencils and legal tablets and directed him to that office.

After a brief phone search Ken found General Ascani in Dr. Brockway McMillian's office (Assistant AF Secretary for R&D). He said, "General Ascani, I am in Mr. Zuckert's office and I need some help."

General Ascani replied, "Ken, I'll be there in a minute."

When he arrived Ken explained what had happened. Of course, Ascani hadn't been briefed on the Westinghouse radar and Ken didn't tell him about it, but he did tell him that he was being asked to make a comparison of the Goodyear system and something he knew about but could not talk about.

Ascani replied, "Ken, I can only offer you advice. Be very honest and very careful. Do exactly what the Secretary has asked you to do. Good luck!" He then left Ken to do his work.

That didn't help much, but at least now his immediate boss knew where he was and what he was doing. Ken wrote about ten pages of comparison on each system but carefully avoided the issue of which system to buy. He felt he could guess which system LeMay supported but was unwilling to take the gamble. Ken handed the finished study to Zuckert's secretary and she allowed as how it should be typed. She called in five other secretaries and farmed out the pages. The finished paper was done in no time. Ken waited.

Right on schedule Zuckert returned to the office, was handed the study, and shuffled through it reading quickly. Speed reading at its finest. "You didn't tell me which one to buy," he said.

"No, Sir, it would depend on how long you have for the remaining development. The technical approaches are somewhat different, but either system can be built. I don't see a fatal flaw in either one."

Zuckert replied, "Okay, Major, and thank you. Please don't leave the building as I may want to speak to you again later."

Ken saw to it that all copies and carbons were collected and destroyed. The one copy left with Secretary Zuckert would be retrieved later by Col. Leo Geary. He hung around until after six in the evening when General Ascani finally got through to General Burchinal, who gave Major

Hurley permission to leave. That was the last of that episode. Later David Jones pressed Ken for what Secretary Zuckert had wanted. Ken gave him an RS–70 version of the story. At this time Jones was not briefed on the RS–12 or any of the associated black activities supporting that program. The data generated that day stayed within the Secretary's office and LeMay didn't fry the Radar Major.

First rule of Pentagon briefing—be flexible

One day Ken was working on his B–70 job when he got a call from the Pentagon. It was Colonel David Jones wanting him to get on the Kittyhawk (the military aircraft shuttle that hauled Wright–Patterson people back and forth daily to Andrews AFB.) the next morning and be at the Pentagon to back Jones up on a Recce/Strike briefing to General LeMay in the afternoon.

Ken said, "I don't have any charts. I'm not sure I can get a set put together that fast.

Jones told him, "Don't sweat it. We are going to give the briefing. All you need to do is sit in the back of the room and field any technical questions."

Next morning Ken reported to Jones' office about 09:30, right off the Kittyhawk. The first question Jones asked was, "Where are your charts?"

Ken answered, "What charts? I didn't bring any charts! You told me I wouldn't need any charts."

"Don't worry," Jones said, "We'll get a briefing put together for you."

"What do you mean, me?" Ken asked, "I'm just here to back you up, not give the briefing."

"Well, I decided it would have more impact if you gave it, so we will build your charts for you. Oh, by the way," Jones added, "The briefing is at 14:30."

To his credit, David Jones put his minions to work and they built a fine briefing, flip charts and all, in record time. At 14:30, everyone assembled in the briefing room, charts all set up, and ready to go. In came LeMay with his entourage of aides, brigadiers, and lesser horse holders, plus General Thomas Power, who was the Commander in Chief of SAC at the time.

LeMay said, to no one in particular, "Tommy was in the building so I invited him to sit in. Hope you don't mind."

Ken had the fleeting thought of saying, "Sir, I do mind. Please, send him away." But common sense and thoughts of career preservation prevailed. General LeMay was Chief of Staff of the Air Force at the time.

As the briefing began, Jones stood, flipped the first chart, and then introduced Ken. Ken began to brief from his next chart when almost immediately General Power jumped up and started briefing the charts to The Chief (LeMay). He gave the entire briefing without Ken uttering a single word, but just turning the charts for him. It was obvious that Power had been briefed on the subject, and recently.

Nobody else took part in that briefing except to build and flip the charts. Amazing!

How long can this go on?

The briefing pace continued and conflicts between in–the–open efforts to sell the B–70 and the black RS–12 program got hotter and hotter. Because Jones was told that Ken and Ward were assigned to him full time to support the B–70 sales program, he rightfully expected to see them working on that effort full time. Ken and Ward, as is the case so frequently when people are working a black program, were actually serving two masters. They would hustle the briefings and field questions and make briefing charts for Jones for most of the day. But about mid–afternoon when nothing was scheduled on the B–70 effort, they would drift off and pick up their other work assignments on the RS–12 from Col. Leo Geary, who was also located in the Pentagon. Jones was becoming very frustrated at not being able to find the elusive pair in the afternoons and the two Wright Fielders began to fear for their careers. This was a very valid concern as Jones had the ear of LeMay, and the Air Force Chief of Staff could turn these two into toast with a couple of words to the right person. Finally, Hurley and Protsman went to Leo Geary with a request that David Jones be briefed on the RS–12 program in its entirety. This was to smoothe over the gathering storm of duplicity needed for Hurley and Protsman to faithfully serve their masters on both sides of the street. When Hurley and Protsman asked Jones to go with them to another office but wouldn't tell him why, he wasn't particularly enthusiastic. He finally condescended to give them twenty minutes. After they arrived at Leo's office and he began to speak, Jones became a lot more interested. Jones spent over two hours getting the full story on the Blackbird program. While there are no clues or conclusive evidence available, the resulting timing has got to be more than just coincidental. The RS–12 program died almost immediately after Jones received the full OXCART briefing.

Another LeMay briefing

After the RS–12 death struggle, briefings continued on the fallout aircraft designated the R–12, a pure reconnaissance version. By this time any briefing on the R–model or the SR bird was a best seller in the Pentagon. Many people had been briefed at various clearance levels and it was always easy to draw a crowd when the subject of Mach 3 reconnaissance was mentioned. A briefing was set up for General LeMay and the room soon filled with big shooters and their horseholders. Even General "Spike" Momeyer was there. The black side of the house was represented by Leo Geary, Sid Brewer, Ward Protsman, Temp, and Ken. Temp was briefing how they'd gobbled up GAM–87 navigation system assets and were adapting them to the R–12 design.

LeMay asked, "How much does that system weigh?"

Temp deferred to Ken who began with an explanation. "Sir, It depends on how much of the system can be used. With the cooling system, which we aren't sure…"

LeMay cut him off. "Major, you talk too damn much!"

"Ninety–eight pounds, Sir," was Ken's immediate reply.

The briefing continued without further discussion of navigation system weights. When it was finished, Leo Geary walked up and put his arm over Ken's shoulder. "You were just trying to answer his question. Forget it."

From then on whenever Ken would meet Leo he'd say, "Hello Sir," and Leo would respond, "Major, you talk too damn much."

President Johnson makes a clarifying statement

In February 1964, President Johnson made an announcement about the existence of the SR–71, which no one had ever heard of. The RS–12 terminology had been around for a while as had the name RS–70. The RS–12 and the R–12 had not been discussed outside the black community. How the term SR–71 came about in the President's announcement is still a mystery to the people who were working the program at the time. But once the President named the bird, the name stuck.

At the same time Johnson proclaimed the existence of an aircraft called the A–11, and released photos. The photos were of an aircraft already designated the YF–12. Small wonder that everyone was confused. People within the programs were amazed; the rest of us hadn't a clue, so we just went with the flow.

When all this coming out announcing was done, the YF–12s were being flown out of Area 51, affectionately referred to by program people as the Area, the Sand Pile, or The Ranch, and, in some cases, simply Nowhere Air Force Base. But all the world was told that three of these new "A–11s" were flying out of Edwards AFB. The Air Force entered an immediate screaming panic to clear out a hangar at Edwards (Building 1881), secure the area, and get these three machines established there so the President would be telling the truth. The first YF–12 to arrive at Edwards after the story hit the news was taxied to its hastily prepared nest and rolled directly into the waiting hangar. As the doors were being closed to keep out prying eyes, the heat from the hot aircraft and engines set off the deluge sprinkler system inside the hangar. The water came so fast and so hard and there was so much of it, it felt like you were standing waist deep in a lake, with a monsoon storm from there up. It was strange to see that much water in the desert. The YF got a proper bath. Within fifteen minutes of the aircraft's arrival at Edwards the program had the first uncleared person to visit the hangar. The Edwards fire chief came down to shut off the sprinkler system. This was not the last time the sprinklers were set off, but after the initial soaking, the support crews learned how to shut the system off themselves.

Let's all share this technology

One of the results of the RS–12 study effort was the realization that both this program, (whatever it would eventually be called, and the B–70 program, whatever version might survive, were both government programs, and there ought to be a way to share knowledge gained on one program with the other program without acknowledging the existence of the black program.

Ken was elected to be that common denominator. He was to provide data across programs but was not to violate any security conditions. He was to provide the B–70 program managers and engineers with information on how to fix things but was not to reveal how he knew that the fixes would work. All this time many thought that the B–70 program contributed technology advances used by Lockheed in the development of the SR–71 but, as it turned out, that was flat wrong. It was predominantly the Lockheed advanced techniques and processes that were infused into the B–70 program. Amazingly, when this technology transfer idea was presented to Kelly Johnson, he did not explode. He spent the next two days personally guiding Ken around the production floor of the Skunk Works, showing how they had solved some of their toughest fabrication problems.

One example of Kelly's innovations was in the area of welding hydraulic tubing and fittings. North American had spent months and plenty of money to get tubing welded to fittings in a manner that could survive vibration tests. The tubing invariably cracked right at the weld during vibration testing. Kelly had solved that problem and was routinely fabricating welded tube and fittings with no problem. The secret was a portable furnace brazier that wrapped around the tube and fitting to make a nice filleted braze. The brazed area was then shot–peened with .020 glass beads to surface harden it. (Shot–peening is a fancy name for air blasting something with lots of little round balls. In this particular case the little round balls were very tiny glass beads.) No cracks! Kelly also revealed how they solved the titanium spring–back problem in their forming jigs by using annealed stock and heated dies. Kelly showed Ken how they were spot–welding titanium, something that was unknown at the time. And one last thing, Kelly was absolutely sure that North American would never make their welded honeycomb work. As history shows, that problem transcended the plagued and short–lived B–70 program and gave the General Dynamics engineers and production people fits in their honeycomb efforts on the F–111.

Ken played the role for many months. Here he was, an electronics weenie in possession of key data very foreign to his area of expertise, trying to convince experts in other fields to implement processes they just knew would not work. It was like possessing knowledge of the future and not being able to explain how you knew the suggested fixes had already been tried and proved.

This was a time when things really began to move. Hardware and systems came together from all over the country. Section II, *Origins*, traces some of the major pieces and how they got to the right place at the right time.

Chapter 3

The 665A Program

"This work has broad application for future tactical and strategic weapons systems, and the cost for 1964 will be $19.3 million."
Congressional Record, 1962

"My strong suit was not necessarily technical excellence in any particular scientific or engineering discipline, but it was knowledge of how Wright Field worked and how to play the game."
Col. Donn A. Byrnes, reflecting on the program, 1998

In retrospect it is difficult to convey the climate of defensive urgency present in the early 1960s, an urgency not commonly embraced by all. We were still filled with adrenaline from our scrape with the Russians over their missiles in Cuba. In Southeast Asia, our political mouth was leading us on a downward spiral of involvement from which it would take years to recover. The Soviet Union was aggressively moving into space. They were strong, determined, and willing to make the needed economic and national sacrifices to meet any challenge or counter any move the U.S. might make. We were not as strong as we needed to be. As a nation we were far from united with respect to our role in the international family of nations. Our strategic reconnaissance eyes had recently been poked out because of the U–2's vulnerability to Russian SA–2 ground–to–air missiles. The only hope for a penetrating and survivable U.S. strategic bomber lay in the B–70, or in a more sophisticated smart missile/guided weapon deploying version listed in the talking papers of the planners as the RS–70. Technology was just arriving that could provide navigation guidance systems and the necessary sensors for an effective reconnaissance–strike capability within hostile airspace. Program

665A was funded to provide an R&D platform with integrated hardware dedicated to the exploration of these concepts.

At the end of January and throughout February 1963, the House Armed Services Hearings on Military Posture and Appropriations for FY64 were held. Those hearings quantified weapon system funding and political and military baselines for existing operational systems, as well as those systems in R&D at the time. A distillation of the printed record documenting those proceedings provides the following testimonial tea leaves. The bottom line to all the discussions was that the GAM–87 Skybolt was finally and completely sentenced to die. The B–70 would be quite limited, maybe three aircraft at the most, with the remainder of B–70 program funds appropriated by the Congress for FY63 to be held back.

Buried down near the bottom of Page 1,286 of this document is an entry titled Reconnaissance/Strike Program. The last sentence of the paragraph says it all:

"This work has broad application for future tactical and strategic weapons systems, and the cost for 1964 will be $19.3 million."

This funding poured new resources and enthusiasm into the 665A effort, which now became the seed development program for the sensor systems of the R–12 a.k.a. the SR–71.

What did this effort entail?

There had been multispectral sensor reconnaissance programs in the near past, but 665A represented a significant turn of philosophy. For the first time, Congress and the Air Force were willing to fund a development program that combined the elements of a classic multispectral sensor recce suite with a near–real–time strike application. The task was to develop sensors, integrate their outputs with navigational avionics, and mix with that weapon laying methodologies so a single vehicle could do its own seek and kill missions. It was to be an all weather–capable system. The intended operational weapon system for a fully functional hardware package was the Mach 3 B/RS–70, then under design and development by North American Aviation. But even while 665A was being funded by the Congress, the entire B/RS–70 program was fighting a losing battle for life.

A multispectral reconnaissance program first named MONTICELLO and later called QUICK CHECK, was the test bed for early integrated hardware development and application. Mounted in an oversized B–58 weapons/ fuel pod, a combined system was developed for collecting information in every spectrum. QUICK CHECK was the first USAF program established for pulling together photography, side–looking radar imagery, infrared imagery, electronic intelligence, and communication intelligence in one collection vehicle. Imagery from the B–58 was used extensively to support Ken and Ward's briefings on the B–70 and RS–70 in the Pentagon. This B–58's home base was the General Dynamics plant at Carswell AFB, Fort Worth, Texas. An excellent home for this kind of activity because this plant was also supporting the world wide program, BIG SAFARI, and various long–wing versions of the B–57.

How do you know where this stuff comes from?

To make effective use of collected data and allow for critical analysis, another subsystem had been added to the QUICK CHECK mix. It was a data block system which provided the ability to record aircraft geographical position and aircraft speed, direction of travel, aircraft attitude in pitch and roll, and aircraft altitude above the ground at the time. By tagging information gathered by all sensors, a common baseline in time and position was established so each sensor's take could be used to amplify and validate the information presented by other sensors. Data block information came from the navigational system, the air data computer, the aircraft's radar altimeter, and in some cases the sensors themselves. All this information was assembled by an electronic filing system that converted the facts into one simple data block and either flashed it on the border of each frame of film or electronically imprinted it on magnetic tape used to store information collected by the electronic listening sensors.

The greatest reconnaissance data in the world is no good if you do not know where you were when you got it. Plus the value of any one sensor's output is multiplied immeasurably by the inputs from other sensor samplings of their spectrum of interest at the same time.

The QUICK CHECK system provided a truly integrated reconnaissance output. This was the first step in getting data needed for an operational all weather mission. While the real–time processing and analysis capability was to come along later in 665A, the application of covering the same area with several types of overlaying synchronized sensors in a high speed vehicle was benchmarked by the systems in QUICK CHECK.

In 1962, the QUICK CHECK program and its sensor suite blended nicely into the emerging 665A Program. The job of 665A was to build on current technology and add the elements of near–real–time in–flight processing to enable target detection, identification, assessment, and weapons deployment, on the fly. To accomplish the RS role, sensor and navigation data were processed to derive instantaneous aircraft position and the relative coordinates of targets with respect to the mission aircraft. This task accomplished, an inertially guided missile could be told the coordinates of its starting point at the aircraft and the coordinates of the target at the ending point of its flight. All this was to be done by a weapon system operator as the aircraft flew at 70,000 feet or higher, and flashed along at one–half mile per second. These were challenges that made designers salivate and gave systems integration people and human factors specialists migraine headaches.

Once the funding for 665A was authorized and a high priority assigned, QUICK CHECK was quietly folded and its program assets were directed into the Recce–Strike Program. The pod, the sensor hardware, support equipment, and experimental aircraft systems were stripped from the B–58 and everything was shipped via C–124 and C–54 aircraft and rail cars to Wright–Patterson AFB, Ohio.

Fragile—handle with care

The B–58 Hustler program at Fort Worth was supported by a dedicated C–54 nicknamed *The Hustler's Mother*. On one flight, *Hustler's Mother* brought the optical correlator for the side looking radar to Patterson Field. This was the one and only correlator available at the time. It was large, heavy, and optically delicate. If damaged, the radar segment of the program would instantly be a year behind. When the time came to unload our precious correlator, the duty forklift operator was indoctrinated as to how critically important this piece of hardware was and how the safety of the free world depended on his forklifting and loading skills. He nodded that he fully understood the gravity of the situation, turned his forklift around, took a great stab at the six–by–eight–foot correlator crate, and speared it well above the pallet cutouts. We all stood in horror as he then extracted the crate from the aircraft cargo door, spun it around and, in one smooth coordinated movement, slammed the box down in the back of a waiting six–by–six cargo truck as if it were just so much crated rubble. No one spoke. All who watched were convinced that every piece of optical glass in the system was at the bottom of the crate like so many crushed coke bottles. Actually, the machine survived in remarkable condition. It was driven carefully to the project photo processing facility, and forklifted out by one of the program people, our facilities and hardware wizard Chuck Hughes. Later it was painstakingly uncrated and calibrated by Don Beckerleg of Goodyear Aerospace. We had just experienced our first program miracle.

665A's Operational Concept Demonstration

To prove the concept of Recce–Strike, a multispectral sensor system, a sensor output – target detection – target identification display console, and a weapons laying computer simulation system were integrated with necessary aircraft systems. This package was to be installed and flown in the project KC–135. With refueling tanks removed, refueling boom removed, and a huge radome the size of a Ford station wagon mounted on the right side of the forward fuselage, the test bed began to take shape. The staffers at SAC Headquarters were not enthusiastic about getting one of their aircraft stolen by a bunch of goofy tinkerers at Wright Field; but because it was a program directly supporting the RS–70, permission was granted and the aircraft, now designated a JKC–135[1], tail number 596, was delivered to Patterson Field to begin an in–house modification program.

The 665A's charter was to demonstrate the capability of the system to detect targets, overlay the sensor information from several sources, and display that information on large, high–definition (at the time) CRTs. The operator would review the information presented as it rolled down

---

[1]The "J" added to the designation announced to the world that this aircraft could be returned to its original configuration as a tanker, but *very creative* re-assembly required.

the screen and make a decision about the targets detected, and when and if to launch a pretend—missile at the target under consideration. To accomplish all this, information from all on board sensors had to be exposed on film, the film processed, the image scanned, and the results properly scaled and presented on the operator's console.

Each sensor had a different reaction time. Boiled down this means that without "adjustment" of the processing and image manipulation times, none of the information would appear for the same area at the same time. These differences were compensated for by varying film path lengths. The film was driven by the aircraft ground speed with certain other processing parameters remaining independent of ground speed. The long pole in the tent was the side looking radar (SLR) which had to process two films to produce an image readable by humans. The first process was to develop, read, and correlate the data film to produce a map film and then process, scan, and project the map film to produce the CRT image. The all—weather recce—strike mission was absolutely dependent on the availability of SLR data in near real time. At the time photo processing in flight was the only practical solution to that problem.

Enter the In—flight Correlator Processor (ICP)

For engineers and technicians who love a challenge, the ICP was it. It was the crankiest of the cranky. It gave its handlers and feeders continuous fits. But lucky for the program, in addition to the Goodyear people who were skilled and patient beyond belief, along came a couple of quirky Air Force aerial photographers to join our flight crew. While I cannot remember their real names, their nicknames still stick after all these years. We called them "Tom Terrific" and "Mighty Manfred." Nothing seemed to bother these guys. They worked the ICP hardware, dealing with all its distasteful and leaking habits. They just went with the flow, you might say. Just like my friend Glen Chapman, Driftsight Dragon Emeritus, Air Force technician extraordinaire, and author of *Me and U—2*, there are some marriages made in heaven. Glen loved and hated the U—2 driftsight in the very same and capable way that Tom Terrific and Mighty Manfred took to the 665A ICP and the Ansco in—flight film processors. The presence of liquid—filled film processing systems in an aircraft that bumps along through rough air causing chemical baths high in hydroxides to spill on the aircraft's tender aluminum skin, does nothing for one's sense of self preservation. After every flight all the plumbing had to be purged and cleaned including the processing heads and other system paraphernalia. I can still remember the look of Mighty Manfred's hands with the peeling skin. He was unfortunate enough to be allergic to photo chemicals. Not good for an aerial photographer, no matter what your nickname is.

Let's design an experiment

The basic idea was to present the operator with information on two big TV–like screens mounted side by side on a console. The operator would have the capability of selecting either radar, infrared (IR), electro–optical (EO), or electronic intelligence (ELINT) information on the screens, and also had the ability to overlay one sensor's output on another. Once a specific target had been identified, the operator would move a set of crosshairs to that location and lock the system onto the target. The crosshairs would then track that target. At this point the operator had to decide to attack the target or let it pass. Our simulated recce–strike aircraft carried three types of simulated missiles—short range, mid range, and long range. The console operator was told, through a system of beeping sounds in the headset, which missile or missiles were available to hit the selected target. In a sense this was the very first high tech, high flying, high stakes, high stress, video game, and not everyone could play it well.

Oops, we forgot the hand control

Right in the middle of all the preparations, Litton Industries, the console/display contractor, realized it did not have a suitable militarized hand control for manipulating the crosshairs on the displays. So I was launched by my boss to find such an animal and told, "Don't return without it."

There was an old B–36 sitting at the far west end of the Wright Field runway layout and after searching everywhere I finally crawled up inside. There in the bomb–nav station was the very hand control we needed. Back to the office, write letters to the Air Force Museum, flaunt our priority, promise the world, and presto!

"You may remove the hand control for your use if you promise to return it when you are finished."

I promised, in writing, and the deed was done. Returning to the old B–36 with no more than a Swiss Army knife and good intentions, I removed the hand control and associated wiring. (The device was still being used daily in the 665A aircraft when I left for Edwards. Don't ask me if it ever got back to the museum.)

Get me some guinea pigs

Testing the concept involved human subjects and that meant psychologists and behavioral scientists, and a list of fighter pilots from Langley AFB, Virginia. Our resident psychologist was a lady named Barbara Van Ausdall. Her supervisor was Lee Griffin. The two made a great team and flew frequently in the back of aircraft number 596. Lee was an Army pilot on the weekends and had access to an L–20 Beaver which we used for flying here and there. Barbara turned out to be the very best at finding and identifying targets as the imagery scrolled down the faces of the two huge console CRTs. The Langley pilots were a great mix of really good and not–so–good, target finders. Everybody wanted to understand why the differences.

The solution was to make the test subjects at the console wear a special helmet with a camera mounted on top. This camera photographed the CRT screens on which were superimposed small light spots showing where the subject's eyes were looking. By following the dots, the headshrinkers could determine what each subject's personal search pattern was and how that related to individual success or failure at finding targets. The results were statistically inconclusive; however, we did get a lot of complaints about wearing a ten pound, top heavy, helmet for hours at a time, especially comments about the small crutch–like support resting on the subject's nose bridge to keep the camera and optics aligned.

The first glimmer on an integrated sensor system

This flight test period in the JKC–135 represented a major step forward in integrating the outputs of several sensors and combining that information for a single purpose. It's where the sensor suite for the SR–71 really began its gestation period. It is also the timeframe where the system for data block definition and application reached another level of sophistication.

There were limited resources for the technologies involved, so when the push for sensor system development and integration began, those companies with histories that included work with QUICK CHECK had a real foothold in the door toward being credible providers of systems for the 665A suite. Those companies turned out to be:[2]

Goodyear Aerospace for the side looking radar—it had provided the SLR system for QUICK CHECK

HRB–Singer for the infrared and electro optical system, also a QUICK CHECK hardware provider.

Air Products for the closed–cycle IR detector cooling system. This was a first time for everyone on this system.

ITT for the data block system; came from QUICK CHECK.

Litton Industries for the in–flight and ground display consoles and target–tracking methodology, a new requirement originating with 665A.

AIL for the ELINT/COMINT system, another QUICK CHECK provider.

Fairchild Industries for the ground track camera, a stabilized standard T–11, same as the vertical camera on QUICK CHECK.

Kollsman Industries for the astro–tracker.

Ansco for the in–flight semi–instant film processing equipment and chemistry. The methodology for in–flight processing used in 665A ICP and later the SR–71 RCD was the brainchild of Charlie Dotson (Goodyear Aerospace). The ICP provided a great source of wonder and excitement for all of us who flew in the back half of aircraft 596.

---

[2]The final SR–71 sensor configuration reaching the Category II test program at Edwards included SLR (Goodyear), IR (HRB–Singer), the ground track camera (Fairchild Industries), and the ELINT/COMINT system (AIL). Additional cameras were added by HYCON and ITEK. The individual sensors and results are described later in the sections titled *Origins* and *Cat II Testing*.

Ansco Films for the multitude of film sizes, emulsions, and specialty handling. This company was extremely helpful and responsive to a struggling program with large requirements and small film budgets. (Our large variety of emulsions and small quantities of each did not interest Eastman Kodak.)

665A was a right–handed system with all sensors and antennas oriented to collect data from directly beneath the aircraft to beyond the horizon on the right side of the aircraft. The SR–71, of course, carried an ambidextrous system.

I arrived at the 665A Office through a long line of coincidental happenings and was assigned as SLR and IR development engineer, camera person, support facilities and supplies person, and general cook and bottle washer. This was perfect training ground for the developing Blackbird program. The 665A people, except for my boss Jim Singer, were clueless about the onrushing SR–71 (really R–12 prior to Johnson's announcement). My strong suit was not necessarily technical excellence in any particular scientific or engineering discipline, but knowledge of how Wright Field worked and how to play the game. I knew how to "play Wright Field" and get things done. Early on, I ran into a Major Kenneth Hurley, allegedly assigned to the B–70 System Program Office. Ken was very nosey and very knowledgeable about the 665A hardware. I found his knowledge of our technology comprehensive and unnerving. He flew with us frequently during test flights, allegedly, to meet his monthly flying time. He proved to be an astute observer, and not one of the dreaded guest tweakers.

Now doesn't that look better?

In–flight observers of the real–time film processing equipment were the motivating force for the development of a series of what became known as executive knobs. On some of the film processing equipment certain parameters could be varied, within reason, to enhance or decrease contrast or change basic film background density. These adjustments would be made in the name of projecting a better console CRT image. On one particular flight a big shooter visiting firemen from Air Force Systems Command was riding along and adjusting things to improve the pictures. He optimized the system so well that it ceased to function.

Once we were back on the ground at Patterson Field, returning the system to working order took several hours. At that point Charlie Dotson and Don Beckerleg of Goodyear asked whether it would be okay to disconnect the control panel knobs but leave them there for the visitors to play with. They proposed actual system adjustments be made only through small obscure holes using long skinny screwdrivers. From that point on the system remained operational through most of the flights and VIPs marveled at how the operator could make adjustments to improve the CRT images.

Don't ask, just do what I say

Early in the flight test program I was instructed by my boss, Mr. James Singer, that if ever Major Hurley asked for something, it would be provided without question, even if it was the best we had and even if it was classified. No questions asked. Just hand him whatever he wants.

"I can't do that without a hand receipt," I said.

Jim looked me straight in the eye and said, "Yes you will, Captain."

The only correct answer was "Yes, Sir."

Almost immediately Ken showed increased interest in the goings–on in the back of the JKC–135 where sensor films were instantly processed, scanned, and projected onto the operator's console CRTs. (And we all thought he was just riding along to get flying time in the navigator's seat up front.) Without fail, Ken would select the finest imagery we produced and request, after it had been reviewed to assess system performance, that it be delivered to him at his office at the B–70.

"Just in case I'm not there," he would say, "You can leave it with my secretary."

I balked at leaving these SECRET materials with the secretary in case Major Hurley was not there. Back to question Jim Singer. Same answer. "Yes you will, Captain."

I did what I was told.

The bottom line to this story is that Major Hurley was never there. Major Hurley was never anywhere. Yes, he flew with us, and yes, he stopped by to ask all sorts of prying questions. He was ever so polite and proper but undeniably pushy. But no, he was never anywhere when we went looking.

Years later Ken and I were laughing about this and his wife Jeanne added, "You were not the only one frustrated by Ken's elusive behavior. Even Ken's B–70 office boss would frequently call me, his wife, to try to track him down."

Ken was doing his RS–12 business and we were not the only ones frustrated by his frequent disappearing act.

Looking back at how it was

On the surface, 665A struggled along in full and direct support of a technological steamroller called the RS–70. Concept formulation and proof were the avowed charter. We even flew 350 knots at 500 feet above the ground to simulate image rates of a Mach 3 attack. While this sounds impressive and was indeed fun to fly, about all we ever proved at that speed and altitude was that central Ohio was not ready or willing to have a huge JKC–135 blasting along close to the ground at full bore frightening chickens, and spooking horses.

On the black side, 665A was mixing a batter that would cook up to be one of the best all–spectrum recce cakes ever baked, and we didn't even know it!

Part II

Origins

Chapter 4

The J-58 Legend
Digging up roots and dirty laundry

"The engine manufacturer always gives the Air Force
one part of the engine for free. It's the shaft."
Lloyd Wenzel, Wright Field, on any given day.

"The engine failed because of foreign object damage. It
appears that something about the size of
a flashlight went through the engine."
Kelly Johnson, Skunk Works
message to Wright Field, 1964

"No Sir, that part did not fail. However, many of its pieces
did display signs of extreme mechanical distress."
Unknown engine tech rep, West Palm Beach, 1969

To discover the roots of a spooky engine and uncover the spooky people involved, the researcher needs to start with old friends and experts in the engine business. This endeavor leads, sometimes not directly, but interestingly, backward in time to the creation of a new life form on the production floor at the Pratt and Whitney Alligator Farm west of West Palm Beach, Florida. To put the entire episode in perspective, it helps to start at the beginning and march forward from there.

Asking for favors

I called Lloyd Wenzel to ask about the J–58 and where its creation may have started. He did not have any specific knowledge about the engine but did know about the people. Lloyd is an old P–38 pilot, by now I guess all P–38 pilots are old. He was originally assigned to Wright Field shortly after World War II because he was fluent in

German, having grown up in the little German town of Seguin, Texas. He became a propulsion expert with Air Force R&D and knows Pratt like the back of his hand. When he retired from the Air Force he went to work for Pratt's International Division. Lloyd and I shared an office when we were both assigned to the F–15 Program. Lloyd was a colonel and I was a major fresh back from the South Atlantic. Lloyd is the consummate storyteller and can remember where all the political bones are buried on many engines and airplane programs.

I asked Lloyd whether he was ever involved with the J–58 and how it got from the Navy to the Air Force SR–71. He said, "First of all, Navy engines at the time were all even numbered and Air Force engines were odd numbered." He told me that it could have been some little offbeat development program started by the Navy that died or almost died and was then picked up by the CIA or whomever for the Blackbird. He mentioned a few names and promised to see what he could find out.

Grabbing the early end of the string

John F. McDermott (most everyone calls him Jack), from Pratt, was the program manager on the J–58. (B. N. Bellis later asked for Jack to be put on the F–15's F–100 engine because Bellis knew Jack from the J–58 days.) Jack is retired now. Wenzel called him and pleaded my case for engine origin research.

Another name Lloyd mentioned was Fred Parker, an engineer at Pratt on the J–58 and the F–100 engine programs. Fred was the guy who always got the job of telling the government every time the engine did something untoward in the test program, i.e., when it managed to disassemble itself or catch on fire or burn out part of the aft section or whatever. Fred was dead honest and he would stare you right in the eyes and tell you the truth… but only as much as you asked for.

The third person was someone whose name Wenzel could not remember. He was an Air Force captain, who had been grounded after he broke both legs in an ejection from a T–33 when his knees hit the bow over the front windscreen.[1] This captain's job was to take briefcases full of cash in large denominations down to Pratt at the Alligator Farm

---

[1] Many of the contributors to this book remember this man but none could supply his name.

and dump it into their financial hopper. He was a bag man in the same sense as the guys who carried cash to Kelly's Skunk Works in the early days.

Above all, don't snoop

From his position of oversight at Wright Field, Wenzel could see piles of Air Force dollars disappearing into Pratt with no apparent benefit to Air Force programs at the Florida plant. Lloyd sent his contracting officer, Bob Swisher, down to the Alligator Farm. Bob was great at sniffing out where money went.

Lloyd's instructions were, "Don't come back until you find out where the money is coming from and where it is going."

About three days after Bob arrived and started rooting around in West Palm Beach, Lloyd received a phone call from "some general" in the Office of the Secretary of the Air Force. This general told Lloyd to get his nose out of that business and recall his minion from Pratt. The general instructed Colonel Wenzel to get on with his life while there was still a chance that he had an Air Force career left and a potential retirement to look forward to. Lloyd recalled Bob and the case was closed… at least from their perspective.

The J—58 breathed its first in Hartford, Connecticut

I called Mr. Jack McDermott and discovered that he had been the program manager on the J—58 engine all along. First at East Hartford, Connecticut and then he was transferred to West Palm, out to the Pratt Alligator Farm. This place got its name from the fact that in addition to being out in a remote area of the Everglades, there were alligators all over the place. There was a very large cooling pond out in the front of the main building and the lunch hour sport was to walk out to the pond and throw the rest of your brown bag contents to the waiting alligators as a treat.

One event during a J—58 run in one of the outlying engine test cells adds further depth to the alligator legend. For some reason the gators seemed to think these big engines were the ultimate bull alligator and were not the least put off by the sound or smell. It was winter in Florida and the evenings get cool if you are a reptile. So the concrete pads of the test cells which heated during the engine runs, attracted the gators. They would crawl up on the warm concrete and snooze. Late one dark swamp moonless night a couple of Pratt engineers were doing some engine runs. One of the guys left the control booth and stepped into the dark to check something on the test engine. Wham, he tripped over a rather large alligator and fell headlong across the floor of the test cell. The gator, unruffled by the engine noise, was equally undisturbed by the human doing a "pratfall" across its back. (Sorry, just could not resist that!) The engineer quickly retreated to the safety of the control booth.

Back to the engine story

Jack said that in the late 1950s, before McNamara, the engine community used to look ahead and plan the next series or capability of engines without having a specific airframe in mind. This is an important issue in the weapon system development philosophy. Since McNamara, there must be a waiting airframe or one under development contract to produce a new engine. There is a significant difficulty with this latter approach. The gestation period for a modern jet engine is about eight years and as the materials technology continues to expand, the time may actually take longer. Using the same initial ground rules, the average development period for an airframe is three–to–five years. With computer technology and other electronic design and simulation, the lead time for a new airframe could conceivably be reduced in the future. Philosophize all you please, but there is no way to narrow the disparity in development times between a new engine and a new airframe. This is a chicken and egg problem that is essentially without solution within the current Department of Defense management policies and procurement ground rules applied by the Congress.

The first J–58 design and development was funded by the Navy in search of an engine capable of Mach 3 dash. That was how the Blackbird future engine got a Navy number designation. At that time the U.S. military aircraft inventory already contained Mach 1 engines and Mach 2–capable inlets and engines. The B–58 Hustler (no connection between the numbers) was the dominant Mach 2 airframe in operational service. The next quantum jump was planned to be Mach 3. This initial J–58 was designed for short times at Mach 3 and had no capability for sustained cruise at that speed. The determining factor between a dash engine and a Mach 3 cruise engine lay in the rotating disks (in the compressor and in the turbine). These parts take the longest to heat up and, in the case of a quick run at Mach 3 and back to subsonic cruise, there would be insufficient time to significantly increase their temperature.

When did all this start?

The original J–58 design was run for the first time at East Hartford on 24 December 1957. That engine did not resemble the final J–58 and had no bypass system at all. There were strenuous efforts on the part of Pratt to sell the engine to the B–70. That aircraft was designed for sprints to Mach 3 but was not intended for extended cruise at that speed. Even at that time, the J–58 was too large in diameter to fit within the B–70 internal engine envelope. The North American engineers and designers were too far along on the existing configuration using the General Electric J–93 to seriously entertain the early J–58. Development and testing continued in Connecticut, and Pratt tried mightily to sell its design to North American. In the end it was not to be. The design more or less faltered along without any real emphasis on the final output. This early version finally died on the vine at East Hartford.

On 29 August 1959, the U.S. accepted the design for the A–12 and that program began to move forward. In September, 1959, Jack McDermott and a core of engineers moved to the Pratt facility located in the boonies just west of West Palm Beach, Florida. Once situated and operating in Florida, the Pratt team started over on the design of an engine with true Mach 3 cruise capability. While the engine designation remained the same, J–58, in the vernacular of the engine builder, "We laid down a new center line." That means a fresh piece of paper and a brand new start. This engine was now to be designed to meet the needs of the A–12, and that created a whole new series of issues. The compressor was the first problem. No matter what they did, they could not efficiently accommodate the subsonic requirements and the high Mach requirements. A compressor design that could provide acceptable performance at both the high and the low end of the airspeed scale was elusive. Finally, the engineers decided they would use an internal bypass system that took excess air from the compressor at the high Mach numbers and passed it around the engine then dumping it into the exhaust path upstream of the afterburner. This was not the only design problem, but it was the refinement that resulted in bypass tubes along the exterior of the J–58 as we know it today. The J–58 is the only operational engine to ever employ this design feature.

With the design of the engine progressing and a known thrust profile defined, the engineers at Pratt and Lockheed pressed hard to get things done. The Mach 3 cruise J–58 engine passed its Preliminary Flight Rating Test (PFRT) on 30 July 1962. A quick look back at the other side of the program, the A–12 airframe, shows that it flew first on 26 April 1962. That first flight, and many others, were powered by the J–75 engine. (The J–75 was the power plant for the Air Force F–105.)

It was not until 31 January 1963 that the first J–58 flew in an A–12. This flight was made with one J–58 engine and one J–75 engine. While the J–75 did an admirable job in pushing the A–12 design around in the early phases of the flight test program, it was not until the J–58s arrived that the aircraft could reach its design Mach number.

A very expensive vacuum cleaner

During the initial period of marrying the engine to the airframe and getting the mechanical bugs worked out there was a string of Foreign Object Damage (FOD) problems. This problem was not unique to the Blackbird and is present to some extent in every marriage between engine and airframe. Anything left loose in the inlet or any part of the inlet bypass passages was ultimately sucked into the engine and in many cases caused serious engine damage. Engines like the J–58 move a tremendous amount of air through the inlet duct when they are operating at high power settings and low forward speeds. When the aircraft is tied down on a thrust stand and the engine run at full power, inrushing air can literally suck poorly seated rivets out of the sheet metal and into the engine. Any loose manufacturing debris left in nooks and crannies of the inlet makes its way into and through the engine. Small things sometime make it through without causing a major engine failure. The airframe manufacturer's inspectors spend literally hundreds of hours looking for potential FOD in all parts of the aircraft. Kelly even hired a group of midgets to inspect the inner fuel tanks for pieces and parts left over after assembly. Loose things in the fuel system are just as threatening to the plumbing system as scraps and rivets in the inlets are to engines. And some days it just does not work out.

A particular reporting requirement placed on the Skunk Works was to notify the Program Office at Wright Field by teletype every time there was an engine incident, no matter what the cause. One of these messages is notable for its thoroughness and especially for the final one liner. The teletype goes on and on about the technical details of this major engine failure. The engine essentially ate itself right there inside the aircraft. After pages and pages of hypertechnical description, Kelly added a final comment at the bottom of the message, "The engine failed because of foreign object damage. It appears that something about the size of a flashlight went through the engine."

The readers at the Program Office were left mentally picturing a Ray–O–Vac battery label imbedded in a painfully contorted fan or compressor blade.

Historical note

The J–58 that had its early beginnings in 1957, is the very Wrst identiWable piece of the eventual SR–71 aircraft system that became hardware. We have traced the side looking radar back to the monticello Program in 1959 but it does not have the direct relationship with the Wnal product like the engine does. The Pratt and Whitney J–58 engine is, indeed, the bottom of the root system that grew to be the Blackbird.

Chapter 5

The Navigation System

"Now we're gonna lay all the printouts down side by side, tape them to the floor, and nobody leaves until we figure this out."

Bruce Hartman, hangar floor, 1 A.M.,
Beale AFB, 1968

One system on board the aircraft could be considered the heart of mission accomplishment, it was the navigation system. It is conceivably possible for an accomplished crew to have successfully completed a full–up reconnaissance mission without the Astro–inertial Navigation System (ANS) operating, but it was not a likely scenario. The idea of traveling a distance of 4,000 miles or so to photograph a specific pinpoint target located in hostile territory without the capabilities provided by a functional nav system, seems a little farfetched even by today's standards. In the 1960s, before the Global Positioning System (GPS) and other technological advances it would have been a near impossibility. Maintaining a preplanned ground track and being able to point and click the cameras when the time spread for accuracy could be as small as a two–second window out of a three or four hour flight would have been a remarkable feat. And this does not even consider finding the tanker in the middle of nowhere on a dark night. In the case of finding the tanker, there were other systems that aided location once you were in the ballpark. But without the ANS system to get you close enough for the others to work, the SR and her crew would be in a world of hurt.

The SR–71's navigation system was as much a part of the mission accomplishment scenario as were the crew, the airframe, the engines, the sensors, the tanker crews, and a legion of ground support people. It navigated, provided the primary attitude reference for the autopilot, furnished information to key cockpit instruments, and supplied information for very accurate aircraft pitch control. As they say, "Don't leave home without it!" — and they didn't!

The anatomy of an Astro–inertial Navigation System

To understand the SR–71 test program and how the aircraft was operated and employed, it helps to have at least a rudimentary understanding of what a generic inertial navigation system contains and generally how such a system would operate.

The platform

In most cases the platform is a metaphorical expression used to describe an assembly of hardware containing gyros, accelerometers, and their associated electronics and integrators. The platform is a three–axis, three–gimbal system, with each axis being 90 degrees from the plane defined by the other two axes. Once properly aligned and stabilized, the gyros provide a known relationship to space and the center of the earth. This relationship is dependent upon a known geographical starting point. Another way to view this is to envision the platform acting like a very long pendulum with its bob weight located at the center of the earth and having its pivot point fastened to the local position on the surface of the earth. With the platform, this is all accomplished mathematically within the system's computer.

A little physics

If a pendulum is disturbed, it will swing at a frequency based upon the length between the pivot point and the bob weight at the opposite end. The period (time for one cycle) of a pretend–pendulum with its pivot at the surface and its bob at the center of the earth is eighty–plus minutes, and is called the Schuler Period. The effects of this Schuler Period phenomenon are present with, and must be considered in, all inertial systems. The way an inertial system responds to this influence is to pretend that its bob is fixed at the center of the earth and the pivot point waves back and forth. What happens with a stationary operating system is that it will appear to move its location in a cyclic fashion with a period of about 84 minutes.[1]

Getting aligned

No matter how good an inertial system might be, to work properly it must first be meticulously aligned with the local vertical, and platform oscillations damped out. If the platform is perfect and the alignment is perfect, then the platform can track any motion experienced by the platform with great precision while its mythical plumb bob remains locked at the center of the earth. This initial alignment of the platform to the local vertical is crucial to system performance. Any error (and there is always some) in alignment causes the pendulum to start to swing. This shows itself in an ever–increasing oscillatory error in position data put out by the inertial system. The problem is compounded by uncompensated mechanical errors like friction and other system tolerance bands. These linear effects produce a non–cyclic error that adds to the Schuler Period sinusoidal problem. In the real world of the 1960s, the very best pure inertial systems displayed a position error drift rate of about one nautical mile per hour.

The process of alignment took about 30 minutes on a good day. The platform erected itself to the local vertical and then was able to sense the earth's rotation. This type of alignment was called gyro compassing and was the preferred method.

Characteristics of a pure inertial system

The above is referred to as a pure inertial system. Many aircraft and missiles operate and are guided by pure inertial systems. The A–11/12 navigational system was a pure inertial system made by Honeywell. In the short term, the ability of a pure inertial system to measure small variations from its norm is excellent. However in the long term, errors of alignment and hardware implementation introduce errors that lead to unacceptable inaccuracies. Here is how those errors develop.

---

[1]Most inertial systems at the time had cyclic periods of eighty-four to eighty-six minutes due to platform damping. Damping was applied to assure oscillations did not increase in magnitude.

Assume you have the perfect aircraft proceeding along a straight line, actually a great circle course over the earth's surface. The pure inertial system on board this aircraft thinks it is following the exact intended path called for in its program. But, in actuality it is causing its airplane to diverge from this preplanned straight line at a rate of about one nautical mile per hour. In addition the platform is oscillating at the Schuler Period of 84 minutes. This adds additional displacement from the desired ground track which appears as a sine wave added to the fixed error of one nautical mile per hour. At the start of the flight these displacements are small and the aircraft does not depart from the intended track by much. But without some correcting information from another source, these position errors grow with time. If the autopilot is tied to the inertial system for its heading information and control, the aircraft will fly a long sinusoidal path that departs at some constant rate from the planned course rather than following a pre–planned straight line or great circle route. With careful testing one can predict the magnitude of the linear error–induced variations. However, on a particular day, at a particular time, at the start of a particular flight path, one cannot predict sufficiently where the inertial system might be on the Schuler curve.

A pre–GPS 1960s solution to inertial divergence

One choice for minimizing cyclic errors was to externally update the nav system with correct velocity vector data and/or position data. This could be done by the navigator inserting in–flight position updates or it could be accomplished by using Doppler radar or other active velocity measuring techniques. Any kind of active radar device such as a Doppler system could be detected at long ranges so it was a poor option when trying to sneak through the enemy's airspace.

Another and the most effective method of updating an inertial navigation system concerning its real position was collecting information from the stars. As navigators always say, "Nobody can jam or shoot down the sun, the moon, the planets, or the stars." Adding the capability of tracking stars day or night and then computing star fixes narrows the wander observed in inertial systems down to almost nothing. This was the system chosen for the SR–71.

Proof of the pudding

During Category II testing, the value of the SR–71 Astro–inertial Navigation System was demonstrated many times. A course was set up to evaluate how well the aircraft and nav system adhered to the planned and programmed ground track. One of the typical routes started about 800 miles off the west coast of California, roared across the southern U.S., over the center of Phoenix, south of Dallas, south of Memphis, and then turned to decelerate along the west coast of Florida toward Key West for a rendezvous with the tanker. After that, the aircraft accelerated up the Gulf Coast of Florida, made a long curving turn toward the west to repeat the exact eastbound flight path of a few minutes earlier.

One of the best surveyed and most frequently photographed places along the path was the central portion of downtown Phoenix, Arizona. It had been carefully surveyed by Army teams for the purpose of positioning the Blackbird on both the outbound and return legs of several missions. The largest distance ever measured between the outbound and return legs over the city of Phoenix was 1,200 feet. This was a navigational feat that could be reproduced by no other air–breather in service in the mid–1960s. Star tracking combined with an excellent ANS platform, and a clever computer program did the job every time.

How the navigation system hardware got there

While organ transplants from one weapon system to another are not generally associated with aircraft design and development, the story that follows is exactly that. It happens with today's systems much as it did then.

The Skybolt (GAM–87), a ballistic missile designed to be carried by and launched from a B–52, was canceled—declared dead—in about 1963. That coincided with the RS–12 studies going on at the time, which recognized a need for an effective star–tracking system for navigation. The RS–12 design mission demanded extreme accuracy because of the intended aircraft speed, the anticipated distances involved, and the pinpoint accuracy required for successful target acquisition and attack.

The GAM–87 navigation system had almost everything needed for the RS–12 (which later evolved into the R–12), and which Lyndon

Johnson publicly labeled the SR–71, everything except the necessary computer capacity. The system had a 4,000 word memory. Excellent for the ballistic mission of the day, but insufficient for mission management tasks associated with a long–legged reconnaissance aircraft, traveling where there were no radio navigational aids available to update system position. After the GAM–87 program was declared dead, fourteen complete astro–inertial navigation systems were placed in bonded storage in a screen room at Northrop. Using the mystical powers of those in black programs, Ken Hurley and Ward Protsman were able to capture those systems and divert them to the RS–12 study assets. Other R&D programs had their eyes on these systems but were outgunned by the Blackbird priority.

Computer memory capacity became a big deal

To really understand the way things were in the computer memory business in the early 1960s, one needs to look at the various memory storage technologies at the time. Following this path leads directly to one of the more defining developments in the SR–71 ANS.

Some six or seven years before the RS–12 came on the scene, IBM had invented a storage device called ferrite cores. These were little iron doughnuts (toruses) that carried a charge or no charge so they could be a one or a zero as the circumstances required at the moment. When the system read the memory, the charge on the individual cores was reduced. As soon as the memory was read that value had to be replaced by re–charging that particular torus. This was an important issue and we will revisit it later. The ratio of how much energy was removed from the memory element and how much was used to recharge that element was called the drive ratio. Ken Hurley had been well grounded in this particular technology through his RS–70 job and had a pretty good knowledge of how it was supposed to work. Drive ratio became a sticking point in the SR–71 ANS memory development. This same characteristic of read and re–write is not unique to only one kind of memory and was a factor in solid state, disk, and drum memory as well. Because IBM's market was ground–based computers and the company had to satisfy that market, they developed a 4,000 word standard memory storage cube—16x16x16, or a 4,096–bit memory. It was one of the earliest random access memory devices.

In the late 1950s and early 1960s, contractors began to digitize information and speak about the transition from analog to digital systems. Ken Hurley's question to IBM was, "Who on earth is going to convert the entire world into ones and zeros?" Even today he talks about missed opportunities and his lack of forward thinking.

This was a time when developmental bomb/nav systems built by IBM, known as the MA–2, or the ASB–4 and the ASB–9, were doing well. It was a period of transition from pure analog to digital technology in airborne systems. Digital and solid state technology had progressed sufficiently so developers decided to start incorporating this new science into B–52 systems currently in production.

Selling digital to LeMay

The engineers and program managers at Wright Field gathered together a briefing team and flew to Omaha to brief General LeMay. The B–52 production line was at about aircraft number 382 or so. In the briefing the team recommended the new systems be incorporated in B–52s immediately, and the old ASB–4 systems be scrapped and K system production halted.[2]

A couple of the attendees invited to this meeting were the pilot and co–pilot (student officers at the Air Force Institute of Technology getting their flying time) of the Gooney Bird (C–47) that had flown the briefing team from Wright Field to Omaha. They had no other connection with the team. This was a fairly normal practice. What followed, however, was not normal. As in all meetings there was an attendance sheet with everyone's name, rank, office symbol, and location. LeMay asked for the signup sheet for this particular meeting and then said, "You have told me to interrupt the production line, terminate installation of the K system, cease K system production, and began installing a brand new bomb–nav system in the B–52."[3] Holding the briefing attendance sheet

---

[2]K systems were the standard Air Force bomb/nav system currently in use in the B–47, and B–52s and were part of every new B–52 as it came off the production line.

[3]Digital technology, while not extremely new was still in its infancy. The specifics of digital computing and its advantages were not generally agreed to by all companies operating in the field. Obviously there was significant risk involved.

up LeMay announced, "If this turns out wrong, I want every man in this room identified, located, and fired!" Later he wrote and distributed a letter to that effect. Fortunately all turned out well enough to stave off a mass manhunt and firing!

Though Ken Hurley was not a member of that august briefing body, he did see the letter. Later Ken had the opportunity to brief LeMay on subjects related to the RS–12 and the SR–71. He clearly felt the overpowering presence of the General.

Back to ANS system memory

Emerging at the same time was the drum memory system and the disk memory system. The drum was simpler because all tracks were the same length and an equal distance from each other. The disk system presented problems of different track lengths and different bit rates at different distances from the rim. Finding data on the drum was much easier than on a disk. (As we know now, those problems were solved later to great effect.)

The drum was the favored mechanization because of the ease of finding data. In fact the Weapon System 110A, which eventually became the B–70, was originally defined with a bomb/nav system using a 32K drum memory system. When the ASG–18 radar system was designed and built by Hughes for the YF–12A, it had a drum memory system. Keep in mind that the YF–12 system led the SR–71 system by only a few months. This was a Hughes developed drum and not the IBM device. From there on, the memory trail led to solid state. That brings us to the departure point for the SR–71–based improvements to the GAM–87's astro–inertial navigation system computer.

How the SR–71 ANS got its memory

The GAM–87 nav system problem–solving needs were relatively simple compared to the computations required from the SR–71 nav system computer. The GAM–87 needed to store the necessary stars for its particular mission, needed to incorporate a ballistic table so it could back fit from the target's coordinates to the launch point, and be able to guide the B–52, acting as the missile's first stage, to that launch point. In contrast, the SR–71 nav system computer needed to store a particular mission course, all its way points, and store the intended reconnaissance target coordinates so the cameras could be pointed and operated. The system needed to incorporate any flight path modifications to avoid threat areas. It was to include the capacity to output velocity and attitude information to on–board systems and sensors. It was to store and process information needed to facilitate a proper rendezvous with refueling tankers.

The SR's mission demanded more than the original 4,000–word memory. It needed additional memory and computational capacity so the managers at Wright Field approached Hughes Aircraft. After all, they were already on the program, and there was no need to bring in another contractor to this small classified group. Hughes already had the necessary connections with Lockheed and was deeply involved in the YF–12's missile and radar. Hughes was the natural choice to do the job. So the Air Force contracted with Hughes to do the SR–71 ANS computer and memory development for incorporation in the Nortronics GAM–87 ANS system.

Things did not go well

Hughes was provided the necessary assets to start development of a computer and memory combination needed to do the SR reconnaissance job. That memory capacity was estimated by Ken Hurley and Ward Protsman and Hughes to be on the order of 8,000 words. This was about twice the capacity of the Nortronics computer used in the original GAM–87 system. Time lines were short, and the stakes were extremely high, so the Air Force kept a very close watch on the progress of each contractor. When Ken and Ward got down into the nuts and bolts of the Hughes memory design, they discovered a potentially serious problem of dropping bits when memory was being read. Further exploration of this issue led to the examination of drive ratios being used by Hughes to read and then replace the memory signals. At that point, and even now, it is not clear whether there was simply a design philosophy or an implementation concept that needed refining, but the Air Force was more goal–oriented than wanting to explore technology limitations. The U.S. needed the Blackbird capabilities and this was a time for decision making. Ken and Ward took what little information Hughes would share with them back to Wright Field and discussed it with Col. Templeton. Temp asked how they would determine whether this design approach was an acceptable risk.

Asking the experts

Because the black side of any operation has many advantages and usually cuts to the quick without messing about, Ken called a friend at IBM, an engineering manager named Del Babb. They had worked together in the 1950s with the MA–2 systems. "Del, would you mind if I came up and asked you some questions without explaining why I am asking?"

Del said, "Sure, come on up and let's talk."

Ken and Ward went to IBM and laid out everything they knew about solid state memory. They discussed drive ratios and implementation of read/write technology with Del. Without mentioning any specific program, they asked what he and his associates thought. This was a time when IBM was quite successful at the read/write business and had many cutting–edge operating systems in the field. Ken and Ward gathered all the comments and returned to Wright Field.

When they explained what they had learned at IBM. Temp said, "Take this information out to Hughes. See if you can sway them into changing their design approach in the drive ratio area." Clearly a mission to bell the cat. Hughes refused to budge on the company's design approach. Ward and Ken returned without hanging the bell. They both explained how antzy they felt and expressed their doubts. They weren't sure where to go from here.

Temp was decisive. He said, "We'll terminate Hughes." And Hughes was terminated for cause—the first time in anyone's memory that had been done to a major manufacturer. The Air Force took steps to recapture all the program assets associated with this computer development effort, the test equipment, bonded stores, spares, working bench–stock, whatever program materials there were. They effectively bundled all that material in a big box and took it over to Nortronics. They placed the box, figuratively speaking, on the desk of one George Fritzel and said, "You guys make this stuff work." This all took place in late 1961 or early 1962. It was before the R program (R–12), but at a time when design efforts for the RS–12 were under a full court press. This was not new ground for Nortronics. They were deeply involved in enabling digital conversation between digital inertial platforms managed by small digital computers. The Air Force did not tell Nortronics what size the computer had to be; they just told them what the computer had to do. Nortronics started with the 8,000–word memory but quickly decided that this was still a marginal size even with Nortronics' capability in half–word programming. Half–word programming is a technique where the accuracy of specific values can be relaxed at the benefit of having more apparent memory. This technique could significantly increase memory capacity on any particular machine at the time.

Almost coincident with this activity, Denny White arrived at the SPO at Wright Field just in time to become deeply involved in the asset capture at Hughes. Denny quickly assumed the reins and the memory was driven to 16K before the first flight of the SR–71 in December, 1964. The memory storage medium was solid state. Memory state of the art had progressed to non–destructive memory which by this time did not have to be re–charged after being read. As an interesting side point—the size of the original box set aside to house the Hughes computer was about the size of a standard shoe box. Development in memory and computer technology was progressing so rapidly during this period that the final volume occupied by the Nortronics computer was half of the original shoe box.

What about the star tracker?

The tracker came with the system and never seemed to give anyone much trouble. To assure the greatest possible line of sight, stability, and pointing accuracy, the tracker telescope was mounted on the outer gimbal of the platform. Because of its narrow field of view, it could track stars in broad daylight, a significant improvement over other systems of that day. The ANS was located immediately behind the RSO's cockpit. The tracker looked out a window on the top of the unit. When the system was mounted in the aircraft, the tracker telescope had to look out through the ANS window plus a second window mounted in the aircraft skin. The ANS could acquire and track stars before the aircraft ever left its parking place on the ramp at Edwards. During preflight for each test mission the ANS ground crew would go over to the aircrew van and let them know that the system was tracking stars and they could get ready to leave anytime.

The tracking system would be told what stars to use for that particular mission and the star catalog for only those stars would be stored in the memory. Later the navigational stars were broken up into groups needed for navigation in different geographical areas. If one was not going to be flying in the southern hemisphere, then the navigational stars used in that area of the world were not loaded.

One of the refinements within the tracking system was a reference star. This was a little bit of glow in the dark material Carbon 14 (C14)— about the size of a grain of rice—precisely located within ANS tracker compartment. Periodically the tracker telescope would seek out this star to check its mechanical alignment calibration and to be sure that its ability to determine the proper brightness and spectral color of a star was still functional and calibrated. This glowing material was slightly radioactive, comparable to what was on a wrist watch at the time. However the public health officials at Edwards had a complete hissy fit about this radioactive material. So all the ANS boxes and containers and shop doors and work areas and anything else that might be involved with this little bit of glowing material had to have huge bright yellow RADIOACTIVE MATERIAL decals pasted on them. Whenever one of the ANS systems was shipped from one location to another, even if being "shipped" aboard a deploying SR–71, the system had to be tested for leaks by using a special material rubbed over the system's integral window (a swipe test). That material was then sent to Northrop, with additional samples to Norton AFB, and a reference sample to the Edwards AFB hospital. The problem was more complex because a back–up sample was kept in the ANS shop and a sample went with the hardware, wherever that might be. All of these samples and reports were classified and required handling as classified material. Imagine everyone having to do that every time they changed the location of their glow in the dark watch. It must have made sense to someone but in retrospect it seems rather silly.

Getting the ANS ready for a flight

In a testing environment the need for full knowledge of what the ANS was doing and thinking was paramount. Actually in the operational environment the same is true because of the critical nature of ANS performance in the execution of any mission, test or operational.

The mission planning effort defined the various hot leg profiles, the coordinates of all the targets or test conditions or test points, the exact flight paths, coordinates for turn points, and other mission sensitive particulars. The mission planning cycle output directly involving the ANS was the mission tape. This was a mylar–based punched tape. With the mission tape ready and having been verified as being correct, flight preparations could begin.

The day before the flight

Warm–up, alignment, and loading of the ANS mission tape took only twenty to thirty minutes, with aircraft power supplied by an external source and air readily available supplied by an external air conditioning cart. This was normally accomplished the day before the aircraft was scheduled to fly, and was called an ANS Configuration. An ANS Configuration entailed loading the mission tape, verifying the correct mission number on the Navigation Control and Display (NCD) panel, and obtaining a quick indication the system had initialized and its internal self–test worked as advertised.

The day of the mission

The actual flight mission alignment involved approximately two hours and two ANS specialists. The ANS techs removed the star tracker window cover, installed a fully charged battery, and time hacked the chronometer in the back cockpit. They connected cooling air, power and the telemetry unit. It rarely took more than four to five minutes in southern California. After the temperature light went out, which also indicated the completion of the coarse gyro compass alignment, the NCD mode switch was put in the NAV position, beginning the internal star tracking. The ANS computer did not have sufficient memory for an exhaustive self–test program. Self–test routines were done by very sophisticated ground equipment prior to system release for the mission.

What really goes on inside?

Most single platform systems are erected by placing them in the gyro compass mode. The term erected as used here means to erect or align the platform with the local vertical. This gyro compass mode can be one of east seeking, which means that during the period of alignment the system begins to be affected by the earth's rotation. This alignment period, in the early days of inertial system development, could take hours and hours. With a pure inertial system, if the alignment is not properly done, the expectations of accurate navigation are dismal to non–existent.

A way to quickly align a system is to slave the platform to a plumb bob. The term plumb bob as used here does not mean a real one, just some sort of vertical reference such as a bubble. A system aligned using some sort of vertical reference comes up more quickly but initially is not as accurate as one erected in the gyro–compass mode. In practice some combination of the two methods is usually used.

Looking to the stars

With a system coupled with a star tracker the object is to get the platform aligned enough to acquire stars and then it can correct itself. In the test program at the later stages the average alignment time for the SR nav system was about thirty minutes. The tracker had a very narrow rectangular search pattern. It would go to the expected azimuth and elevation predicted in the loaded star tables and begin the search for whatever magnitude star it was supposed to find and track. The tracker would set up a search pattern and proceed until it had found the star it was assigned. Failing that, it would go to the next star in the program and search again. Once an assigned star was found it would begin to track that star and indicate on the RSO's control panel that it was indeed tracking a star.

Watching the system on taxi–out

Given the requirement for star acquisition and tracking before taxi–out, there was little for the system to do other than maintain star track and simply follow the aircraft change in position as the distance from the Cat II hangar the takeoff end of Runway 05 at Edwards is several miles. When the aircraft reached the takeoff end of the runway the RSO, who knew the coordinates of that spot, would compare those numbers with the present position readout from the ANS. They almost always agreed exactly.

Chapter 6

Where Does Side Looking Radar (SLR) Come From?

"If you want to invent a new radar, just give Don Beckerleg an empty black box and say 'It doesn't work.'"
Charlie Dotson, Goodyear Aerospace, 1967

"I'm sure the problem is caused by this little transistor right here. Oops, I guess we'll never know."
Don Beckerleg, Carswell AFB, flight line, 1962

T he history and development of side looking radar (SLR) is treated in more detail here because, unlike other sensors carried by the Blackbird, this sensor technology and the SR–71 came of age together, operationally speaking. Side looking radar and synthetic aperture radar offer today's recce community the best all–weather imaging sensor ever produced.

By way of clarification, side looking radar can be either coherent or non–coherent. When it is coherent, it is called synthetic aperture radar (SAR). A SAR can operate in a side–looking geometry or be "squinted" to look ahead of the aircraft beam. These modes are referred to as push broom modes, in which the physical antenna is pointed precisely to the side of the aircraft and the image is generated as the aircraft moves forward. The SAR systems that have evolved since can operate in "spotlight mode," in which the real antenna beam dwells on the target area to produce very high resolution imagery.

The SAR concept

SAR is coherent, Doppler, synthetic aperture, mapping radar. Coherent as applied here means the system remembers the frequency and phase content of every single pulse it sends out. When a pulse returns, the system compares the frequency and phase of the returned pulse with what it contained going out. Changes in phase and frequency caused by the Doppler effect are then recorded and later summed up to produce a radar image of the ground called a map.

The term synthetic aperture is used to describe the apparent length of the electronic antenna which is much longer than the physical antenna because of the way the radar signals are processed and stored. The longer the synthetic antenna, the narrower the beam width, the better the azimuth resolution of the system. The shorter the radar pulse width and the more acute the timing capabilities of the system, the better the range resolution.

In its basic form, SAR looks out at 90 degrees to its velocity vector. Remember that the velocity vector is no always exactly where the aircraft is pointed. Nailing down this true velocity vector is a significant problem in itself. One of the laws of physics says that at the instant you are exactly 90 degrees from the path of a moving body, it is getting neither closer to you nor farther away. The object's velocity along the line between it and you is exactly zero. If that body were emitting sound or electronic waves you would perceive them as exactly the same frequency as when they were transmitted by the body. At any angle other than 90 degrees, the frequency being received would be altered upward—approaching—or downward—moving away. The classic example is the pitch change of a train whistle as it approaches and then recedes. This change in apparent frequency is called a Doppler shift.

As the Blackbird screams along with its radar beam sticking out at 90 degrees, objects illuminated by that beam would return a radar pulse of exactly the same frequency as the one transmitted. Now just ahead or just behind this 90 degree beam the pulse coming back from a specific reflective object has its initial frequency changed due to the Doppler phenomenon. If the reflecting object is a little ahead of 90 degrees, then when the pulse returns, its frequency had been altered upward. That is how the word Doppler gets into the description of the radar and what happens during flight.

When the system compares (subtracts, in this case) the original frequency and its phase from the returning pulse's phase and frequency, the resulting product is called a phase history of the reflective point in question. The phase history of the point, as the beam sweeps past, is recorded on film or some magnetic media. Because these systems can only handle so much information at a time, the width of ground having its phase histories recorded is limited to a specific swath width. This is done by selecting how long after the radar pulse is sent that the radar starts to listen for the returning pulse and how long it keeps listening. The radar pulses and then only listens when the reflections are returning from a particular time segment. This time segment or swath width can be selected can be changed to obtain radar coverage of different areas of interest within the range capabilities of the system.

What makes optical correlation possible

A phase history recorded on a piece of film appears as a string of alternating opaque and transparent dots that move closer together as the reflective point making that particular phase history moves farther away from the center of the beam (either in front of or behind the beam). This set of dots becomes a frequency modulated diffraction grating. The important thing to remember from all this is that as collimated (light rays parallel to each other), monochromatic (all the same frequency or color) light is passed through a diffraction grating, it is bent (just as it would be if passed through a lens). Now if that diffraction grating is FM'ed (frequency modulated) or displays changes in the relative spacing in a consistent way, not only will the monochromatic light be bent at a predictable angle but the light passing through the grating will be focused to a point at the focal length of that grating. This phenomenon was first demonstrated by Sir Isaac Newton during his studies of optics.

So what does all that have to do with anything?

Putting all this together, here's how it works. The radar sends out a pulse and remembers that pulse's phase and frequency. When the echo from that pulse returns, it is compared to (subtracted from) the original pulse and the result is a phase history of whatever reflected that pulse in the first place. That phase history is then recorded on data film. When the data film is passed through a beam of monochromatic light and the results projected through a slit to filter (select) the angular information wanted, each phase history on the data film is projected as a point (collapsed or focused) onto another piece of film called a map film and that is what is normally seen when someone shows us a SLR map. The process of collapsing phase histories written on the data film to expose tiny tiny dots on the map film representing individual points of reflection on the ground is called optical correlation.

At the time of the SR–71 test program all the data collection from the radar and correlation was done using film as the data storage media. The ratio of data film to map film was ten inches of data film to one inch of map film. Modern systems do this all electronically. Today these signals are digitized and telemetered back to the waiting customer.

How the Blackbird SLR (GA–531) evolved

Back in 1948, the U.S. Navy wanted to detect moving things like periscopes or snorkels. Initial work was carried on at the University of Illinois where researchers discovered that one could read the difference in frequency (the Doppler shift observed in the returning pulse) caused by objects moving against a background of relatively calm sea state. These early experiments were able to show that "out there in that general direction and distance" was something moving differently from the surrounding sea. Interesting but not terribly informative. That enterprise never advanced much from the gee–whiz–look–at–that stage, nor did it spread into other research for the Navy.

The Navy also funded a companion study with experiments that attempted to use Doppler–shifted radar returns to see whether they could separate non–random events from the random sea activity. Normal sea surface activity was assumed to be random. The hope was to detect a submarine lurking just beneath the surface. Like the previous effort for periscope detection, it sank from sight.

About this same time the U.S. Air Force wanted to use radar for terminal guidance of ICBM projectiles. Just one problem: in the final phases of flight, ICBM warheads tended to tumble. This attitude instability dictated the need to create radar images of the ground without scanning or using beamed antennas.

Some guys were really clever

In 1950 Carl Wiley looked at the problem in a different way. He realized that the warhead itself might not be stable but the flight path was very predictable (a ballistic trajectory). If radar returns were collected a little at a time and then added up based on the predicted flight path, then a system could make sense out of the information. This gave rise to a coherent system nicknamed DOUSER (Doppler, Unbeamed Search Radar). Remember, a coherent radar system is nothing more than one that can remember each pulse individually so that each particular transmitted pulse and its reflected return can be compared for phase and frequency shift.

Carl was an employee of the Goodyear Aircraft Co., Akron, Ohio, when he had this revelation. He was a free spirit sort, but a deep thinker, and while maybe not the ideal employee, he did have some great ideas and unique ways of viewing various physical phenomenon.

While Carl dabbled in Doppler, a man of considerable World War I Zeppelin experience, Dr. Karl Arnstein, was sought out and recruited by Goodyear. The Ohio–based company had significant interests in the dirigible market. Arnstrum became a chief scientist at the Goodyear Aircraft Co. of Akron and recognized Carl as a real rare asset. Arnstrum arranged to have Carl moved to the Goodyear facility at Litchfield Park, Arizona, before higher–ups in the company fired him or the other employees did him serious bodily harm. As I said, he was not the ideal employee.

This sleepy little town was the center for Goodyear's flight test operations. Goodyear Aircraft Co. was located beside the runways of Litchfield Park Naval Air Station. In this new and less bureaucratic environment Carl had considerable freedom to think and work on his new radar concept. The DOUSER was tested as a terminal guidance system for Atlas ICBMs. First test–flown in a C–47, it was without a doubt, the primary ancestor of modern coherent side looking radars. Various versions of DOUSER were tested from 1955 through 1962.

Charlie Dotson transferred from Goodyear, Akron, to the company operation at Litchfield Park to participate in flight test programs on early radars. An Akron employee since August, 1951, he arrived at Litchfield Park in March, 1954. Charlie signed on as employee number thirteen for Goodyear's Arizona–based operation. In June, 1954 Charlie became the flight test engineer for DOUSER.

Don Beckerleg applied at Goodyear's Litchfield Park facility for any job having to do with flight test. There were no openings, but because he listed photography as a hobby on his application, the company offered him a job as a photographer's assistant. Don signed on with the company in September, 1951.

These two men's careers embody the life and development of side looking radar as we know it today.

Climbing the stairs to technical complexity

The DOUSER radar did not use photographic film as a storage medium or an optical correlator to process the stored information. None of that had been invented yet. It wrote, electronically speaking, radar pulse Doppler histories on a storage tube vertically and then read the results horizontally, in effect summing up the Doppler history of many pulses from a particular range. The system used two storage tubes in tandem, while one was being read, the other was having the next histories written on it.

While Carl had breathed life into the initial DOUSER, he got itchy feet and moved on to join a venture capitalist and faded from the scene to form his own company and pursue other interests. His system patents were owned by Goodyear and assigned to the Government, so the world moved ahead without him.

E.O. Hartig, Ph.D., tells it like it is

Coherent–Doppler radar had always been described and explained in the arcane language and terms of physics. The concepts had been thought out and explored by physicists and technical papers of the time presented coherent radar as a wholly owned phenomenon of physics. Much was published in the scientific journals of the time and many papers were presented at academic symposia.

Then a significant event occurred, not in hardware development nor in the mechanization of radar systems, but in the way coherent radar and signal characteristics were viewed. Enter Dr. E.O. Hartig. E.O. left his University of Michigan (UofM) position and came to work for the Goodyear Aircraft Co. The company readily admits that E.O. perpetrated one of the greatest acts of assistance to every Goodyear radar competitor. He explained coherent Doppler radar, not in the convoluted jargon of the physicist, but for the first time, in terms of what really was taking place. He pictured the system as effectively having this great long synthetic (imaginary) array (antenna) and the pulses were summed up piece by piece for the length of this make–believe antenna as it moved along at 90 degrees to the major axis of the antenna. To E.O. 's credit he was able to visualize and describe the system's operational physics in a way that engineers and technicians could understand and implement. This is the same E.O. Hartig who had been a part of the MANHATTAN Project during World War II. When Ken briefed him on the SR–71 program, he commented that this was a better kept secret than the MANHATTAN program had been. He hadn't a clue about what was going on right under his nose at Litchfield Park. Even his own people had not leaked the story to him.

Emmit Leith, working for the University of Michigan, invented the concept of optical correlation and the optical correlator. The UofM built the finest correlators known to man, but it was Goodyear who designed and built correlators that were practical for operational use. This was a major step forward in converting a clever concept to something with hard cold applications throughout the military world.

The Army, Navy, and Air Force all rowed the boat

All three services pushed system designs but individual objectives varied the direction and results of their research. The Navy fell out quite early when it could not find a cast iron application in their search to distinguish random sea surfaces from non–random sea surfaces caused by submarines or other underwater disturbances.

The Army had by far the best long–range plans for SLR. They had well–defined goals and applications but fell short on funding. Although the Army's continued development of radar systems and introduction into the operational inventory fell by the wayside in favor of cannons, tanks, and other more immediately needed weapons, it did field some good systems made by Motorola. The APS–94 was mounted in the Army's OV–1D Mohawk. The Army also funded development of a Philco radar which used an acoustic delay line processor. The Philco system was flown in twin–engine Beech aircraft. In reality, the Army was much more interested in detecting moving objects, especially tanks moving toward them, than in generating displayable, high definition radar–generated maps of the ground. Their early systems produced no humanly readable output such as a map or other representational product. The outputs were electronic in nature and served as comparisons to other electronic signal matrixes.

The Air Force and big–time radar

The Air Force was interested in making radar maps for map–matching terminal guidance for ICBMs as well as IRBMs. The cruise missile, Mace, was another example. Mission planners were looking ahead toward increased offensive capacity. They wanted to develop an air–to–ground, "find'em–shoot'em" capability in a single aircraft. This system would use airborne coherent imaging radar to discover, identify, assess, and guide a missile to kill enemy ground targets. These concepts were at the root of RS–12 application studies. This same find–and–kill idea was basic to implementation of the RS–70. Much was at stake operationally for the Air Force and it looked to this new radar capability as the key to new survivable methods of accurately delivering standoff offensive weapons. (It was 1962, during the RS–12 studies, when Ken Hurley brought a bag of money, figuratively speaking, to the Goodyear plant at Litchfield Park and first met Charlie Dotson.)

Technology began to catch up with the need

Next came refinement in storing phase histories on film instead of storage tubes or magnetic drums and integrating those phase histories (correlating) into a useable radar image of the ground. A major push was initiated to refine this capability with the Air Force taking the lead role.

A series of radars, based on the design principals flowing from DOUSER and the concept of coherence, burst to life from the Goodyear plant. A family of experimental radars designated APS–73 was funded through a progression of Air Force research and development efforts. These technology steps and demonstration systems were designated the APS–73, XH–1 through the XH–4.

The XH–1 first flew in a B–29. If it had a project name or nickname it has been forgotten.

The XH–2, with some refinements, flew in a B–50. No identifying project name was found for this experimental program either.

The XH–3, which followed the –2, was first flown in a C–97 for system operational evaluation. This was the system that generated the short strip of 35mm film that Charlie showed Ken on that first visit in 1962. After a period of flight testing to prove the system to be functional, the XH–3 was modified to a five–inch film–based system and installed in a B–58 weapons system pod. The B–58 and its other pod–mounted sensor systems began life as a program known as MONTICELLO. The initial intent of this program was to quickly make radar maps of large expanses of territory. The XH–3 system capabilities reflected that desire. It could map both sides of the flight path at the same time with large swath widths.

Some history from Charlie Dotson

"The XH–3 utilized the first airborne inertial navigation system (INS). This INS was developed by Draper Labs for submarine applications, was painted Navy Gray (naturally) and weighed close to one ton. The C–97 was selected for the SAR/INS flight test because it was one of the few aircraft that could handle the size and weight of the equipment.

"This INS used a mechanical analog computer consisting of many motors, gear trains, and resolvers. It never failed, but then on the other hand, I'm not too sure we ever got it to work."

Meanwhile back at the…

Air Force interest in the reconnaissance–strike role was building. The RS–70 was being talked about in the Pentagon and the Congress. And as so often happens, the R&D community hooks its sled to the fastest moving program. The Congress was talking about money to explore RS concepts. To accommodate this shift in the political wind, MONTICELLO became QUICK CHECK and was ultimately flown on a Mach 2 demonstration mission against Cuba.

When the radar imagery from this flight was collected and processed it was classified SECRET. Don Beckerleg was instructed to get this film to the project manager at Wright Field ASAP. After an all–night processing binge and taking the red eye to Dayton, and with this SECRET material chained to his wrist (figuratively speaking), he finally reached the desk of the Wright Field engineer. To Don's consternation the engineer briefly looked at the map film and said in a rather dismissive manner, "The data blocks are crooked."

Wright Field will always be Wright Field and every contractor has experienced this turnoff in one way or another.

The APS–73 flight test programs except the B–58, MONTICELLO/ QUICK CHECK, were based at the Litchfield Naval Air Station. During the early days Ken was able to funnel money into the flagging C–97 program to keep it flying and generating data while the RS–12 study progressed.

Jump on the 665A sled for the next ride

With a few refinements and some additional improvements the XH–3 was converted to the XH–4 system when QUICK CHECK breathed its last. All the assets were taken from the QUICK CHECK B–58 operation at Fort Worth directly to W–PAFB and many of those pieces of hardware went directly into the XH–4, which was installed in a JKC–135, tail number 596.

By 1963 the art and science of optical correlation was firmly founded. Goodyear was building SLR systems for the RF–4. The Air Force threw itself headlong into multispectral sensor exploration and behind the scenes was a black program benefiting from all that had gone on in the open. The RS–12 people pulled strings and pumped up priorities for relevant research programs.

Enter the In–flight Correlator Processor (ICP)

An essential part of the recce–strike concept and implementation was the development of an in–flight, near–real–time ability to collect, process and display radar ground maps. It would have been simpler to do instant photo or electro–optical processing but that was no good in the dark or through the clouds and the same problem was true with infrared. So the In–flight Correlator Processor (ICP) was born. This device recorded and processed SLR data film, performed optical correlation, exposed a map film, processed that map film, and displayed the result on an airborne console in the same aircraft.

As Norm Drake, one of the pillars of the SR–71 Cat II test program, used to say about other things, "If there was ever a case of twenty–seven pounds of technological malorganite in a five–pound bag, this was it."

Because Goodyear, in general, and Charlie Dotson and Don Beckerleg, in particular, were on the advancing flood to marry in–flight correlation and rapid film development technology, the task of ICP fabrication, and flight test support fell to them.

Working both sides of the street

Like the rest of the 665A sensor contractors, Goodyear developed the APS–73, XH–4 in parallel with the onrushing black development of sensors for the RS–12, later the R–12, and finally announced as the SR–71.

The black program radar was named the Goodyear Aerospace–531, or GA–531.

Every program at Goodyear was assigned a block of numbers to identify that program's drawings. The number 531 was nothing more than the first group of the assigned drawing number series. So now you know.

One last bit of trivia. The center frequency of the GA–531 radar was chosen to be a little different from the then–operational APQ–102, a small side looker flown on RF–4s. It was a little different, but not enough to allow enemy ECM operators to readily distinguish the 531 as a unique system.

Chapter 7

Electronic Intelligence

"Instead of having this two day discussion, to avoid the alpha–numerics coming out backwards and then having them come out backwards anyway, why don't we just see how they come out and if they're backwards or mirror image, we can fix it on the spot by reversing two wires."
Don Beckerleg, Goodyear Aerospace, 1962

"We'll just fly this system against the emitters on Wake Island and then no one will get confused about what is on the ground."
Clint Butler, 665A Program, 1963

While there were some attempts to incorporate electronic signal collection and analysis in QUICK CHECK, there is little historical data around to describe the system or the results. The family origins for the Electronic Intelligence System (ELINT) in the SR–71 first appear in the sensor suite of 665A. The bloodline flows from one contractor.

Airborne Instrument Laboratories (AIL) was contracted to build a companion electronic signal collection system for the 665A program. Their design was compatible with other sensor systems and target acquisition methods intended for the prototype reconnaissance/strike system in support of various RS–70 studies.

How hard can this be?

The concept in 665A was a simple one. The AIL system would detect emitters, classify them as antiaircraft radars (AAA), search or surveillance radars, or tracking radars used for ground–to–air missile guidance. The information from the AIL system was processed and each type of emitter intended for display was given a letter of the alphabet. If emitters were similar in characteristics to a threat emitter but not classifiable, they would be shown on the film as a "U." All other emitters were to be rejected by this system. These letter designators were exposed on film, processed through one of the onboard processing systems, scanned, and then projected electronically on the operator's display console. Through electronic magic based upon antenna patterns, signal strength, and number of samples, the AIL system could approximate the distance and location of the sensed emitters. Geographical position was reflected by where and when the letter representing the emitter was written on the moving film.

When the emitter–designating letter was projected on the console display it would be superimposed over the radar, or electro–optical, or infrared ground map. The intent was to provide a clue to the observer that something was in that location and further examination of the other sensor outputs covering that area was needed. It would help the operator make a decision as to whether the imaged target area and the emitter belonged together. The ELINT information provided another clue to identify the target and its level of threat to the sensing aircraft or desirability as a target to be attacked with one of the computer–resident–only missiles carried by the 665A JKC–135.

Information overload

The application of ELINT output was simple, the mechanization of getting the output to the operator for decision–making was direct, but there were too many emitters along the test flight paths within the U.S. to be able to sort out all that information. The JKC–135 was flown against a known family of emitters at Rome Air Development Center (RADC). These select emitters had every characteristic and signal nuance assigned to the AIL box for detection and classification. Again, there were too many other emitters in the Rome, New York, area and the system became confused or just plain refused to provide the appropriate letter code in the right geographic location on the display.

After about ten frustrating flights, Captain Clint Butler, a C–124 pilot with many hours cruising the Pacific, decided the only place to go was Wake Island so there would be no emitters around except those on the island, and we could narrow those down for each test flight. This plan for our winter vacation in the tropics was nixed by one of the supervisory civil servants as too risky. It would involve long overwater flights.

"What will you do if you lose an engine?"

"Fly on the other three, "Clint answered.

It was not to be. Throughout the 665A program we continued the unsuccessful struggle to sort out the threat emitters from the literally hundreds of other emitters the system would pick up.

At one point Clint directed AIL to print out the results of a particular series of flights against RADC and identify the emitters and characteristics stored in the 665A system tapes. They dutifully brought the printouts to Wright Field and dropped them on his desk. It was all in hex and octal. It was just as meaningless to us in the comfort of our offices as it had been in the air during the missions.

Other AIL ELINT efforts were much more successful. There was another system under development at the same time. This was no five–foot tall, two–foot–wide gray box with a few blinking lights on the front like its poor 665A cousin. The new system filled an entire C–135 and weighed a little over 10,000 pounds. It was designated the ASD–1. Probably because it was contracted for and managed under the careful guidance of the Aeronautical Systems Division. The ASD–1 went from development prototype to operational duty in short order.

The ASD–1 system was filled with state of the art electronics, magical antennas, and tape recorders. It flew the world collecting electronic intelligence and communication signals. It was a roaring success in collecting information. The problem fell in the area of reducing the taped data to something useable by the intelligence community, mission planners, and specialists who made assessments of enemy capabilities.

When the SR–71 ELINT system arrived at Edwards for flight test in 1966 it was a miniaturized version of the ASD–1. The system was divided into two major boxes and mounted on two SR–71 sensor bay doors, one left side and one right side. It weighed ten times less than the original ASD–1, was about twenty times smaller in volume, was designed to fly seven times faster than its parent system, and operate at two times the mission altitude. By integrating the electronic collection system with the highly accurate SR–71 navigation system and the stability of the Blackbird as a platform at cruise, many of the ASD–1 problems disappeared. The Blackbird's EW systems were flown in both Cat I and Cat II aircraft.

One final comparison

During a series of missions off the Vietnam coast, the ASD–1 was flown against a certain area and detected five emitters of a particular category. At the same time the SR–71 covered that same area and detected and documented twenty–four emitters of the same class. The Blackbird's ears showed a significant improvement over the listening capabilities of its parent system. And you can take that to the bank!

Chapter 8

How the SR-71 got its Infrared (IR) System

*"We called Air Products in Allentown and asked about the
availability of liquid neon. When I told him how much we needed,
he said there was not that much liquid neon in the entire U.S."*
Dean Poeth, talking of the early days at HRB,[1] 1999

*"We tech reps were sent into the field to make things work.
The phrase 'Make it work' was a gross understatement"*
**Jerry Hogan, retired HRB tech rep,
reflecting on a life well spent, 1999**

I magine a long horizontal box with a crosswise slit in the bottom at
one end. Directly above this slit is a front surface scanning mirror.
The angled mirror spins on a horizontal axis. For high altitude
systems there is only one surface on the mirror at 45 degrees to the
rotating axis. Now imagine a series of other mirrors and lenses to focus
the image of the ground reflected from the scanning mirror. The image
of that spot is then optically projected onto the surface of the detector.
The detector instantaneously senses the relative intensity of the IR
radiation emanating from that particular spot on the ground. As the
mirror spins, the viewable spot flies from one side of the scan to the
other, across the flight path of the aircraft. As the aircraft advances, so
does the film used to record the detector output from a single line on
the face of a cathode ray tube. The film advances at a rate proportional
to the speed and the altitude of the aircraft. The film's rate of advance
is driven by the ratio of velocity over height (V/H). The rotational rate

---

[1]Haller, Raymond, and Brown (HRB) started out as a small company in State College, Pennsylvania,
founded by three Penn Staters. Their specialties were ELINT and infrared imaging systems.

of the mirror remains constant, generating a single scan of the ground for every revolution.

Infrared imaging systems are judged in their performance by two primary measurements, how little is the scanned spot size, the smaller the better, and how small a temperature difference can be detected. The differences in temperature to an IR system are analogous to the differences in shades of gray to a camera and film operating in the visual portion of the spectrum. One very important thing to remember is that an IR map (the output image on the film) looks deceptively like an optical photograph. It is not. What is presented on the film is a thermal map of the ground. The image contrast is made by temperature differences between one piece of ground and the next.

The HRB–Singer IR system lineage

In the 1960s there were three serious providers of IR mapping systems, Honeywell, Texas Instruments, and HRB–Singer. The Blackbird line of the IR family comes from HRB–Singer ancestry, and the nearest traceable relative began its life in the QUICK CHECK B–58 pod–borne system. That system was a non–complex system cooled by liquid nitrogen and operated pretty much as the system–in–a–box described above. Using that experience, HRB was able to successfully bid on and capture an R&D contract to design and develop a side-looking IR system to be installed in the 665A aircraft. From there, in a seemingly unrelated (but someone knew it was related) twist of fate, came the eventual hardware that served in the SR–71. An additional side trip was made into the X–15 program where the window material, IRTRAN IV, was tested to see how it behaved at high heats and in a stressful aerodynamic environment. But we are getting ahead of the story.

Dave Harris, a program manager at HRB–Singer, got his first taste of the Blackbird way of doing business one evening. Looking back we recognize the modus operandi. I spoke to Dave on the phone, and here is how he described the first steps toward the SR–71's IR system.

"In mid 1963 I got a phone call one night from Bob Riddle, who was involved with the ELINT side of the HRB–Singer Corporation. He asked if he could come over and talk to me that evening. When I answered his knock on my door he led me back out to the street. We sat in his car and he explained what sort of system might be needed by something that might appear at some time in the future and what the environment might be like aboard that something. He suggested that we, HRB–Singer and I, write an unsolicited proposal about an IR system with some cutting–edge capabilities that would satisfy those conditions. Then he further suggested (it was considerably stronger than a suggestion) that I hand–carry the proposal down to Wright Field and deliver it to someone named Ken Hurley."

Dave said he did not remember any formal submission process. They just delivered the study/proposal to this guy at Wright Field down in the basement of some building.

Very shortly after delivery of the proposal the company was notified that it might be a good thing if they were to start work on their proposed system. A contract followed. The first prototype was delivered to Lockheed for integration into the SR–71 in 1964.

Life really began with 665A

While in the overall scheme of things the IR system was one of the least troublesome, it did provide several of the most interesting activities and anecdotes of the entire program. More are discussed in the *Category II* Section.

Engineers are funny people. Some are very conservative and are always telling exactly why something is too tough or cannot be done. Others are cursed with an optimistic imagination that says, "Hey, there just might be a way to do that." It is because of this latter bunch that we went to the moon, to the bottom of the Marianas Trench, and we cruised an aircraft at Mach 3.2 at 80,000 feet.

Some equally creative engineers at Air Products in Philadelphia, Pennsylvania, took on a 665A Program requirement for the IR system to hold the detector at liquid nitrogen (LN_2) temperature ($-196°c$) for a full twelve–hour mission by designing a closed–cycle cooling system. This unit would keep exactly one strawberry sized object super cold for an almost indefinite period. It had two operating gases and was a two–stage system taking advantage of the individual gas properties. One of the gases was neon, the other was nitrogen. When I went to pick up a large bottle of neon at the local welding supply in Dayton (about the third purchase that week), the man behind the counter asked, "Just how many signs are you making anyway?"

The good news was this clever system took only about thirty to forty minutes to cool the detector down to its operating temperature. The bad news was that early on, the mean time to failure of this little system, the size of a vw engine, was about thirty minutes. Sometimes it lasted longer and other times it failed sooner. Very seldom did it start a mission let alone finish one but that is not the point. That effort proved beyond a doubt that a closed–cycle system was not practical for liquid helium systems, and therefore provided motivation to design and build liquid helium detector/dewars that would last for an eight–hour SR–71 mission. Later, under the kind and loving care of Jerry Hogan, the HRB field rep to 665A, this little system became more reliable.

In the 665A aircraft pre–flight prep sequence, one of the steps was to fire up the closed–cycle cooler to see whether it was going to get with the program that day. This aircraft, a JKC–135, tail number 596, and support systems were located on the ramp at Patterson Field while the program office and engineers were situated at Wright Field. The two locations were separated by only a few miles but still remained a barrier to various activities needed to support the flight test. Operation of the HRB–Singer IR system was one of those.

The pre–flight plan, if the cooler failed, was for the sensor engineer (Byrnes) to pick up a couple of thermos jugs of LN_2 as a substitute for the installed cooling system and bring them to Patterson Field in time for the mission takeoff. This plan B also required changing the detector and cooling assembly.

While you're up, would you please hand me that jug of LN_2

Picking up a thermos or two of LN_2 was not like getting a Coke at the local convenience store. It went something like this:

At Wright Field there was an environmental chamber wherein cameras could be subjected to conditions expected in outer space. It was a rather large vacuum chamber with a window for the camera to look out and many feet of tubing to run liquid nitrogen through to simulate the cold of outer space. The other side of the inner part of this chamber had heating elements to simulate the direct thermal radiation effects of the sun. The work and the chamber were the brainchild of one Wright Field engineer named Haley. Thus the machine itself was nicknamed Haley's Comet. The engineers at Haley's Comet always had plenty of LN_2 stored in huge thermo–trailers out back. The man in charge of the trailer and chief dispenser of LN_2 was casual to a fault. The spigot, outlet spout if you will, on one of those trailers was about an inch and a half in diameter. It was always a thrill to get a couple of small–necked thermos bottles filled. You always wore boots. We would usually show up in a great hurry and ask to have our two half–gallon vacuum bottles filled. The hole in the tops of the jugs was almost as large as the truck valve opening.

"Just set one of them down there," he would say, while pointing at a spot just below the spigot. "Now stand back." When he opened the valve there was a great hissing and fizzing sound as the stream of cryogenic liquid hit the warm jug and the ground around it. There was no point in trying to see what was happening. Everything below our waists was fogged out of view by the vaporous cloud caused by the liquid nitrogen. After a minute or two he would shut it off and wave away the clouds to find our poor little jug caked in icy stalagmites and frozen to the ground. Using heavy gloves we retrieved the filled jug and put the second in its place to repeat the process. "That ought to do it," he would say after deluging the second thermos with a fire–hose stream of liquid nitrogen. Once both were filled, the containers were lightly capped and put in a cardboard box on the passenger side of the car so they wouldn't spill, and we were off to Patterson Field and the waiting JKC–135.

The system in 665A had another wrinkle. The output film, after being exposed by a single line scan across a cathode ray tube, was instantly processed on board the aircraft. The processed and still wet film was passed through a liquid gate, which amounted to a sealed (but a few drips here and there as the film passed through) area with glass on both top and bottom. A light on the bottom of this gate illuminated the film passing through and a TV camera on the upper side captured the image which was then displayed on the operator's console along with images from other sensors. The film processors were made by ANSCO, a film and photo hardware company located in Binghamton, New York, and were more or less off the shelf.

To meet the needs of the reconnaissance–strike concept demonstration study, the Air Force had taken a perfectly good scanning infrared system and turned it into a nightmare of leaking chemicals and cranky electronics. The film needed for recording the IR signals from a CRT had, of course, a non–standard emulsion and was patiently provided by ANSCO. As is pretty much the case under such circumstances, the film was too slow, i.e., the emulsion was not sensitive enough in the color given off by the CRT phosphor that would produce the smallest spot sizes. This was not a shortcoming of the ANSCO product, this was just the way things were with respect to the laws of physics, P–11 phosphor, and the world of film chemistry. The only available answer was to drive the electron gun at the back of the CRT with a higher voltage making the spot brighter. This worked most of the time but if the scan input stopped and the spot lingered in one place on the tube face for a while, it would overheat the face of the CRT and cause the tube face to crack. The CRTs were $5,000 a pop (no pun intended). We went through a few of those. Finally, Dave Harris, back at the HRB ranch, designed and produced a circuit board that blanked the CRT when the spot–sweep failed.

Things continued to roll along in the back of the 665A aircraft, while at the home office in State College, Pennsylvania, and out at the Skunk Works, people were pressing on with another scanning IR system. As always, the environment to be experienced in the aircraft gave the designers and engineers fits.

Seeing the ground might be a problem

While Harris and friends started on the new system design and prototype fabrication, they voiced their concerns as to how this heat–sensitive system was going to be looking out of a window heated to about 450° Fahrenheit. Imagine trying to see something on a dark night while holding a burning magnesium flare next to your eye. Others were working and thinking about this problem as well.

When Kelly Johnson was approached with the idea that an open slit could be used to avoid the window problem all together, he was skeptical. A cavity and slit for specific aerodynamic conditions could conceivably be designed. However, Kelly said, "For all other conditions you would have the world's fastest whistle." That shot a hole in the open–slit concept!

Ordinary light need not pass through an IR window

The criteria for an IR window is that it be transparent to the infrared wavelengths to be seen by the detector and also that it not generate radiation in the same wavelength band. There is no requirement for this material to pass the visual spectrum. There were several window materials around. Their proprietary names were IRTRAN I through V. Each was a different composition to be transparent to different wavelengths of infrared radiation. There was one material that seemed to have the correct characteristics. The material was zinc selenide. (IRTRAN IV). It came in a powder and had to be pressed under great pressure to form a solid material. The output of this process were disks about six inches in diameter and about ½–inch thick. Eastman Kodak was the only U.S. company with the capability to press and produce this material, so a contract was let to get the disks done. The pressed disks were sent to the Skunk Works where they were trimmed into rectangular pieces and mounted in a titanium frame to make a window of about four inches wide by roughly twenty inches long. Each window had four segments and cost about $10,000. There was no easy way to bond the segments, so they were carefully polished on the edges and butted against each other. Then a high–temperature epoxy was used to hold them together. The seams became a problem later and the epoxy bonding, because it radiated in the wrong IR wavelength when heated, was abandoned early on in favor of a very close–fitting process without any added material.

Additional problem solving required

By the summer of 1964, Jerry Hogan had been freed from bondage as a 665A slave riding in the back of a JKC–135 on ten–hour missions and was assigned as the HRB tech rep on the X–15 IR system being flown out of the NASA facility at Edwards. His buddy and fellow 1964 T–Bird driver was Bill Engle, the HRB tech rep on the SR–71 system.

Together these two, with engineering help from the HRB at State College, Pennsylvania, worked the early problems of window and system compatibility. Lockheed rigged up a window in their lab in Burbank so it could be heated and the spectral emissions measured. This test program and initial flights in the X–15 and SR–71 showed that the window did radiate in the wrong frequency. Yes, the seams in the windows did cause a problem and yes, the detector could see its own reflection in the back surface of the window. The solution, an elegant one, to the window radiation problem was the brainchild of Dave Harris. He saw from measurements made in the Lockheed lab that a dual detector with sensitivities in two wavelengths would solve the problem. One detector saw the window radiation and "subtracted" that from the output of the main detector. Presto—clean IR video signals. The problem of the detector seeing its reflection in the back of the window was corrected by tilting the detector/dewar slightly.

These changes came as a direct result of the data collected on the X–15 program and testing in the Skunk Works lab. Another interesting aspect of the X–15 program was that the HRB system had to be installed and buttoned up three days before the flight. This left no opportunity to top off the level of cryogenic coolant in the detector dewar. The solution was to substitute liquid neon for liquid helium. It just was not possible to retain sufficient liquid helium (–269°C) over that period of time and still have enough remaining to fly the mission. The boil–off rate was less than that for liquid helium and the temperature of liquid neon (–246°C) was sufficiently low to put the detector into its proper sensitivity range. There were three or four system flights made on the X–15 before sufficient information was collected and the experiment dropped.

The remainder of the IR story is told in the Category II Testing Section.

Chapter 9

The Pressure Suit Story

*"There we were, Scotty Crossfield and I, in the bomb bay
of this B–29 at 30,000 feet, dressing Marion Carl
in his pressure suit so he could set a world
altitude record in the D558–2."*
Joe Ruseckas, remembering past events, 1999

*"If there is anyone who can tell you about pressure
suits and the early days, it's Jack Bassick
at the David Clark Company."*
Tom Bowen, long–time pressure suit
support legend, Beale AFB, 1998

T he quest started with a phone call to a long–time friend, Scott
Willey, docent at the Garber and Dulles Facilities of the
Smithsonian's National Air and Space Museum. Scott asked
Tom Alison, Chief, Collections Division at the National Air and Space
Museum for help. Tom is an ex–Blackbird pilot. Tom said to call Tom
Bowen at Beale.

I spoke to Tom Bowen.

He said, "There is one guy that can really tell you about pressure suits
and their history, it is Jack Bassick at David Clark Company in Worcester,
Massachussetts. Jack was the David Clark suit rep at the Ranch back in the
early, early days. He finally moved back east to work at the company plant.
Ended up as Executive Vice President or something. Just tell him Tom
Bowen said to call. He knows the whole thing inside and out."

I called and Jack invited me to visit David Clark in Worcester and
am I glad I did.

103

Basic altitude physiology

There are two great absolutes associated with man's exploration of the lower pressure realms in the upper atmosphere. The first one occurs about 43,000 feet and the second kills the unprotected above 63,000 feet.

The first number is the altitude at which even 100 percent oxygen will not allow the lungs to absorb enough oxygen to sustain consciousness and eventually life. Without what is called pressure breathing, there is no way the average pilot can live above the 43,000 foot level in an unpressurized compartment. The good news is, if a little extra pressure is applied to the breather's mask and forces the oxygen into the lungs at a positive pressure, the problem of insufficient oxygen in the blood can be delayed to a higher altitude. The bad news is the breather must exhale forcefully to expel his breath and then relax to let the next breath be jammed into his lungs from the pressurized mask. This pressure breathing is conducted under very low mask pressures, usually equivalent to the weight of a column of water about five inches high. Imagine blowing a five–inch plug of water out of your snorkel in the swimming pool each time you exhaled, and doing that for a couple hours or more. It represents a complete reversal of man's physiology with respect to breathing. Even the most skilled and hardened aircrew members cannot pressure–breathe for extended periods of time before becoming fatigued.

The higher number, 63,000 feet, is the altitude at which blood boils at body temperature. At that altitude bubbles form in the blood and death results almost instantly. No creature can survive such a situation. Clearly, the answer to safe, reasonably comfortable, and sustainable aircrew protection for high altitude flight lay in the development of a device that would pressurize the body so it never experienced the need to pressure–breathe for extended periods or be exposed to low pressures causing boiling blood.

Events leading to the solution of these issues and a search by Mr. David M. Clark for the perfect G–suit leads us to discovering how pressure suits were developed and in particular how the Blackbird family of full pressure suits (FPS) evolved.

It didn't start with a full pressure suit

Well, actually it did start with a full pressure suit. It started in 1935 with Wiley Post and the very first high altitude suit ever invented and used in an aircraft. The development of the FPS showcases a who's who of remarkable individuals in the aerospace industry. Our story would not be complete without a brief discussion of the very first full pressure suit. That suit, developed jointly by B.F. Goodrich and aviation pioneer Wiley Post, highlighted the primary truths about full pressure suits.

B. F. Goodrich and Wiley Post take the first steps

Just being inside a big thick pressurized rubber bag was not the right answer for someone needing finger dexterity and reasonable mobility of the body extremities for aircraft flying. Wiley's Suit Number One was little more than a vulcanized rubber deep sea diver's suit with a specialized helmet attached at the neck ring. When this suit was inflated to the necessary pressure, Wiley became almost immobile. There was also an issue of suit ventilation or venting. It is no fun sitting in a hot stinky rubber bag for hours at a time when there is little or no airflow to provide cooling and moisture removal. With that knowledge under their belts, they moved on.

Wiley's Suit Number Two illustrated that making the suit fit tighter around the body, so when inflated it did not impede movement of the arms and legs, was not only a step in the wrong direction but created a whole new set of inner suit environmental problems. During testing, the ventilation problem had still not been addressed. As Wiley's body heated up the confined space of this non–vented, non–breathable rubber bag, he began to sweat, his body swelled, and out popped some low level claustrophobic tendencies. He became quite agitated and displayed considerable stress. And, because of the tight fitting suit, his increasing body heat, and slight body swelling, he could not get out of the suit the same way he got in. Have you ever tried to get out of a scuba wet suit when you were hot and sweaty? Wiley demanded the ability to be removed from the suit quickly. As he became more and more distraught, the solution was not to struggle more but to quickly cut the suit away from his body. So much for Suit Number Two.

Suit Number Three, the one he eventually flew with, highlighted the ability of Mr. Post and the Goodrich people to learn and improve based on experience. That third and final suit embodied some of the basic FPS elements present in current pressure suits used by everyone, from SR–71 and U-2R aircrews to moon–exploring astronauts.

The really basic FPS elements

Some form of longjohns to help absorb or wick away body moisture and to prevent body contact with the pressure layer.

A ventilating system inside the pressure layer to deal with the buildup of body heat and moisture in this small confined space was a must to provide airflow paths for suit venting.

On top of all that, literally, a bladder–restraint garment to hold the inflated pressure suit in the proper geometry around the joints of the arms, legs, and fingers, to permit useful movement and mobility.

And finally, an overgarment to protect the inner layers and restraint system from dirt, abrasion, tearing, puncture, and any other mechanical damage that would compromise the physical integrity of the pressure layer.

Suit Number Three incorporated all that and worked. Wiley Post flew and set records. And in these early developments, he and B.F. Goodrich of Akron, Ohio, laid the first cornerstones for full pressure suit technology.

SR–71 pressure suits grew from three roots

First came the partial pressure suit (PPS). Actually the PPS began with an idea to place a bladder across the chest to pressurize the outside of the chest cavity at the same pressure as the inbound pressurized breathing oxygen, thus alleviating the pressure imbalance between inside and outside the chest cavity. This was to solve the problem of early fatigue with pressure breathing. The concept was successfully demonstrated in an altitude chamber and delayed serious hypoxia to about 55,000 feet or so.

Giving credit where credit is due

No story about full pressure suits in general, or SR–71 pressure suits in particular, can be told without acknowledging the pivotal role played by a small company situated in the heart of New England. The roots of all Blackbird suits start at the David Clark Company. There in the quiet unassuming mill town of Worcester, Massachussetts, in a building constructed in 1890, is a remarkable operation combining leading edge technology and personal dedication that has sustained American high altitude aircrews in all their endeavors. David Clark Co. is the only game in town if you want to fly a high altitude aircraft. If you need a full pressure suit to fly an aircraft or ride a spacecraft this is the only place in the western world where you can get a fully matured, quality suit. That is the way it was then and that is the way it is today.

On the fourth floor of this building with its high bays, where the echoes of both leather manufacturing and knitting machines died decades ago, on creaky wooden floors stained by years and years of lanolin and sweeping compound, resides one of the most remarkable enterprises in the aerospace industry. The pressure suit business is not one of high volume but one of excruciatingly careful preparation and extremely high–quality one–at–a–time production. Because of this, there are essentially no subcontractors. The David Clark Co. makes and refurbishes every piece, every part, every helmet, every visor, every neck ring, and on and on. Time after time, subcontractors and vendors have learned all they wanted to know about exacting quality standards and difficult design problems. One by one they bowed out leaving the David Clark Co. to pick up the slack.

Ultimately the result is good for the customer. This little company turns to and succeeds in producing a better, safer, lighter, more user friendly piece of protective equipment. This small company still does some things because "it is the right thing to do." This organization represents the very embodiment of spirit and dedication permeating the companies and individuals involved throughout the Blackbird's development and operational life.

The David Clark Co. is the only company involved in the original development of the Blackbird that still goes by the same name. It is privately owned by a group of employees. Their goal is to make the best product humanly possible, sustain their sterling reputation, and provide service to their aircrew and astronaut customers worldwide. If you have ever done any flying at high altitude then your life has literally been in the hands of this small group of dedicated people in Worcester, Massachussetts.

Aircrews are indoctrinated and familiarized with their suits in an altitude chamber. One set of conditions everyone must experience is an explosive decompression to about 78,000 feet. In this situation there is only the pressure suit between the person in the chamber and certain death. That may sound a little overdramatic, but in the final analysis that is the way it is. From an aviator's point of view, these are the kind of people you want making and maintaining your personal equipment when your life literally depends on it. Above 63,000 feet if the suit makes one little hiccup, your blood boils and you are instantly dead. These suit makers take their responsibility to aircrews very, very seriously. Some aircrew members have had their lives sustained high above 60,000 feet when they lost cockpit pressure and could not descend for four hours or more until they reached a safe location. These flyers didn't want to hear low bidder or bottom-line decision. They just wanted to hear the soft, comforting hiss of oxygen as it kept their suit pressurized and them alive until they reached friendly territory and could descend to lower altitude without getting shot down. Today's high altitude aircrews and astronauts are no different in their trust of this company and the suit systems they provide.

Some guys have a lotta class

Here is a story about the company's founder, David M. Clark, which highlights his philosophy. On one contract, the company figured a way to make items much more efficiently than envisioned when the fixed-price contract was signed. They made a great deal more profit than Mr. Clark thought was right. He tried to return the money to Department of Defense, but of course, the Government was incapable of reacting to the truly honest person's need to keep a fair deal. David stewed about the situation. He referred to it as tainted money and finally donated what he considered to be the excessive profit to charity. His concept of doing business has stuck with the current owners and managers. The same dead–honest approach continues today. Their profit margins are not as high as they could be, and they don't have a big fountain in a fancy tiled front lobby, but they are the only company in the western world that can and does produce pressure suits that work and that aircrews trust. Nobody else is currently doing that job and many have really tried. There has got to be a message in there somewhere.

Let's talk pressure suits

Pound for pound, the maturing of the full pressure suit as an integral part of the overall Blackbird development is arguably one of the least heralded and most understated technological accomplishments of the entire program. Because pressure suits are so often dismissed with only a casual mention, it is important to go into some detail about what they do and how they are made. We want the reader to have a good understanding of the complexity associated with pressure suit design and construction.

All Blackbird suits (A–12, YF–12 and SR–71) were full pressure suits and were designated PPAs for pilot's protective assembly. The PPA was a piece of flying gear that must not fail when the chips are down. None has ever failed to protect when the Blackbird crews' lives depended on the suit. The dedication of the people who make these suits and the USAF Personal Equipment people who maintain the hardware in the field are unquestioned. You will never hear any of them complain when asked about a helmet fit, or how the regulators are working, or when requested to adjust a parachute harness or readjust some part of the suit. There is a bond among individuals who design and make personal equipment for aircrews, the field people who maintain it, and the crews who use it on a daily basis. These people are a breed apart and we feel compelled to call attention to all those behind the scenes men and women who contributed so richly to the success of this facet of the A–12, YF–12, and the SR–71 programs. There have been bailouts from Blackbirds at all altitudes from ground level to nearly 80,000 feet and at speeds in excess of Mach 3. The suit has always been there to protect.

Here is what the suit does.

There are three easily definable levels of performance that any full pressure suit must perform to be successful and responsive to the needs of the wearer.

Level one requirements directly affect the crewmember's performance on every single mission. The suit must be easy to get into and out. It has to be comfortable and provide good mobility when unpressurized. The wearer must be afforded excellent visibility under all flight conditions. The gloves, while being an integral part of the pressure garment, must allow good dexterity to manipulate small switches, push buttons, and dials within the cockpit. The suit and helmet must provide the oxygen breathing system, facilitate clearing the ears during climbs and descents and, of course, provide a communications capability. This same suit must provide thermal protection under both hot and cold conditions. And it goes without saying that the suit and all its connections must be compatible with the aircraft, parachute, seat, emergency oxygen system, and seat kit. These suits allow the crew to do everything needed to fly the aircraft and supply a little pressure bubble that keeps them alive in an emergency, and, keep them alive under just normal operating circumstances. The cabin pressure in the SR–71 generally followed the outside altitude until the aircraft climbed above 27,000 feet. Above that altitude the cabin pressure remained constant no matter how high the aircraft went. The suit kept the crew alive at 27,000 feet altitude throughout a normal flight profile.

Level two requirements appear with an intermediate frequency. The suit must provide for eating and drinking without compromising the integrity of the pressure envelope and it must enable urine collection. It must provide absolute hypobaric protection affording necessary mobility, comfort, dexterity, and structural integrity when pressurized.

Level three requirements must be satisfied on a very infrequent basis under extreme or emergency conditions. The suit must protect the wearer in the event of explosive decompression, protect from high temperature and high–speed air blast during ejection, and maintain compatibility with the parachute and survival kit. There is a parachute harness integrated into the suit. The suit must protect its wearer during water immersion, provide automatic flotation that keeps the downed flyer right side up even if unconscious, and assure anti–suffocation for the aircrew until they have managed to collect themselves and open the visor. The suit must also furnish protection against open flames and impacts or penetrations.

A lot is taken for granted

We do not think about a lot of the things pressure suits do. Just breathing out, all that breath has to go somewhere. Flotation, anti–suffocation protection, ventilation, the communications equipment, and more, a whole laundry list of things the suit must do to support the aircrew at the right time. It provides the extra protection needed in case of an unexpected event like cockpit depressurization or ejection. To be sure all these capabilities are as advertised, several adventurous souls have actually tested these features. The tests run the gamut from ground level compatibility testing, to endless altitude chamber rides, plunging into water to be sure one floats properly, and finally an extensive series of live parachute jump tests.

Different parts do different jobs

The suit performs by assigning different responsibilities to different layers of the suit. To illustrate how this is done, let's walk through a sample suit made up of five generic layers. In real–life full pressure suits, these individual layers may be combined in a variety of ways. But the basic functional layers are always present.

The first layer for the wearer is the ventilation layer and incorporates some form of longjohns and socks and glove liners with additional materials to allow ventilating air throughout the entire garment. This keeps the wearer warm or cool as required and carries moisture away from the skin.

The second layer is the pressure layer, sometimes called the gas container. This layer is really the pressure vessel that surrounds the entire body, and in the case of decompression, inflates to maintain an internal pressure that sustains the flyer's life. This layer includes the helmet and visor seals, neck rings, gloves and wrist rings, booties and seals, and various valves and connectors that penetrate this pressure vessel to pass needed ventilating air from the aircraft's environmental system into the suit and allow entry of oxygen from the aircraft's liquid oxygen system.

The third layer is the restraint layer and a cover. This layer provides the necessary confinement of the pressure layer so that the aircrew can move and continue to function as needed to fly the airplane when the suit is inflated. It is this restraint layer that keeps the wearer from looking like a little kid in a bulky snowsuit with arms and legs extended, while the eyes are barely visible between the neck scarf and the woolly cap. The entire restraint layer is protected by its own outer cover.

The fourth layer in our generic suit is the exterior coverall. This coverall protects the other layers of the suit from abrasion, and keeps it clean and free of unwanted particles. This exterior coverall provides the first layer of windblast, heat, and flame protection. The fourth layer accounts for the suit color we see when the aircrew walks out to get into the aircraft.

The fifth and final layer is an abbreviated vest type garment that integrates the parachute and survival kit harness with the automatic flotation system. This garment is donned separately over the other four layers of the suit. One cannot be bailing out with the parachute simply safety–pinned to one's longjohns.

A complete suit, integral harness, helmet, gloves, boots, and all, weighs about forty pounds.

Let's look at the SR–71 suit bloodline

In 1949–1950 the U.S. Navy wanted to develop a full pressure suit capability for the Douglas A4D Skyray. At a conference at the Douglas plant in Long Beach, California, the original requirements were laid down. Joe Ruseckas of the David Clark Co. was there, as was Scott Crossfield, later of X–15 fame. Following close on the heels of this meeting was the Navy's desire to set an altitude record in an aircraft designated the Douglas D–558–2, better known to some as the Douglas Skyrocket.

Although unbeknownst at the time, the Blackbird suit development really started at this point. The people most intimately associated were NACA's Scott Crossfield, a Marine test pilot and World War II fighter ace, Colonel Marion Carl, and two David Clark Company reps, Joe

Ruseckas and John Flagg. Scott Crossfield was deeply involved in the suit development and in the many suit trials and improvements. It was the plan all along that Scott Crossfield would set the altitude record with the Skyrocket. Suddenly there was a change in plans by the Navy. Crossfield was dropped in favor of Marion Carl.[1]

This Marine flyer was first measured at the David Clark Company in late 1951. In the meantime Crossfield was getting plenty of altitude chamber rides to qualify the suit design at Mustin Field located on the old Navy Yard in Philadelphia. Designated unofficially as DC Model 7 Suit, it was identified to the outside world as the NACA–Navy–Clark Suit. In June, 1953, Marion Carl was fitted with his full pressure suit in Worcester and took it to Edwards AFB. Carl's suit was the Model 7 style and performance qualified by Crossfield at Mustin Field. But each suit was a little different because everyone took advantage of the learning curve as designs progressed. Carl's custom suit was referred to as Model 13. A fact of life in these early days was that all suits were custom made for the intended wearer after an extensive body measurement session.

The big event arrives

July, 1953 found Joe Ruseckas, Scott Crossfield, and Marion Carl, airborne for several flights in the bomb bay of a B–29 mothership flying out of Edwards AFB. The D–558–2 aircraft was carried half submerged, tucked into the belly of the B–29. When the mother ship reached the proper altitude, about 30,000 feet in this case, Joe and Scott would dress Marion Carl in the full pressure suit, check it all out for proper operation, and then install him in the cockpit of the D–558–2. Wearing his Suit Number Thirteen, Marion Carl finally rode the Douglas Skyrocket to an altitude record of more than 83,000 feet in the fall of 1953.

Next step, the X–15

Scott Crossfield carried his D–558–2 pressure suit knowledge and understanding to the X–15 Program. He and North American, working with the David Clark Co., defined the next developmental branch on the family tree which led to the A–12/YF–12/SR–71 Blackbird full pressure suits. The X–15 suits were a continuation of the effort started from the Marion Carl suit. The X–15 suits (the first Air Force–funded

---

[1] There are many stories and rumors as to why this happened but none could be verified so none of the stories are presented here.

full pressure suit development) were a slight departure from the status quo. Up until this time, the Navy had specialized in full pressure suits and the Air Force in partial pressure suits. The X–15 Program broke that tradition and the Air Force got into the FPS business in spades. The X–15 suits were made by the David Clark Co. but initially incorporated a government furnished helmet made by the Bill Jack Co.[2]

The X–15 suits, like all prior X–plane suits, were custom–made and individually fitted. Each test pilot visited the David Clark Co. and was measured so a suit could be made and fitted to provide optimum performance, comfort, mobility, and protection.

The Air Force had bigger fish to fry

Arrival of more capable interceptors like the F–101, F–102, and F–106, that could perform what is called a pop–up maneuver to altitudes above 50,000 feet, drove the Air Force to develop and acquire its first standardized full pressure suits. These suits were designated the A/P225–2 High Altitude Full Pressure Flying Outfits. This number designation identified the entire assembly including all the components associated with the suit including the helmet, gloves and booties. The David Clark Co. designed and manufactured the entire assembly including the helmet with only pressure controls and some connecting rings being outsourced.

They were made in eight standard sizes, based upon USAF–provided anthropomorphic data. While made in the eight standard sizes, each suit was still capable of being custom fitted and adjusted to the specific pilot who would be using the suit.

These suits were used on all high altitude missions of interceptor aircraft listed above as well as the high altitude versions of the B–57 Canberra. Specifically the B–57D, E, and F. In 1962 the Air Force centralized its full pressure suit business for the standardized A/P225–2 suit at Tyndall AFB, Florida. The major customer for the standardized suit was the Air Defense Command, satisfying the pop–up above 50,000 feet requirement. There, at Tyndall, all pressure suit indoctrination was accomplished for all Air Force programs using the standard suit. And that is the way things continued in the open and above board world of USAF programs.

---

[2]Like so many companies in the pressure suit business, the Bill Jack Co. is no longer a player in the aerospace protective equipment business. Full pressure suit helmets are now made by the David Clark Co.

Bob Banks of David Clark was the technical representative at Tyndall for that program. Bob is still with the company as a Program Manager in Worcester. As stated earlier, the U–2 program, both the CIA side and the USAF side, continued to use partial pressure suits and to qualify their suits and to indoctrinate aircrews elsewhere.

Here come the Blackbird suits

During 1958 and 1959 a series of cockpit mockup evaluations were conducted with great secrecy at Lockheed's Skunk Works in Burbank, and requirements for the OXCART A–12 suits were first defined. The cockpit interface arrangements for the seat, parachute, and the suit for the A–12 and the YF–12 were essentially identical. In June, 1960, Lockheed's test pilot Lou Shalk was measured for his suit at Worcester.

Many parallel actions took place about this time in the Blackbird suit development story. The one standout individual was an Air Force Captain named Harry Collins. He was stationed in the Washington area and traveled extensively, like most of the early program people. Harry was the government's go–to guy in the Blackbird suit/seat/chute and aircrew oxygen equipment efforts. He worked very closely with the Skunk Works personal equipment and cockpit people. Harry not only did a monumental job of coordinating, he also participated (literally) with Dick Markum in jump testing the A–12 parachutes and pressure suits. When he didn't have anything else to do, he was riding the altitude chamber in Buffalo, New York, at Firewell Co. to collect data on suit performance and gather time to qualify the suit design.

While the Air Force had a rather large scale standardized suit program and low pressure chamber facilities at Tyndall AFB, none of the Blackbird suits or equipment ever went through that facility. The A–12 was a very closely held black program and the contractors were told not to fraternize with the subjects that were sent out to be measured and tested—no dinners, no talking, no invites to the theater, no nothing. "Just measure'em and make their suits," and that was it. During the early time in the A–12 program the David Clark Co was a subcontractor to the Firewell Co. of Buffalo, who made and supplied the oxygen system and other components for the A–12 and the YF–12 aircraft.

The OXCART pilots, both CIA people and Lockheed test pilots, got their suits in Worcester and then were flown to Buffalo by Joe Ruseckas in the company's Bonanza. There they were run through a chamber at Firewell, later ARO, and now Carleton Technologies. This chamber at Buffalo not only had the required high altitude capability and the facility for explosive decompression, but it could expose the suited person to radiant heat, simulating interior cockpit heat of the new Mach 3 vehicle. This simulation allowed the subjects to experience the added heat they could expect in flight and to see how their suits performed the difficult task of keeping them relatively comfortable. There was a surprising difference between subjects in tolerance for heat and the confines of the chamber over long periods. Some never made it past the heat stress and chamber rides. They were filtered out of the program accordingly.

The foundational suit

The first Blackbird–specific suit was ordered on 7 March 1960. The company records show the model number as S–901 and that it was custom made for Subject Number One (the A–12 program). This first suit was made for Capt. Harry Collins, who endured through many early chamber tests as the designated guinea pig.

The S–901 PPA qualification jumps were done by Dick Marcum and Harry Collins at El Centro NAS, California, in 1961. The time between entries for the first S–901 suit for Collins and the second suit, S–901A, ordered on 28 June 1962 for Subject Number Two (Lockheed test pilot Lew Schalk) would imply plenty of testing and work done between the birth dates of these two suits.

The S–901 suit went through continued development as the A–12 program progressed, S–901A through H, and a suit designated the S–970. The S–970 suit was developed with the entry zippers configured to allow donning from the rear. Earlier models used a U–shaped zipper at the upper front body/chest area. These suits were all custom made and served the needs of both the A–12 and the YF–12 programs.

The SR gets its own suits

An entirely new suit designated the S–901J, PPA, was developed for the SR–71 aircraft. The SR–71 suits were non–custom and available in twelve standard sizes based upon USAF–provided anthropomorphic data. The first of this series of standard sized operational suits (S–901J) was produced in 1965. Learning from A–12 and YF–12 experience, designers incorporated numerous improvements into the SR suits. The suit/seat interface fittings were streamlined and the bailout oxygen supply was moved from inside the parachute backpack into the seat kit. The suit pressure controls were simplified. Continual helmets improvements were made throughout the Blackbird program. There were some interesting developments with the helmet visor/faceplate.

How am I supposed to see through that?

Sooner or later, most suit components wound up being produced and improved by the David Clark Co.

In the early test program at Edwards and Area 51 there was a problem with glare in the cockpit and reflections within the faceplates (visors). This was not a simple problem to solve. To eliminate or at least minimize the amount of internal fogging of the faceplate from the flyer's breath, one of the layers of the visor had a vacuum–deposited layer of gold about a molecule or two thick. You could see through it just fine. This coating accounted for the gold cast seen on so many pressure suit helmet faceplates. On each side of the faceplate there was an electrical connection allowing the passage of current through the gold coating to provide a small amount of heating. This heating dissipated the fogging caused by the crew's breath. On the downside, the gold coating tended to produce a mirror effect.

The visor's shape was semi–spherical. It acted as a concave reflecting surface so crew members could see themselves peering back from their own visor. To most of the crews this was no big deal and they looked right past the face staring back at them. Some, however, tended to be bugged by this reflection. Bugged or no, reflections created a serious problem for the pilots because the suit exteriors were silver for heat reflection. The instruments on the panel acted like little mirrors sometimes, and the sun was quite strong at altitude. All these reflections were picked up in the visor and bounced around some more. It was tough for pilots to deal with tanker hookups at certain sun angles. The problem did not go away at night. The instrument lights lit up the suit which reflected off the instrument glass covers into the gold mirror in front of the pilot's face, creating very confusing images and obscuring the outside view during night operations such as refuelings and landing approaches.

The resulting solution was to ask Pittsburgh Plate Glass (PPG) to make some clear glass visors with very small heating wires embedded between layers of glass and an anti–reflective coating on the visor's surfaces. They made and delivered a number of visors that met specifications but eventually gave up far short of the total quantity requested, acknowledging the great difficulty in manufacturing such an item.

After struggling with the visor production problems, PPG finally told the David Clark Co., "We've learned all we want to know about making electrically heated, optically correct, curved glass visors."

PPA helmet visor manufacture, once again, defaulted to Worcester where they are still made today.

A little about the suit colors.

The suit's interior layers have generally been whatever color material such as Nomex was available from DuPont. Most materials have been and continue to be supplied in olive or sage green with some supplied in dark blue. Whatever the color of inner layers, those are not what one sees when the crew walks out to the aircraft. The outer coverall layers of SR–71 suits on the other hand, have been purposely manufactured in a number of different colors, including in a reflective silver, white, very dark brown, golden, and blue.

Silver

The first outer coveralls were silver colored because of a layer of aluminum vacuum deposited on HT–1 material. The HT stood for high temperature and that material went on to be called Nomex. It is a fire–resistant fabric used in all military flying suits and for many other high temperature applications. The idea behind the silver suits was primarily heat rejection, both inside the cockpit where the inner surfaces of the windows reach a temperature of 250°F at cruise, and to protect against the instant heat pulse received by the aircrew during an ejection at Mach 3. These silver suits did just fine at heat rejection but their

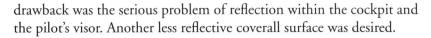

drawback was the serious problem of reflection within the cockpit and the pilot's visor. Another less reflective coverall surface was desired.

White

A white coverall was developed to both reduce reflections, and at the same time eliminate the problem of the vacuum–deposited aluminum surface cover wearing off. However, the white outside coverall, was made from a white dacron material and was not fireproof and still created some serious cockpit reflections. Nonetheless, these white coveralls saw a considerable amount of service.

Very dark brown

The David Clark Co. developed a proprietary process to produce a material they called Fypro. The Fypro process actually did some molecular rearrangement within the Nomex yarns which enhanced the fire resistance of original Nomex and changed its color. When olive green Nomex fabric was put through the Fypro process it turned a very dark brown or almost black. That was how the near–black suits arrived. This was great for the reflection problem within the cockpit but did absolutely nothing for the radiant heat rejection needed at normal cruise conditions. Black suits were not a big item on the pressure suit scene.

Golden

The next coverall color was a golden color and has been the predominant follow–on color to the original silver suits. Almost all of the Blackbird suits in service until the program was shut down were golden tan. It was not a reflective gold as the silver suits were, but simply a non–glossy gold colored cloth. Starting with natural (white) colored Nomex fibers and applying the Fypro process, the material turns a nice golden color. This was a reasonable compromise between reflection reduction and the ability to reject the cockpit radiant heat loading at cruise.

Blue

In the mid–1980s interest renewed in changing the suit color again. Some of the drive behind this quest was a search for the optimum color to contrast with surroundings in the event the aircrew was down and awaiting pickup by rescue forces. There were even some reversible outer garments made with high–visibility color on one side and a low–visibility color on the other. An extensive study was undertaken to determine the single color providing the best contrast with the earth's surface world–wide. It turned out to be tan, very close to the color of Fypro processed natural Nomex fiber. Later DuPont did produce some desert–tan Nomex for Gulf War applications and some outer covers for pressure suits were made for evaluation of this color. An additional suit was made in dark blue for evaluation. These later non–gold, non–Fypro'ed suits were made of dyed Nomex but the dyed material was not color–fast and showed the effects of bleaching out, particularly on the shoulders and other locations exposed to the sun at high altitude.

In the end, though there were many combinations and colors tried, the gold colored, Fyproed, natural Nomex suits were the predominant outer garment color used during the SR–71's operational life.

Time for a human interest story

In the early Blackbird days at Area 51, the pressure suit tech reps did it all. They maintained the suits, dressed the pilots for the A–12s, and assisted the aircrews in and out of the cockpits with all the connections and checkout before and after each flight. Everything was super–secret and the reps were flown from Burbank to the Ranch on Mondays and returned to Burbank on Fridays. They were not at Area 51 if not needed.

Tom Smith was one of these reps and floated between Burbank, the Area, and other locations as required. He and his company partner were also custodians of the suits when they had to be transported to different locations. On one weekend the two young reps found themselves close to the Mexican border so they just drove across to have a meal and a few drinks before going on their way.

When returning, the U.S. Border Patrol demanded a look in the trunk. When the guard saw two locked and suspicious cases he demanded they be unlocked for inspection. Tom and his friend refused. Stalemate!

To cover unplanned situations, every program member had been given a phone number to call for help. Tom called the number and explained. They waited for a couple of hours while confined at the

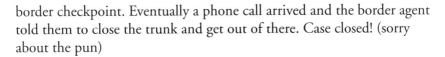

border checkpoint. Eventually a phone call arrived and the border agent told them to close the trunk and get out of there. Case closed! (sorry about the pun)

Throughout the program there were incidents occurring where serious security problems could have arisen but everyone kept their cool. Tom still works for the David Clark Co. as a product manager.

Here's how it all shook out

As the SR–71 program came on line in 1968 with S–901J suits, the A–12 program wound down. At that same time the new U-2R aircraft began to roll off the production line. The U-2R, the first of the U–2 line to incorporate a full pressure suit, took a page from the SR–71 suits and began to go its own way as the S–1010 suit was developed specifically to satisfy the long—fourteen hours unrefueled—flights and other cockpit constraints.

In 1977 the first SR–71 suits, the S–901Js, were replaced by the next generation S–1030–series suits.

By the early 1980s the second generation full pressure suit for the U-2R and TR–1 was developed and designated the S–1031. By the mid–1980s the S–1031C suit arrived on the high altitude protection scene as a common suit (almost) for both the U-2R and the SR–71. The final configuration of pressure suits worn by the last operational SR–71 crews was the S–1031C. Now, all those suits, like the aircraft they were designed for, are scattered around the country in museums and dusty remote storage places quietly waiting for their crews. And it is a crying shame!

The story of the partial pressure suit is every bit as fascinating as the FPS story. The PPS development began in the 1940s and one might intuitively conclude that in the black airplane world the PPS was the foundational suit for the Blackbird FPS. Based upon logic and chronology, it would be easy to assume that the OXCART and Blackbird suits grew out of the information and hardware experience gained in the U–2 Program. After all, the missions were similar, the operating agencies involved were the same, and many of the personnel in one program gravitated to the other. That assumption would be dead wrong.

Pressure suit development for the Blackbird's stablemate, the U–2, was an earlier and parallel effort following the course of partial pressure suits. Throughout the U–2 program from 1955 to 1989, all versions, including the U–2C, used the partial pressure suit. It was not until the advent of the U-2R (TR–1) that a full pressure suit was incorporated. The building blocks for the U-2R's S–1010 suit were drawn from the SR–71 suits, not the reverse, as might be suspected.

Part III

Category II Testing

Birds of a Feather Flock to Edwards

SR-71 Flight Test Program

Security Was Everyone's Business

Inlets, Unstarts and High Speed Air

Cat II Camera Testing

Supplies, Spares and Consumables

SLR Flight Test at Edwards

Flight Testing the HRB-454

The 2,500 Mile Micrometer

The SR-71 Had Big Ears

Number Three Dies

Anatomy of a Rendezvous

Mission Planning

Chapter 10

Birds of a Feather
Flock to Edwards

"Captain, if I had wanted a Goddamn weather
report I would have asked for it"
Lt.Col Dan Andre, Edwards AFB, 1964

"Now you get together with all those guys from up there
and coordinate with the others from down south or this
thing is gonna sink like a chicken wire submarine."
Col. Robert L. Stephens, Edwards AFB, 1964

B
y early 1964 events began to zip along. President Johnson had
made the A–11 (really the YF–12) public knowledge. The
implications were that the SR–71, a super secret Mach 3 plus
reconnaissance aircraft, was not far behind. There were Blackbirds at Edwards
and now it was time to organize a test force to do an Air Force testing job.

Col. Robert L. "Fox" Stephens was designated the Test Force Director
and senior Air Force test pilot on the YF–12 program, however the test
force would not be officially designated for nearly a year, so Fox had to
be satisfied being the head of FTTA. That was the organizational cubby
hole used to collect and administer the members of the team as well as
an address to send those who were yet to arrive.

The Edwards connection began much earlier

The Air Force Flight Test Center (AFFTC) participation in the YF–12/
SR–71 activities started in 1961 when OXCART clearances were authorized
for Brig. General "Twig" Branch, Center Commander, and Captain
James Irwin. The intent behind providing early clearances for Edwards

people was the anticipated increased flying activity at Area 51. Key AFFTC players were to keep an eye out for potential breaches in security. In addition, Edwards AFB was one of the bases in southwestern U.S. to be used as part of a cover plan should there be an aircraft accident. (Remember the alleged F–105 crashes in the northern reaches of the Nellis AFB, Nevada gunnery range?)

In early 1963, Headquarters Systems Command assigned additional manpower slots to Col. Guy Townsend, Director of Flight Test at AFFTC. These additional people were to be used in conjunction with a BRICKBAT priority for developing a test program foundation and plan for a combined YF–12/SR–71 test force. To proceed with this activity without giving away any secrets, Townsend established a "plans" organization. This group grew from a handful at the start to over four hundred strong during the height of flight test activity. The organization included personnel from Air Force Systems Command (AFSC), Air Defense Command (ADC), and Strategic Air Command (SAC). This plans office, headed by Fox Stephens, was assigned the organizational symbol FTTA. All activities were cloaked in black even after the President's announcement. Stephens was supported by Colonel Vernon Henderson from ADC and Colonel Frenchy Bennett from SAC.

As the SAC and ADC personnel began to arrive in 1963 and 1964 before the program surfaced, there was no visible program for them to support. To avoid giving something away, all SAC and ADC patches and markings were removed from uniforms and flight suits. These personnel were assigned to Col. Townsend's ever-expanding "plans" shop.

By mid summer 1964 the FTTA assignees working for Col. Stephens were:

Lt.Col. Norman S. Drake—Chief of Test Engineering

Lt.Col. Daniel Andre—Chief of Security and all other form of cats and dogs

Major Walter F. Daniels—YF–12 Performance, Stability and Control Test Pilot and Operations Officer

Major James Cooney—YF–12 Fire Control Officer

Major Noel Warner—YF–12 Fire Control Officer

Major James Irwin—Backup YF–12 Test Pilot (Later went to the moon for NASA)

Major William Shipley—Supply Officer Extraordinaire

Major Douglas Dodge—Maintenance (and extremely talented artistic welder)

Major Douglas Boteler—Maintenance

Wilma Fields—Secretary

By mid July 1964 the second contingent of the SR–71 test force began to arrive. Maj. Ken Hurley and Maj Harold Chapman arrived from the SR–71 System Program Office (SPO) at Wright Field. I arrived fresh from the 665A Program Office at Wright Field.

Captain Bruce Hartman checked in with FTTA about the same time. Bruce, like me, had never dealt with a program involving such momentum and stature, so he wanted to make a good impression on the FTTA residents. On his first day he showed up at a quarter after seven with the intention of making a good impression as an early arrival and all-around eager beaver. He told me later that he was surprised to find everyone there already hard at work. Coming down the hall he met Lt.Col. Dan Andre.

"Good morning, Sir," Bruce said with a big smile.

Andre stepped right in front of Bruce, fixed him with one of his famous stares, and replied in his usual vein, "Captain, if I had wanted a goddamn weather report I would have asked for it." Then he just marched on down the hall without another comment.

Bruce's first day was about like everyone else's. Andre got on their case big time. It was not for another three or four months that we junior weenies would be able to cope with this World War II, P–61 radar observer and veteran of three bailouts. The last bailout had been from a jet interceptor (don't know if it was F–89 or F–94), but it was at very high speed. Andre's face reflected the facial rearrangement that often comes from such an event.

Bruce gathered his waning self confidence and entered the office to report in. No one bit him. My experience was not much different. As I entered the office on my first day, I was stopped at the door by Wilma Fields, the secretary and resident interrogator. After being questioned at length about my background, showing my orders, and answering questions covering everything from my birthplace to when my last acne pimples faded, she finally allowed as how I might be permitted to sit in the chair next to her desk. She made it painfully clear that I was to proceed no farther until she had completed the required paperwork. All this time I sat and watched the rest of the inhabitants of my new FTTA office home go on with their work as if I did not exist. About midway through my initial "Wilma interrogation," I was wondering whether I would ever be able to pass myself off as a real engineer and gain access to the rest of the room. Life can be tough for FNGs (frigging new guys).

Without warning there was a huge crash behind me and some one yelled, "Gotcha! You SOB." When I finally gained the nerve to turn and look, there stood this really mean looking Lieutenant Colonel and a Major, staring up at the smudge of a huge bug on the ceiling. On the floor in front of them lay the rumpled yellow pages from the LA phone book. Not one person in the rest of the group even missed a beat. The entire episode that set my adrenaline at full overload was simply passed off as business as usual. Andre picked up his phone book and Maj. Jim Cooney said, "Nice shot, Colonel." And that was it. I told myself this was going to be a tough group to fit in with. Nothing could have been further from the truth. Eccentric, yes, but a great bunch of people.

Maj. Ken Hurley arrived about the same time I did; and, as he was one of the initial old timers in the SR enterprise, I felt reassured that things could not go too far south. Ken would be there if things really went around the bend. By the same token Bruce Hartman had been selected for this job by Norm Drake, so here were two FNG engineers who simply had to learn the ropes and not do anything really dumb in the process. Both of us were comforted by the knowledge that at least one person at Edwards actually wanted us to be there.

One morning that first week I arrived in my khakis and was greeted by Andre in his dress blues. "You're outta uniform, Captain," he shouted from about six inches from my face. That man could get in front of you and stare without blinking or moving a muscle and just remain that way until the "stare-ee" folded. "So," he continued, "you're gonna get a lesson in penmanship."

This is terribly unnerving for a junior officer so I just said, "Yes, Sir." He backed away from my face, picked up a piece of chalk in each hand and proceeded to the center of a wall–mounted blackboard. Without further comment he began writing outward from the middle with both hands. His right hand wrote Daniel Andre from left to right while his left hand wrote the mirror image, Leinad Erdna. I prayed he would not hand me the chalk and expect me to repeat that test. He didn't, he just smiled, turned without a word, put away the chalk, and walked to his office. I was beginning to wonder how I would ever make the grade here at FTTA. No one else seemed to notice or care.

Ken Hurley had an advantage none of us knew. Both he and Andre grew up in Memphis, Tennessee. Here is how Ken described one of their conversations.

"There are many Andre stories that should be told, if we can remember them.

"The day Dan first heard that I came from South Memphis, he said, 'Did you go to South Side?'

"I said, 'Yes.'

"He said, 'That's the roughest part of Memphis, and you played football with all those Fort Pickering guys?'

"I said, 'Yes.'

"He said, 'That was the year South Side placed first in the State and second in the Southeast?'

"I said, 'Yes.'

129

"He said, 'From now on I won't mess with you.'"

"And he didn't! He had gone to another school in East Memphis–Messick. We got along fine!"

At last, maybe Bruce and I would survive after all.

Mid 1964 was a time in high pressure growth for the young test force and people began to show up from everywhere. Because the YF–12 was a prototype only and the SR–71 was a production program, there were some initial struggles as to which aircraft and priorities should come first. The YF was at Edwards and flying, while the SRs were still being put together at Burbank with nothing scheduled to show up on the desert until very late in the year. It was a time for planning, learning from the A–12 program at Area 51, and setting our ducks in a row for what was to come.

Chapter 11

SR-71 Flight Test Program at Edwards Air Force Base

"This was the most integrated test force I can remember.
We really had good cooperation with Dick Miller of
Lockheed and the rest of the contractors."
Art Lusby, 1999

"Merv Evanson and I rode Aircraft 953 out to Mach 3.22
at 89,650 feet altitude. That was the upper right
hand corner of the envelope at the time."
Ken Hurley, reflecting on the
Cat II Program at Edwards

It all began in the final days of 1964. The Air Force Test Pilot School at Edwards AFB is devoted primarily to the training of pilots who conduct this sort of testing. In addition to the test pilot, a flight test engineer (FTE) is usually assigned to each project. The FTE helps in managing the test plan, assists the pilot in the conduct of the test card, and in the end has a significant responsibility in documenting and reporting the test results. Many Ph.Ds have been granted in the fields of Performance, Stability and Control. For obvious reasons this book will not treat these subjects in any exhaustive manner. However, using just plain English words, we hope to give the reader an appreciation for the job done in this area for the SR–71 program.

Aerodynamic testing of a modern aircraft is not a rudder kicking, stick jerking, leather helmet, silk scarf, and sunglasses, kind of operation. These programs produce an inundating mountain of data points and individual samples from all sorts of interrelated information. The skills and dedication needed by aircrews and engineers, both on the ground and in the air, is monumental. The detailed planning of data points and flight conditions, the precise execution, and the painstaking analysis both via computer and human technical judgments are extremely taxing. Time to complete flight testing is always compressed in order to deliver the aircraft to the user as quickly as possible. If there were ever a single portion of any aircraft test program that would qualify as the Excedrin headache generator of the century, it is the performance, stability, and control testing. The stakes are high and, to the unwary, the risks are heart–stopping, literally.

The final product that comes out includes a bunch of spots and dots on graph paper charts with clever little lines and curves going through the middle of scattered blasts of data points. The final results are published in detail in a flight test report. Key results appear in paragraphs or tables in the flight manual. Each one of those data points was the product of countless hours of sweat and correlation between what the collected data said and what the existing conditions should have produced based on modeling done and engineering judgments made before the flight was conducted. Once sufficient correlation is established between the modeling and the flight test data, engineers can calculate performance, stability, and control information throughout the flight envelope with confidence.

In today's aircraft testing environment there are many more sophisticated computer simulations and modeling techniques that further strengthen the test crew's and engineers' knowledge of just how a particular configuration will react under specific conditions. The SR–71 test program was only on the early edges of this technology so a more cautious approach was followed. "Anticipate the rough spots and find'em before you hit'em" was the name of the game. The search required patience, caution, courage, dedication, and the ability to sift the fly specs out of the data pepper, a very demanding job. The road to success was littered with frustration and do–it–overs. Every operational aircrew member owes his or her hat, fanny, and spats to the pros that conduct these flight test programs and the data in the flight manual.

At the start of the Blackbird flight test program this aircraft's operating envelope was a virtually unexplored aerodynamic world. There were no high–speed cruise (Mach 3) aircraft flying at the time. Even today there are no operational Mach 3 cruise aircraft in service. Nothing has come along to fill the huge hole left by the deactivation of the SR–71. The X–15 was flying at bursts of speed well above Mach 3 and at altitudes far higher than anyone else had flown before in an aerodynamic vehicle. The B–70, whose intended flight envelope included a Mach 3 dash in hostile areas but really was not intended for sustained cruise at those speeds, was waiting in the wings to try its luck at the Mach 3 regime. The first flight of the B–70 occurred on 21 September 1964 and by 1 July 1965 it had only flown fourteen flights. It was not until 12 April 1966 that the B–70 reached its highest speed of Mach 3.08. Both the X–15 and the B–70 were made by North American Rockwell, who had chosen steel or Inconel to address the issues of airframe strength at the higher aerodynamic temperatures. Lockheed selected titanium. Sustained Mach 3 plus cruise was a very hostile thermal environment where the inside of the cockpit windows rose to 250°. Temperatures in the fuel tanks exceeded 300°, and stagnation temperatures at cruise Mach number exceeded 800° F. No other airbreather had ever dealt with this hostile flight environment under sustained conditions.

In normal flight test programs there are usually other aircraft available with similar speed and altitude performance capabilities. For example, B–58s could be paced with F–104s throughout their flight envelopes, making it easier to calibrate flight test instrumentation and visually observe and photograph the more exciting tests. With the SR–71 there was no airplane with known performance that could be used in this role. The only others around were the A–12 and the YF–12, unsuitable as chase aircraft because they were involved in their own testing and evaluation programs. In addition, most of the ground–based instrumentation systems of the day, such as long lens camera systems, could not acquire and track the SR at altitude and speed. Also, there were few wind tunnels that could perform instrumentation calibration at Mach 3 and above 75,000 feet.

During the world speed record attempts on 1 May 1965, each YF–12 aircraft setting the records had huge white crosses painted on their undersides so they could be photographed at the checkpoints. The cameras were slaved to radar tracking antennas. All that was visible when the photos were processed was a white cross against the dark black background of outer space.

Rivalry between black and white airplanes

Because the SR–71 program flight information was very closely held, and the B–70 was a paint–it–on–the–wall sort of thing with respect to getting information out to the public, there developed a significant rivalry between the YF–12/SR–71 flight test crews and those of the B–70 program. The North American PR people even had an evening news spot on one of the local Palmdale radio stations. Every day or so they would toot their horn about how well, how high, and how fast the B–70 was going. They would talk about how many minutes of accumulated time above Mach 2, above Mach 2.5, and Mach 3 their number one airframe had under its belt, and on and on about the wonders of high speed and high altitude flight. These announcements said little about one of the B–70's structural problems, which was a tendency to lose large pieces of the aircraft when in flight. As you might suspect all this bragging about high Mach time stuck in the craw of the Lockheed test pilots who regularly flew more Mach 3 time on a single flight than the B–70 program was likely to fly in its entire lifetime.

There was a watering hole in the Palmdale area called Hernando's Hide–a–Way where the test pilots of Edwards programs got together in the evenings over a few beers or Scotches for professional discussions about their relative test accomplishments or whatever. One particular evening, Al White, of B–70 fame, was raving on about his high Mach number time. Nearby, Lockheed test pilot Jim Eastham, who had flown both the A–12 and YF–12 extensively and had been flying the YF–12 that day, could stand it no longer. He turned to White and said, "Al, we do more Mach 3 time during a single YF–12 mission than you guys have flown in your entire program." Al looked over at Jim and without hesitation retorted, "Yes that's true Jim, but we lose bigger pieces than you fly!"

Flight Test 101

Flight test programs are more than how high, how fast, and do the wheels go up and down when you want. As aircraft sophistication increased, the test programs to identify and document what and how well the aircraft performed were expanded. There were many functional objectives of the standard aircraft test program. In the 1960s the phases of an Air Force flight test program were called out in Air Force Regulation 80–14 and labeled Category I, Category II, and Category III.

The Category I program was the very first step in flight testing. This part was conducted by the contractor under close observation of the System Program Office at Wright–Patterson AFB. On–site observers at Edwards AFB were the Air Force Category II test team. They were the eyes and ears for the SPO. The contractor was allowed to fly the first aircraft (the number of Cat I aircraft depended on the program and available resources). In the SR–71 program Lockheed was allotted three.

The contractor was to collect, reduce, analyze, and present data to demonstrate it was delivering what the Air Force had purchased. The contractor develops and begins writing the flight handbook and maintenance manuals. The airframe contractor demonstrates the vehicle is safe to fly, is controllable, and that all aircraft systems function properly and in concert with the anticipated use of the aircraft.

In the Blackbird flight test program at least one Air Force flight crew participated in flying Category I aircraft and accomplishing some of the Category I flight test objectives. This crew was Col. Fox Stevens and Lt.Col. Ken Hurley.

In conjunction with the engine contractor, the airframe contractor demonstrated that the propulsion system produced the power needed in the right amounts and at the right time to keep the machine in the air and functioning in the manner advertised to the customer. Supported by reams of model test data gathered in the wind tunnel and many many theoretical calculations, one of the first big tasks for the contractor's test pilots was to demonstrate the limits of the flight envelope. It was a program to define how high, how fast, how slow, and how the aircraft handles. It must be controllable within the confines of this envelope. There were also additional aircraft attributes to be demonstrated, structural integrity and flutter, to name a couple.

A stop sign wiggling back and forth in a strong wind is a very benign form of flutter. In an aircraft, true flutter comes on with almost no warning, and unlike the slowly wiggling stop sign, lasts for only a heartbeat or two before the fluttering piece of the airframe is gone. In the case of a fluttering rudder or vertical stabilizer it is wham–bam and it's gone. This is a violent reaction of the structural dynamics to air loadings. During flutter testing, test crews actually performed tests and recorded airframe element responses to determine how close they were to this flutter phenomenon. This was very touchy business as flight crews and engineers defined the problem and its limits, hoping never to experience it.

Checking out stability

Another of the contractor's chores was to define the stability characteristics of the aircraft. Here are a few of the terms defined:

Directional stability samples. One question to answer is: at different speeds, different air loadings, and different aircraft center of gravity (CG) conditions, if you suddenly kick one rudder and bump the nose sideways to the relative wind, or air turbulence does it for you, would the aircraft return to its original condition? i.e., nose into the wind the way it was before the disturbance, or do something really unexpected? It's the unexpected that makes for wild stories and commands large paychecks, except, of course, for the Air Force flight test crews.

Positive directional stability. At any one set of conditions, termed a data point, if the aircraft in our example has positive directional stability, then the nose does indeed eventually return and aim into the relative wind after a few cycles without further pilot input. The higher the stability factor, the fewer cycles needed to return to rest.

Neutral directional stability. If the aircraft is neutrally stable it will just stay where it is with the nose sideways to the airstream until something else happens to make it change again. This almost never happens in real life.

Negative directional stability. If the aircraft is directionally unstable, then it departs from anything you would normally expect an aircraft in its right mind to do. And that is how whifferdills and other unexpected maneuvers take place. These are sudden, exciting, and severe. In high–performance aircraft these can bring catastrophic results to aircraft and crew.

An example of longitudinal (pitch) instability. The F–4 aircraft departs at high angles of attack and other complicating CG and aerodynamic conditions. The aircraft flight path takes on a life of its own: the F–4 stops being controllable and simply becomes a strangely shaped object affected by relative wind and inertial coupling. This is a prime example of an unwanted stability problem that accounted for the loss of more than one airframe.

Here is what Art Lusby, a frequent flyer in the rear seat during the stability and control testing program in SR–71, 953, had to say about one group of test conditions.

"I have a vivid memory of the dynamic lateral–directional test in the SR–71. In the Mach 3 flight regime, the airplane is naturally unstable in the directional axis with the stability augmentation system (SAS) off. With the SAS on there was no problem. However, it was necessary to turn the SAS off and put in a slight rudder pulse to obtain the unaugmented damping derivatives. I can remember watching the flight test instrumentation and seeing the yaw angle slowly increase with each cycle. The inlet spikes began to cycle in and out as the airflow changed direction going into the inlet. We needed several cycles of motion to get enough data. The number of cycles had to be carefully weighed against safety and the flight crew's judgment. Needless to say the pilot had his finger on the SAS re–engagement trigger waiting for a signal to end the test."

The SAS re–engagement trigger referred to was a switch on the pilot's stick that when held down, disengaged the SAS. The SAS was automatically reengaged if the pilot moved his finger.

The above is just a sample of conditions defined in a flight test program. The larger the flight envelope the more data points must be included. Like hanging wall paper, the larger the wall, the more paper, wheat paste, and pain. When fighter aircraft go through a test program, they are tested throughout all the classic aerodynamic parameters—maneuvering, does it spin and when, takeoff and landing performance, shooting, bombing, and on and on. They are like the Swiss Army knives of aircraft because we expect them to do so many things under so many diverse conditions.

The Blackbird was different: she was a thoroughbred from the word go. She was a delicate machine structurally, with the single purpose of carrying herself, her sensors, and her crew wherever on the face of the earth she was directed and returning with the intelligence data needed to get the job done. During the Category I and II flight test program, the maximum maneuvering load factor in a turn was 1.1 Gs. This made for very long and large 180–degree turns. Even with this focused pedigree, her test program was a serious challenge aerodynamically, physically, and sensor–wise. Her flight envelope covered sustained flight conditions and combinations never encountered before on any program. Imagine spending an hour above 75,000 feet while screaming along at 3,300 feet per second. That boils down to an 1,800 nautical mile trip in less time than it takes to wash and wax your car.

The Category II test program was the next step. The Air Force took the machine and data as provided by the contractor and began the task of making the assembled pieces perform as a system and not just individual parts. For the SR–71, the Category II program featured an Air Force team composed of highly experienced test crews. Engineers, technicians, mission and maintenance planners, logistics planners, and support personnel were carefully selected for the task of taking the aircraft and its flight and ground systems to the next level of testing. Night–flying procedures, aerial refueling envelopes, and mission–specific techniques had to be defined. The Air Force test team begin to reconcile the contractors' maintenance practices with the Air Force systems, methods, personnel skills, and ground support equipment.

In most cases the contractor had significant latitude in maintenance techniques, practices, and in the support equipment used. The Air Force test organization was required to operate and maintain the aircraft with the assigned Aerospace Ground Equipment (AGE), the allocated tool kits, and with the same personnel skill levels expected to be available in the operational units. Where there were difficulties, the Cat II personnel were charged with defining the necessary changes to published procedures and coordinating these changes with the contractors who controlled the databases. The operational command then examined its potential resources and made whatever adjustments were possible in anticipation of the bird and support equipment arrival.

In the SR test program, Air Force Systems Command retained responsibility for the testing, but most skilled maintenance personnel came from the Strategic Air Command. These carefully selected and screened individuals were routed through factory training at the various contractors' plants prior to arriving at the test site. They were then assigned for a period of maintenance experience on the test birds at Edwards AFB. This was extremely beneficial to the test force. These people included air crews, maintenance people, planners, film processors, providing every skill and specialty that would be needed at Beale AFB to operate the system. While Systems Command rarely had resources to provide the depth of skilled technicians needed to support testing and maintenance of a soon to be operational aircraft and its systems, it did provide those personnel highly experienced in the testing business. Finally, as the SAC personnel gained experience, they were transferred to Beale to maintain the operational birds and train the additional support personnel. This process was followed like a pipeline as people processed through the contractor plants, to the test force at Edwards, and proceeded on to Beale for their work assignments.

Another task that fell directly at the feet of the Air Force test team was a total demonstration and documentation of sensor package capabilities. The intent was to explore the performance of the sensors delivered for test and not expend time or effort chasing improvements or engineering what–ifs. A fun concept for the engineers, but time was short and the user needed to know current capabilities and not possible performance in the future. A significant part of the Cat II test effort was to also provide the data needed by the SPO at Wright Field for contract performance incentive evaluations. Almost universally, companies working on the SR–71 program had contracts that adjusted their program profits based on the quality and reliability performance of the systems they provided.

The test force was given another task. They were charged with the responsibility of conducting production acceptance flights on new production aircraft from Palmdale. Test force crews were the most experienced available and performed this duty for the first ten or so production aircraft. Production acceptance flights consisted of taking the new airplane out to Mach 3.2 and checking all systems. Most aircraft were flown twice by the test force crews and some required more than two flights before the aircraft was accepted.

Thinking ahead in Cat II

One of the most difficult tasks for the engineers and maintenance people in the Cat II test force was to get inside the head of the operational folks and stick to the business at hand of establishing and documenting the capabilities of the system. Engineers, being creative by nature, become fascinated with making things better. Sometimes this becomes a detractor to completing the immediate task at hand. Avoiding this creative thinking syndrome as the Cat II program progressed was imperative.

Bruce Hartman and I had observed several unusual things happening during some of the test flights and made up our minds to chase this unexpected phenomenon to its source and identify it. We marched into Ken's office and laid out this great plan for "adjusting" several test flights to collect the needed data and were busy selling him on how interesting this might be.

"Does what you have observed have any great impact on aircraft or sensor performance?" Ken asked.

"Not really," we replied. "But it would be nice to identify all the aspects of what is happening here and then move on."

At that point Ken leaned back in his chair and looked at us with his usual fatherly engineer face and said, "We have a very thorough Cat II test plan that has been coordinated with everyone in the program. You two wrote a good bit of that. A well thought–out test plan. It is essential that it be followed closely, the data carefully reduced, and that procedures usable by the operational units be developed. Now you have just said this thing you are chasing does not directly affect either aircraft or sensor performance. True?"

"True," we replied.

"Well, here is what we are going to do. Follow the plan, don't get sidetracked, and when all the things in the plan are done we can talk about this again sometime."

Bruce and I looked at each other, turned to Ken and said, "Yes, Sir." And that was the end of our first sidetrack. In the test environment it is

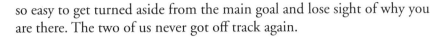
so easy to get turned aside from the main goal and lose sight of why you are there. The two of us never got off track again.

Write that down in the book

In the latter phases of the Cat II program all procedures must stand and die by what is written on the paper. We did maintenance adjustments, equipment repairs, trouble–shooting, and mission preparations by what the manuals said, not what they meant to say. No more tinkering with the film processing in the Mobile Processing Center (MPC) to accommodate less than optimum exposures during flight or compensate for non–standard aperture settings. Process the film by the numbers. Gone were the neat little phrases stenciled on the aircraft's camera–bay doors that read, "If you can't hold up 300 pounds by yourself, don't undo these screws." Everything had to be done by the book. No more logos on the vertical tail fins announcing, "Moon Equipped." Verifying and validating what was written in the manuals was a task the maintenance folks hated. There was a temptation to open the manual and then go about their business as before without much reference to the book.

A simple example

On one occasion I went down to the radar shop where Sgt. Joe McAleer was troubleshooting a radar transmitter. "Are the manual procedures okay?" I asked.

He looked up at me with a pained look and said "They're just fine, Major." And he continued about his business. As I watched him it was obvious that he was not using the manual or even turning the pages to pretend he was following the written procedures.

"I'll tell you what," I said. "Why don't I get a little training here and you can watch me while I check out this box using the manual and its checklists." He nodded okay and turned the book to the beginning of the sequence of tests to be done. I started with step one and went from there.

Abruptly at step four he yelled, "Don't!" and grabbed my arm. "If you hook that probe to that junction you'll blow out the traveling wave tube (TWT) driver. You need to ground this circuit right here first."

"Where does it say that in the manual, Sarge?" I asked.

"It doesn't," he said.

"It needs to," I said, "because some maintenance guy at Beale is going to try to troubleshoot this thing and he's gonna blow out the driver for the TWT. And it will be our fault because you know how to do it right and didn't submit a change to this procedure."

Sgt. McAleer's problem was that he knew that system inside and out, knew every circuit, every board, every screw, and every connector by heart. He could fix it in the dark wearing boxing gloves during a sandstorm. He spent months at the Goodyear plant working on production and assembly lines. (Throughout the Blackbird program Air Force people were introduced to the various plants where they were integrated into the work force as employees.) He was always looking at the manuals but did what he thought they should say and not exactly what they did say. He looked at me for a long time and finally spoke. "I got the message, Major. It won't happen again."

"You promise to read the manual step by step and fix the errors, and I promise not to help you get ready for a mission. Fair enough?"

A big smile crossed his face as we shook hands. "Fair enough, Sir." And the manuals improved very quickly.

Category III testing took place at the Blackbird's main operational base, Beale AFB. There, without all the "help" from the test force, the operational units charged off on their own with the flight handbook, the maintenance manuals, as much support equipment as was available at the time, and the other bits, pieces, and spares needed to start out operating the aircraft as intended. This was, of course, done in parallel with the operational command's desire to show off its new weapon system, demonstrate how well it works, and how they could do the mission better than before. It was not an easy transition. Additional aircrews had to be trained, and ground personnel had to be integrated into the skeleton cadre that had received specialized factory training and hands–on experience at Edwards. The Strategic Air Command operations at Beale were bound by a much more rigid structure. They had the problem of regularizing the flexible personnel and support organizational interrelationships that had worked well at the Cat II site. It was the Category III testing unit's chore to operate and maintain the airplane and its associated systems by the numbers, by the book, and by the written word. Conceptually speaking this was a really keen idea. After all SAC was a by the numbers kind of outfit. But weapons systems are complicated and it was a challenge to weld their care and feeding into a rigid documented framework in such a short time. The supply and logistics support now had to go through the real system. No more borrowing spares from the individual contractor's production line when there were none on the shelf at the depot.

Everything needed to operate must be preplanned and on hand at the site, or the mission didn't go. The mission must go as planned. At Beale there was no longer on–site access to a strong group of experienced engineers the way it had been at Edwards. The using command depended on maintenance data, procedures, and training that was founded on the Cat II testing experience. This made the written word an extremely important element of the transition. All this written documentation had to be as right as it could be.

Before there are any incorrect conclusions drawn here about the test organizational flexibility vs. the operational organization's rigidity, it is necessary to understand the very different objectives of the two groups. One group designs, forges, sharpens, and polishes the knife. The operational folks have to use it in the real world the way it was intended. There are different rules and certainly different consequences. Operational application of the Blackbird and her systems demanded adherence to a structured set of rules and procedures. The aircrews took this lady where the average bear would never be asked to go. (Operationally there were over 100 anti–aircraft missiles fired at the Blackbird and only one bird took a shrapnel hit. There were no knockdowns.) Our hat is off to the operational aircrews and support people. Saying there were structured procedures to be followed in the maintenance and preparation for a mission is in no way intended to diminish their accomplishments, dedication, and courage. They regularly rolled this Thoroughbred out of the barn, wiped her down, and took her where she was designed to go.

On with the story

Now let's look at the SR–71 Category II Performance, Stability, and Control test program as it played out at Edwards AFB from 1964 through 1970.

When the SR–71 test program was being formulated back in early 1963 there were several major decisions to be made regarding what was to be tested, who would do the testing (the Air Force or the contractor) and where the testing would be done. One of Kelly Johnson's ground rules was that the contractor must be allowed to run his own test program and must control his own assets to accomplish this. This concept had been implemented to the ultimate in the CIA–run A–12 Program. Lockheed, mainly because of program security issues, was given complete control of the testing, including the establishment of an entire test site under Lockheed control. Air Force and other government people were involved, but the A–12 Program was run by Lockheed with a minimum of outside participation. In fact, this arrangement worked very well and there was serious consideration given to using the same approach for the SR–71 Program. A major difference between the two aircraft's support and employment strategies, however, demanded a totally different testing approach. The A–12 was never envisioned to be deployed within any standardized Air Force organizational support structure. The unique support for the A–12 was all to be provided by Lockheed and a system of subcontractors and vendors. In an operational sense the A–12 piggy–backed on, or pirated from, the existing Air Force operational infrastructure. (This is the classic manner in which most, if not all, major black programs are supported. Nothing sinful or sinister about that. That is just the way it was and will probably always be.) On the other hand, very early on, it was clear the SR–71 would be supported, operated, and deployed by the Air Force. For the most part this system would have to fit the standard depot, base, maintenance, supply, and personnel structure. There was also the ever–present possibility that other versions of the Blackbird would be produced in significant numbers. Whatever was done in the SR program would have an important effect on those future programs.

The A–12's abbreviated approach to testing was not adequate for the SR–71, although there was certainly a desire to meld the best features of both the contractor–only and the standard Air Force testing approach. In the end there developed an excellent marriage of the two program philosophies. This proved advantageous to both aircraft variants as well as to the Air Force and contractor support teams.

Allocating the SR–71 Flight Test Assets

The following decisions were made with regard to the Lockheed test fleet.

Lockheed would have three airplanes assigned to the Category I test fleet. The first airplane, tail number 950, would be instrumented for conducting performance, stability, and control testing.

The next two airplanes to come off the line, tail numbers 951 and 952, would be assigned to Lockheed for systems testing and other work that Lockheed might need to do.

The Air Force side of the SR–71 test force would receive three aircraft as well. When added to the three YF–12A aircraft that were engaged in a combined Lockheed/Air Force test program, this would bring nine Blackbirds to Edwards AFB for participation in the various flight testing programs. Two additional aircraft were brought into the Cat II fleet later for special reasons.

But all that didn't just happen

With the decision to include a performance airplane in Category II testing, the Air Force test fleet became three airplanes. The fourth airplane off the line, tail number 953, was assigned as the Category II performance airplane. This aircraft would be instrumented by Kelly's Skunk Works using the same instrumentation technology used in 950, the Lockheed performance aircraft. The next two aircraft immediately following down the production line, tail numbers 954 (production number five) and 955 (production number six) were assigned for systems test. The testing life and times of these latter two aircraft is covered elsewhere in this book.

When the configuration of the Category II test fleet was under discussion, there were questions about how data for completion and confirmation of the flight handbook would be done. Lockheed suggested they could do the testing on their instrumented airplane and share the data with the test force. The powers that be at the Air Force Flight Test Center did not like that approach. They characterized the sharing of performance data with Kelly like sharing your lunch with a lion. The decision of whether Air Force Category II program would have its own fully instrumented performance airplane, in addition to two systems test airplanes, was run up the line in the Air Force. Principals in these discussions were Col. Horace A. Templeton, the System Program Director at Wright Patterson Air Force Base, Col. Guy M. Townsend (later Brig. General) Director of the Flight Test Directorate at AFFTC, and Lt.Col. Norman Drake, representing the SR–71 Test Force. One of the stops in the decision process involved briefing Gen. Bernard Schriever, Commander of Air Force Systems Command at the time. The test force people wanted to present their rationale why another performance airplane was needed.

Following is Norm Drake's account of the reasons for a second instrumented aircraft and his description of how the briefing took place.

"There was no doubt in the minds of anyone in the Air Force testing business that without a dedicated Air Force performance aircraft, we, the test force, would simply be out in left field. We would always be begging Kelly and his crew for performance test data. We also felt that there was a complementary nature in having two performance aircraft, an already instrumented and functional aircraft ready to go should something happen to 950 for one thing. Having an additional data collection aircraft to cover more data points would allow the overall performance flight test program to progress more rapidly. We wanted to be able to fill in inside the limiting edges, as Lockheed went about defining the real outside boundaries of the flight envelope. Another instrumented performance bird meant big bucks, and one more test machine to soak up Kelly's aircraft instrumentation resources. Kelly also did not believe it was a worthwhile expenditure of effort and dollars. Plus from a purely proprietary point of view, it loosened his control on program performance data.

"Well, Temp, Guy Townsend, and I trundled off to Systems Command Headquarters at Andrews AFB to brief Schriever. We had scheduled a briefing to plead our case. We felt strongly this second instrumented airframe was the key to a healthy Air Force test program. We arrived at General Schriever's office at the appointed date and hour. His secretary asked us our business and Temp explained that we had an appointment to brief the General but could not really discuss the subject with anyone else.

"'He is over at his quarters having lunch,' the secretary said. 'You should go over there and brief him. General Schriever is expecting you.'

"We grabbed our charts and viewgraphs and assorted other briefing props and beat it over to Schriever's quarters and knocked on the door. Greeted by the General's batman, we were led to the dining room and after reporting in proper military fashion, began our presentation. It was an urgent issue in our minds and we had thoroughly done our homework. We were ready to give the General 'both barrels.'

"Just after the midpoint in the presentation, the general wiped his mouth and hands with his napkin, stood, and said, 'Thank you very much.'

"Without another comment he turned and walked out the front door of his quarters to his waiting car and was gone. There we stood with our charts and our viewgraphs in hand, and absolutely no answer. Not much left to do after that but leave. We all filed out and got in Temp's waiting car and off we went.

"The issue of a second performance airplane, yes or no, just hung in the air for about the next six weeks. Then one day Schriever was out at Edwards visiting on some completely unrelated issue and casually dropped the comment that, 'Yes, the Air Force Flight Test Center would be getting an instrumented performance test aircraft for the SR–71 Category II flight test program.'

"We later asked retired Gen. Guy Townsend if he remembered this meeting and his comment was, 'Vividly.' "

Balancing the Lockheed and Air Force efforts

The decision to put a performance airplane in the Cat II program now required a division of efforts between what Lockheed would do and what the Air Force test crews and aircraft would do. The contractor retained the task of expanding and documenting the aircraft envelope. That means, in general, Lockheed crews would be the first to deliberately fly to the limits of the envelope and the data obtained would be shared with the Category II test force. The test force would be tasked to work within the limits of the Lockheed established envelope and to fill in the data points needed to establish and confirm flight manual data. It was agreed that no changes would be made in the flight manual without the approval of the Category II performance test team. All data was shared and all changes were coordinated.

What on earth is the flight manual?

The aircraft flight manual (the Dash–One) was just one book in a great long series of manuals that cover everything there was to know about a particular aircraft, its limits, its operation, maintenance, depot repair, inspection cycles, time change hardware and components, and on and on.

The flight manual was the basic document for operating the airplane and planning for its use. This manual contains all mission planning data, the pilot and RSO handbook data, checklists for flight, etc. When the airplane was first flown it was operated in accordance with the flight manual developed by the contractor. At this time the manual, of necessity, was based on ground test data and analysis. Because of this, the data was conservative and would not allow full exploitation of the airplane's capabilities. It was only through exhaustive testing and continuous revision that the full potential of the system would be realized. First, the limits of operation were defined and then intermediate data points were established.

The manuals for a specific aircraft represent the ultimate instruction book. The volumes, all designated by dash and a number, fill many a bookshelf. The flight manual makes up just one part of the manual system. If the planner or pilot wants to know how many feet the takeoff roll will be on a particular day, at a particular altitude, at a particular temperature, at the prevailing humidity, with the wind at a certain average velocity coming from a certain angle to the runway, when the aircraft weighs just so many pounds, and the runway slopes at a certain angle, and how far past the starting point aircraft will have to go before it can pass over a fifty foot obstacle, there are charts in the Dash–One to generate that answer. Called chase–around charts, these data sheets have several families of curves on a single page, all of which are geometrically related to each other. You start with your chosen beginning parameter and proceed to its location on Chart 1, and then chase around the page going from chart to chart factoring in parameter after parameter until you reach the last chart in the sequence and hopefully your answer. Using these charts requires skill, judgment, and knowledge. Collecting the mountains of information needed to create these charts is a monumental technical challenge.

The aircraft Dash–One contains many sections that include system and subsystem descriptions, standard operating parameters and conditions, limits for instrument readings, flight operating limitations for airspeed, engine parameters, aircraft CG operating limits, asymmetrical loading limitations, G–limits under all sorts of conditions, and it goes on from there. The flight handbook is a perfect example of the total instruction book. It even contains a section on emergency procedures for every known in–flight and ground emergency ever encountered or likely to be encountered. This book has everything but an 800 number for in–flight tech support. Test flyers and operational aircrews live and die by what is written in this book—literally.

Putting together an accurate and complete set of information in a manual such as the flight manual takes lots and lots of data points, many bottles of aspirin, a zillion hours of sifting data, of re–testing, of adjusting, calculating, doing it over again, and collecting more data. It is an endless job suited for only the most talented and skilled of technically proficient people. Those not interested in excruciating detail, high stakes, and many nights burning the midnight oil need not apply. But the aircrews cannot leave home without this book and the information it contains. Nobody in their right mind flies a modern military aircraft, complex or not, without committing most of the Dash–One to memory. If you're an old gray–haired crew member you know exactly what I mean.

On the ground side of this equation, the maintenance people followed the same obsessive adherence to what is written in their manuals, the Dash–Two, –Three, all the way through –Eight, to –Ten and beyond.

The bottom line here is that these books and the information they contain is tough to get, harder yet to present, and finally, impossible to operate without. During the SR–71 program the contractors and the Air Force teamed together throughout Category I, II, and III testing to generate this information and validate the data presented. Anything less would have been unacceptable.

Basics for the Flight Manual

Here are some of the questions the early part of the flight test program must answer:

What is the range of this airplane? This question alone involves many parts. With full fuel, how far can you fly with takeoff and return from the ground? How far can you go if you takeoff and refuel in flight, returning to the starting point? How far can you go starting with an in–flight refueling and going to another tanker? The answers must be thoroughly verified and then presented in the flight manual.

What happens if you are full of fuel and lose an engine on takeoff? Will the airplane have enough thrust to climb, or will it sink back into the ground? What are the specific effects of temperature and field altitude on performance? Can you operate from high, hot airfields with limited runway lengths? What are the limits?

What is the best climb profile for maximum range? If you know the absolutely best climb profile, can the crew actually perform it? (It was determined during Cat II that the absolutely best profile for climb was too hard to fly to be worth the advantage obtained.)

Are there systems limits that define the way you fly the airplane? Tire limit speeds are a good example of hardware limits to what you can do. Tire limit speed on the SR was just over 230 knots, so any operations that might exceed this speed on the ground must be avoided. Secondary effects of gross weight also must be considered.

If, during a mission, it becomes necessary to depart from the high speed profile, and maybe slow down, what speed should you shoot for and how far can you go at that speed? What are the range numbers at Mach 3.2, 3.0, 2.8, 2.0, etc.? Should you go subsonic, or stay at some supersonic speed? What speed?

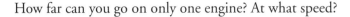

How far can you go on only one engine? At what speed?

These are only a few representative questions facing the performance test program and the trick is to anticipate all the reasonable ones. Test conditions must be defined and flown to generate the necessary data. The questions were simple and direct; getting the answers and proving them to be correct was a bear.

The test hardware arrives

The first of these beautiful machines, 950, we called her Number one, arrived at Edwards in the latter part of 1964. There were several flights flown out of Palmdale prior to that. At least one of those flights was flown by Col. Fox Stephens, Director of the Air Force Cat II Test Force. The test program was officially underway.

To give a sense of the pressure and pace of the test program it is interesting to note that three operational SRs were deployed from Beale Air Force Base to Okinawa in March 1968. They were ready to fly missions over Vietnam by the middle of that month. The monumental effort crammed into that brief intervening period of 38 months included demonstrating everything the aircraft, flight crews, and maintenance crews would need to know and do to carry out the mission. The operational folks at Beale made incredible strides in getting the weapon system fine–tuned. There was a serious difference between the aircraft test and demonstration program and getting this same aircraft and its support structure ready to do the intended job. The combined efforts of all contractors involved, test force personnel, and operational people at Beale compressed the time from first flight to first operational mission to the bare minimum. By way of comparison, the F–111 first flight took place in Ft Worth on 17 December 1964 (Kittyhawk Day), six days before the first flight of SR–71, 950 from Palmdale. The F–111 did not reach its initial operational unit until 1969 and was not deployed until much later.

In defense of the overall F–111 program, the Program Office at Wright Field, and specifically the Edwards F–111 test force, it is important to remember that the F–111 had all the help it could stand from the Secretary of Defense, Mr. Robert McNamara, and the U.S. Navy. The Blackbird was not saddled with that kind of help. To be perfectly fair, the SR–71 did have two cousins flying at the same time with similar internal aircraft systems, the A–12 and the YF–12. Clearly, being a black program, even if much of the SR–71 testing was by then out in the public eye, provided a huge advantage. The spotlighted, joint–service F–111 was forced to suffer the slings and arrows of a normal program with all the political hoorah associated therewith. A piece by piece comparison of the two programs points out the differences.

Test chores assigned to specific Blackbirds

950 — Number One: safety of flight, envelope expansion, aircraft systems performance, engine/inlet compatibility, handling qualities, stability and control, range factor, and whatever else came along in the area of pure aircraft performance. Aircraft 950 was essentially a single–seater, as the entire second station was filled with instrumentation, photo panels, and the like.

A little side trip

During this time there always develops the classic argument between the airplane builder and the engine manufacturer. The airframer says, "I can't meet the specs I promised to the customer because your engines are not putting out the thrust you promised me. And besides your hardware is too heavy."

The engine manufacturer replies, "With the sorry distorted and turbulent air your inlet produces and feeds my engine, it's a wonder they run at all. The extra weight is to keep the engine safe from all the goofy vibrations and other irritations your lousy airframe produces. Then to add insult to injury, you bleed off too much compressor air for cooling the aircraft systems. No wonder the poor engines don't push so hard. And besides that, your sorry fuel system doesn't meet the engine's needs at certain places in the flight envelope."

"With the lack of thrust there are damn few places in the envelope we can reach, so we didn't think fuel flow would be a problem," replies the airframer.

And the conversation goes downhill from there. It sounds funny when it is reduced to a couple of remarks, but the issue is a dead serious one with much hanging in the balance. The performance of the aircraft is the most obvious, but the others are directly related to profit, product sales, corporate pride, and follow–on business.

In the classic weapon system procurement approach at that time the government purchased the engine under separate contract and the airframe was procured under separate contract, so the government became the integrator, stuck between its two contractors and in fact being a customer and supplier to both—not a good position to be in.

951 — Number Two was a systems aircraft with the RSO's second station open and operational as much as it could be at the time. For the most part this aircraft carried someone acting in the capacity of a flight test engineer in the second seat. Inlet and propulsion work were accomplished on this aircraft. Functional sensor bays supported the initial radar and camera flights.

It may sound silly but one of the functions of this aircraft was that of a form–and–fit mockup for late–arriving boxes, especially the offensive and defensive electronics. On one occasion we went down to the hangar floor to watch an electronic jammer box be tested for a trial fit. The questions were, does it fit in the hole, are the mounts in the right place, are the box's connectors in the right place to mate with the aircraft cabling, are the connectors the same kind, do the cooling air inlet and exhaust holes match with the aircraft system, can a maintenance man reach the connectors and can he tighten the mounting bolts? The sample box to be tested was a nice little plywood replica of the real thing, painted black of course, with the connectors, air holes and mounts all attached per the drawing. It did not fit. Would not even go in the hole. Just a seemingly silly little test but one of critical importance. Today all that early pushing and shoving is done by computer in a virtual airplane with a virtual box. Most problems and interferences are ironed out before any metal is bent or connectors soldered to cables.

952 — Number Three rounded out the Lockheed's test aircraft fleet. It was another systems aircraft with functional sensor bays. It carried cameras, radar, and electronic intelligence (ELINT) systems for initial flight testing and performance evaluation. It was performance evaluation

in the sense that the cameras came on when commanded, transported film, the velocity over height (V/H) signals provided were in the ballpark, and the environmental conditions within the sensor bays were within design limits. Initial camera resolution samples were collected and evaluated. In the later phases of the Cat I program a test jammer system and an electronic warning system were installed. This was a marriage of science, engineering, witchcraft, and art. There was no subject shrouded in more blue smoke and black magic than the design and development of electronic warfare equipment and systems. The electronic countermeasures and the counter–counter, and the counter–counter–counter stuff changes so quickly it is the most difficult of disciplines in which to retain currency. There is always a better mouse trap and it is always a different shape. There is only one constant. The new and improved electronics will take more space, more cooling air, and more power. And they will make all the little mice running around on the hangar floor sterile.

953 — Number Four aircraft was the Air Force's equivalent of 950. The instrumentation was essentially the same as that of Number One. The instrumentation was designed and installed by Lockheed – with one significant difference. The photo panels and other recording devices were installed in the sensor bays so that there was room for an RSO/flight engineer in the second station. The presence of a second crewmember was very helpful in reducing the pilot's load in accomplishing the test data points and flying the aircraft at the same time. The Air Force felt that with a two–man crew it could accomplish more data collection per flight. Aircraft 953 carried no sensors but, like all the test aircraft, sported a fully functional astro–inertial navigation system. The presence of an operating ANS assured the collection and recording of continuous data with respect to aircraft altitude, attitude, velocity, in–flight motions, and precise geographic position. It is said that an inertial navigation system always knows where it is. There are times when it does not know where the rest of the world is but there is no doubt in its little mind as to where it is. (This issue is discussed in depth in a later chapter, *The 2,500 Mile Micrometer*.) Ken Hurley had always maintained that the greatest source of aircraft positional and movement data was collected and recorded by the ANS with an accuracy and frequency far superior

to the photo panel data used initially for flight parameter work. Later in the flight test program this concept was fully embraced and proved to be very successful.

954 — Number Five was a systems aircraft with secondary duties covering propulsion, environmental control system (ECS) instrumentation, maintenance procedure verification, egress demonstrations, and emergency procedures in an unpressurized cockpit were all mixed in with a complete menu of full–up sensor test flights.

Bob Gilliland, one of the primary Lockheed test pilots, was a tall fellow with long arms. It was always rumored that Kelly designed the cockpit around someone of his size. He could reach anything inside the pilot's station no matter what. Another of Kelly's pilots, Darrel Greenamyer, was on the other end of the size scale. When Darrel was placed in the cockpit and depressurization simulated (this was done by pumping up his pressure suit to 3.5 psi over atmospheric pressure), his suit became so rigid that he could not reach the ejection seat activation loop mounted on the seat between his knees. The immediate result was to add a second loop that rose above the initial loop. Darrel was happy and so were all the other shorter–than–Gilliland crew members who flew the aircraft. Darrel, by the way, was an avid air racer in the unlimited classes. He still holds the world speed record for a prop driven aircraft. That aircraft, a highly modified Grumman Bearcat, is in the Smithsonian. Greenamyer was also the driving force behind a recently attempted recovery of an almost new B–29 from Greenland. The aircraft made an emergency landing in the boonies and was abandoned just after World War II. After much effort and one unsuccessful recovery attempt, Darrel and crew were taxiing for takeoff on a frozen lake bed when the auxiliary power unit broke a fuel line. The aircraft was consumed by fire. All the crew escaped but a nearly pristine B–29 was lost. Tragic!

955 — Number Six was a systems capable bird with full sensor accommodations. This aircraft flew missions to collect data on sensor performance, establish the reliability and system readiness data needed to assess the sensor contractor's award fee payments, and fill in wherever there were other missions required. In the later stages of the Cat II test program, this aircraft and sister ship, Number Five, flew the Hester routes to simulate operational mission profiles and collect sensor performance data during four hot legs. Aircraft Number Six is one of the few test program birds to have lived a full life. It flew missions out of England with an experimental radar and sported new tail numbers to disguise the fact that she was an old, gray headed lady. But she never needed a cane to get around. The last flight on this airframe was 24 January 1985. Now she sits at the USAF Flight Test Museum at Edwards wishing she were back in harness somewhere.

Later visitors to the test force at Edwards

There were additional aircraft that visited the test program and were used for specific purposes.

956 — Number Seven was the first SR trainer and was flown from Edwards for stability and control testing. Walt Daniels flew the major portion of these flights. Walt went on to bigger and better things. Later he became a general officer and was assigned to the Pentagon. He died of a heart attack at too young an age.

960 — Number Eleven was an updated bird with many of the Cat I revisions driven by results of the flight test and systems testing done in the first few months at Edwards and elsewhere. It was flown from Edwards briefly to evaluate updates and then went to Beale.

967 — Number Eighteen was an updated aircraft assigned to the test force for a time. Its purpose was to evaluate additional changes previously defined in the test program and now implemented in production. This aircraft incorporated many of the cockpit changes driven by the maturing test program.

Number Four gets delivered

The performance airplane, 953, was delivered late to the test force near the end of 1965. Its arrival was delayed due to lay up for instrumentation by Lockheed at Palmdale. Instrumentation consisted primarily of photo panels mounted in the chine areas with state of the art high speed cameras and oscillographs to record the data. The rear cockpit was specifically configured as an engineering station as opposed to the standard RSO station. Those functions from the RSO's systems, such as the ANS, Triple Display Indicator (TDI) etc., were retained for test purposes and some ultimately became keys to testing successes. It must be said that the instrumentation system, though reasonably modern for the time, was a very labor–intensive system that produced data at a snail's pace. Photo panels had to be read frame by frame, with many data points to be recorded from each frame. Each flight produced literally hundreds of these individual frames of data and many all–night sessions were held reading the data from a single flight. As the performance testing progressed Ken Hurley noted that large quantities of the data being produced through the photo panels was probably also being recorded by the ANS on its digital recorder. He suggested that Nortronics be approached about downloading this data in digital form and using it instead of the photo panel data. This was done, and before the program progressed very far, it became the standard procedure to check to see whether the ANS tape was good and, if it was, to simply store the duplicate photo panel data. This change significantly speeded up the data reduction process and improved data accuracy. The photo panel data was still needed for such things as engine conditions and stability and control data.

Some Performance Testing Problems

Probably the most significant problem encountered in performance testing was controlling the configuration of the test airplane. It was not that the configuration could not be tracked, but keeping the change activity consistent with the data being generated was a significant chore. The performance airplane was generating flight manual data while five other SR–71 test airplanes were flying and generating essential changes in the form of Service Bulletins. Not all changes have an effect on airplane performance, but some certainly do. Some of these changes voided large quantities of flight test data and returned the performance flight test program to square one. This is just an example of what happens when there is a high degree of concurrency in a test program. If flight tests were done in serial fashion, none would ever finish.

A good example The loss of 952 near Tucumcari, New Mexico, resulted in a significant aerodynamic change to the SR–71 aircraft. This occurred at a point in the program after a great deal of cruise performance and stability data had been collected by both Lockheed and the Air Force test program.

In the initial design of the SR, the nose of the airplane drooped six degrees below the longitudinal axis of the aircraft. After the loss of 952 it was decided to tilt the nose cone up two degrees to decrease trim drag and adjust the center of lift forward. This change left only a four degree droop and caused all cruise and handling data generated up to that time to be discarded and rerun. Both Lockheed and the test force scrambled to catch up. This was a turning point in data collection and processing philosophy. The use of ANS data instead of photo panels came into its own and saved the day.

A compliment to the performance folks

It wasn't until much later that facilities at Arnold Engineering Development Center, Tullahoma, Tennessee, came on line to confirm early performance data. It is worthy of note that after the flight test program was long gone and the last production aircraft had been delivered to SAC, the errors between the analyses and the tests conducted at Tullahoma were small.

Noteworthy results of Cat I and Cat II performance testing.

A prime performance parameter in any reconnaissance airplane is its range. Early flights were planned very conservatively, usually on the order of 2,000 miles ground to ground with full fuel at takeoff. By the end of Cat II, with the airframe and engine improvements made and operating techniques refined, the ground–to–ground range of the airplane had been extended to over 3,000 miles. Similar improvements were made in refuel–to–refuel range.

Aft transfer of fuel—a case in point

The tragic ending of 952 brought about some very important changes to refine the breed. The change in the nose droop cited before was one, and the accident also highlighted an equally important issue of center of gravity control, the need for a method of transferring fuel aft to adjust the CG for optimum range. This system was installed in production airplanes but never in the test airplanes.

The circumstances surrounding the CG and fuel transfer issue went like this. In the early airplanes Kelly was so paranoid about the potential for aft CG problems that he installed a self–adjusting fuel system that was programmed to transfer fuel from the tanks to the engine in a sequence so the aircraft center of gravity was always within conservative limits. The pilot's only option was to manually transfer fuel forward. In normal subsonic flight the center of pressure (CP) for a delta–like wing is forward of where it would be for that same wing at supersonic flight. Kelly's fuel automatic sequence assumed a normal takeoff, an acceleration to Mach 3, and then a cruise at that condition and altitude. If anything went awry at that configuration and the aircraft was forced to decelerate, the CP would move forward ahead of the aircraft CG. That condition causes an unstable situation in pitch for the aircraft. So when the test aircrews encountered some form of aircraft problem requiring an unplanned deceleration, they immediately began to transfer fuel forward in anticipation of a subsonic CG problem. Good thinking and a good plan, but, if they later solved the problem and wanted to return to supersonic flight, the aircraft was saddled with a terribly inefficient forward CG requiring up–elevon trim to compensate. The resulting high trim drag would mean the aircraft now had too little fuel remaining to reach its destination. The logical solution was an ability to transfer fuel aft to correct this problem without causing other problems. In a testing environment this loss of range capability was merely an inconvenience, but to operational crews it could be the end of everything.

Kelly was adamant, "No," but the test force stuck to its guns and in the end a manual aft–transfer system was installed in the operational aircraft. To satisfy all concerns here is how it was implemented:

The manual aft–transfer rate had to be half of the manual forward fuel transfer rate.

A spring–actuated valve closed and prevented aft transfer in the case of an electrical failure even if the electrical failure occurred during the process of aft transfer.

The pilot's switch to actuate aft transfer had to be held down to accomplish the transfer. This was to assure that if the pilot was distracted (and the

Blackbirds had a million ways to do that) he would not forget and leave the aft transfer on and end up with a terribly out of balance aircraft.

At a Blackbird reunion, Ken Hurley was talking to Rich Graham, an SR–71 pilot, and author of *SR–71 Revealed: The Inside Story*, about the issue of aft transfer and Rich complained, "Yeah, and you had to hold that damn switch down the whole time."

Another thing learned from 952

A system was proposed to minimize the dynamics of an unstart situation. Although the unstart was not particularly dangerous in the straight and level flight, it was certainly dramatic. In other than straight and level conditions it could be downright dangerous. An unstart, in conjunction with a turning situation and an aft CG, were major factors in the loss of 952. The system later installed in all production airplanes caused the good inlet to go into restart configuration sympathetically with the failed inlet. This made the airplane much more symmetrical aerodynamically, so that it would decelerate straight ahead instead of yawing and rolling at the same time. This system was never tested in Cat II.

Some things were too hard to do

The test force devoted many hours and thoughts to determine the climb profile for optimum performance. Finally a profile was developed, refined, and tested during Cat II for the most distance covered with the least fuel while getting to altitude and speed. The initial climb schedule was to hold 400 knots equivalent airspeed for the climb immediately after takeoff, then after a push–over near 31,000 feet where the aircraft went supersonic, continue the climb at 400 knots until reaching the intended cruise Mach. In the end it was determined that 450 knots was a more efficient speed for the first segment of the climb. Many other profiles were tested and a few slightly more efficient ones were defined. These latter profiles were discarded because they were too difficult to fly for the small benefit derived.

Sometimes the using command appreciates your knowledge

Harold Chapman and Ken were sent off to SAC Headquarters to brief the Commander in Chief (CINC) on a spate of control problems that came out of nowhere. Harold was the test force control system expert.

The CINC was General J. D. Ryan, Three–finger Jack to his friends. Frenchy Bennett from the test force was there as well. During the briefing there were a large number of questions asked, many from the CINC himself. When the briefing was concluded, General Ryan got up and said, "We have received countless weapon system briefings from Systems Command people in this Headquarters but you gentlemen know your hardware better than any group we have ever seen here. Thank you!"

Summary–the numbers don't really tell the story

The Cat II performance, stability, and control program flown on aircraft 953 was begun on 9 November 1965. It consisted of 165 instrumented flight hours and 81 flights. A lot of blood, sweat, and tears were crammed into those flights. The countless ground support hours of data reduction and analysis just do not show up in the aircraft flight numbers. It is a pity there is not a way to explain and describe the countless hours spent by Art Lusby, Jim Scheuer, Dick Keller, Bob Suddereth, and an army of others who poured their every waking hour into solving the problems and producing usable and consistent data.

Sometimes the fixes were simple – simple but clever. The problems of heat were ever present. In particular the high temperature at extended cruise would cause the flight path accelerometer in the pitot boom to fail. Frank Doyle and Dick Keller solved that problem by wrapping the instrumentation in Reynolds aluminum foil to reflect the heat.

Almost all test airplanes live hard and die young

To close out this chapter it seems appropriate to tell what happened, where it happened, and when it happened to the original family of nine Blackbirds from the time the first YF–12s arrived at Edwards in 1964.

YF–12 60–6934   This aircraft served honorably during the interceptor testing program and then went on in another life to serve as an SR–71C trainer aircraft. Here is how all that happened. 934 was just sitting around minding its own business, gathering dust in the hangar when the trainer SR–71B #957 crashed at Beale AFB on 11 January 1968. That left only one two–seat trainer aircraft for the entire operational SR fleet. There were only two to begin with. Now then, because McNamara, in his infinite wisdom, had previously directed Lockheed to destroy all the

Blackbird tooling, another trainer could not be built. It could not be built in a conventional sense but it could be assembled from assorted pieces and other birds. The back half of YF–12 #934 was mated with the SR–71 forebody used in static testing and the result was SR–71C #981. This trainer #981 was universally hated by ground crews and aircrews alike. None of the tech data matched and it didn't fly like any of the other aircraft because it was neither YF nor SR. It was the ultimate mechanical equivalent of a high tech titanium shotgun wedding.

Rich Graham always said, "You know, that sucker never even flew straight. It was always a little out of whack. Just enough to keep you guessing."

YF–12 60–6935   This interceptor was transferred along with her sister (936) to a joint Air Force/NASA flight test program in June, 1969. After 145 flights bearing the NASA banner, this only surviving YF–12 airframe was ferried to the Air Force Museum at Wright–Patterson AFB, on 7 November 1979 and is currently on display there.

YF–12 60–6936   On 24 June 1971, after this aircraft had been transferred to NASA for service, pilot Jack Layton and back seater Billy Curtis experienced serious in–flight problems. On return to Edwards the wind was so high that an emergency landing was ruled out as an option. Both Layton and Curtis punched out over the dry lake bed. 936 crashed and burned on Rogers Dry Lake. Layton was picked up rather quickly. Because of the wind, Curtis drifted a considerable distance before reaching the ground. Search and rescue came up empty after Curtis managed to unintentionally evade his rescuers. Finally catching a ride back to the base on his own, he picked up his vehicle and made some brief stops by the flight surgeon's office and elsewhere. Because his parachute had a rescue beacon, which he had neglected to turn off, the rescue crews were finally able to track him down as he made his rounds around the base.

Both crew members returned to duty uninjured.

SR–71A 64–17950   Aircraft Number One died a flaming death on 10 January 1967 during a wet runway test on the main runway at Edwards. The pilot and only occupant, Art Peterson, did a skillful control job but to no avail as the aircraft plunged off the runway overrun and onto the dry lake bed. The nose wheel collapsed and the aircraft caught fire immediately. Art got out with

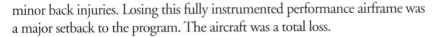

minor back injuries. Losing this fully instrumented performance airframe was a major setback to the program. The aircraft was a total loss.

While 950 was burning just off the end of the runway, Fox Stevens and Ken Hurley arrived in the local area in one of the other SR–71 test aircraft and asked for landing instructions. The Edwards tower informed them that the field was closed and no landings were permitted at this time. When asked what the problem was, the tower would only say, "The Edwards runway is closed until further notice."

Ken and Steve circled over the field and could see the SR burning off the end of the runway and asked for an explanation. "The director of the SR–71 test force is the pilot of this aircraft and we would like to know what is happening down there."

The Edwards tower responded just as their security procedures directed. "The Edwards runway is closed until further notice." To the tower's credit, however, it was not too long before Fox and Ken were allowed to land.

SR–71A 64–17951 Transferred to NASA in July of 1971. As part of the transfer protocol this aircraft received an extensive facelift, became known as a YF–12C, and was given a new tail number 60–6937. She made her first NASA flight in May, 1972. The last flight of this aircraft was to Palmdale on 22 December 1978. The aircraft sat at Palmdale until 1990 when it was moved to a place of honor at the Pima Air and Space Museum in Tucson, Arizona.

SR–71A 64–17952 This aircraft, Number Three, was lost 25 January 1966 resulting in the death of Jim Zwayer, RSO. The Lockheed pilot, Bill Weaver, survived the in–flight breakup. A more definitive description of the accident and circumstances are covered in the chapter *Number Three and Jim Zwayer Died the Same Day*. The remains of 952 lie buried near the riding stables at Edwards AFB.

SR–71A 64–17953 The performance bird, aka Number Four, died an in–flight death on 18 December 1969 near the southern end of Death Valley . The flight crew, pilot Col. Joe Rogers, and RSO Lt.Col. Gary Hidelabugh both ejected safely. In a taped interview, this is how Gary described the sequence of events.

"The aircraft had been in layup for a long time, adding, modifying, or upgrading, some of the aircraft instrumentation. This was the first flight for this bird after quite a long spell of sitting in the hangar. We were just coming off the tanker, heavy, and began to accelerate to supersonic flight when we experienced a pitchup. The nose began to oscillate from side to side rather violently. The aircraft had instantly progressed beyond anything we could ever recover from in the altitude we had to work with. Joe gave the command to punch out and we did. There was apparently some kind of obstruction in the pitot system causing a delay in actual pressure sensing to the stability augmentation system.

"We were floating down near a little town of Shoshone, California, which is about two lanes and a gas station. When I looked down I saw a car parked by the side of the road with two people standing outside. The driver must have heard the explosion on impact and seen the fireball. Here were these two people outside the car, the man taking pictures of us with a 35mm camera as we descended in our chutes. Once I'd landed, I walked over to talk and ask about a lift. I'm from a very small town in North Dakota, and those two tourists who just happened to be there that day, were from the same town. Small world or no?"

SR–71A 64–17954 11 April 1969, Bill Skliar and Noel Warner were on takeoff roll from Edwards at maximum weight. Just at rotation one of the tires or wheels let go and immediately the other two wheels and tires on that main gear failed due to overload. Bill aborted the takeoff. Magnesium wheel fragments ripped through the bottom of the wing rupturing the fuel tank. As the aircraft decelerated a fire began, the fuel ignited by magnesium fragments from the failed wheel rims. The aircraft came to rest in a puddle of burning fuel. The aircraft was totaled.

This accident spelled the end for mag wheels. All SR–71s in operation had their magnesium wheels replaced with aluminum ones.

Bill was one of those guys who was always inventing things, sometimes good for a test program and sometimes not so good. This was one of those times when his tinkering and creative thinking really paid off big.

Blackbird aircrews and F–104 pilots wore attachments to the heels of their flight boots called—as you might suspect—stirrups. The purpose of these stirrups was to allow a connection between the crew's feet and the wind–up cable reels that were part of the ejection seat. In the case of a bailout the crew's feet would be drawn in tight to foot rests at the bottom of the seat and held there until altitude and airspeed sensors separated the man and his parachute and his stirrups from the seat for the next step in the recovery sequence.

Getting the stirrups connected and disconnected while dressed in a full pressure suit was inconvenient to say the least. It was sometimes simple and easy, other times damn near impossible. Getting free of these tethers in a panic during an aircraft emergency on the ground was severely taxing on the crew member. Bill had invented and manufactured a clever little quick disconnect device that he wore on his stirrups all the time. His thinking was that if he ever needed to hop out while the aircraft was on the ground, he could quickly separate himself from the seat's cable tethers.

When 954 finally ground to a halt on the runway at Edwards that day, she was already on fire. When the aircraft came to rest, fire engulfed the plane and crew. Both Bill and Noel went through the emergency egress procedure but because of Bill's nifty little disconnects he was able to exit the front cockpit rather quickly. Noel was still in the back cockpit as the fire continued to rage. Bill returned to help Noel out of the rear seat and both men scrambled away none the worse for wear. Their pressure suits had protected them during their brief encounter with the flames. Shortly after the two had gotten away from the aircraft, a rescue chopper come in low and the downward rotor blast fanned the fire into a real inferno. A valuable lesson learned.

Bill Skliar died some years later while test flying a repair on one of his racing airplanes. A piece of nose cowling came off and smashed the cockpit causing him to crash. Bill and another brainchild of his, an aqua glider, graced the covers of *Popular Mechanics* and *Mechanics Illustrated* magazines in the mid–sixties. I felt honored when Bill let me fly his creation at Lake Isabella, north of Edwards.

SR–71A 64–17955 This aircraft lived a full life in both the testing and operational realms. Her last flight was in January 1985. 955 accumulated nearly 2,000 flying hours during a lifetime of 712 sorties. She is enshrined in the USAF Flight Test Museum at Edwards AFB.

The SR–71 and YF–12 flight test programs at Edwards packed a great deal of effort into a very short time span. When one considers what was accomplished, it is still amazing that it all got done in such a short time.

One last story

All versions of the Blackbird were painted black. The reasons were simple. The radar defeating elements of the Blackbirds were integral parts of the aircraft's frame and this plastic was black. Black paint was used to hide the plastic pieces which otherwise contrasted with the bare titanium skin. Also one of the few paints at the time that would stand the temperatures in flight, and provide the best re–radiation of the heat, was black. It was often said that if the paint with the best emissivity characteristics had been green then we would have been talking about Greenbirds all this time.

The B–70 was painted white. The idea behind the white was that because the B–70 was a Mach 3 dash–only aircraft, it did not have the requirement to re–radiate the heat accumulated during extended Mach 3 cruise. It was painted white so that it could reflect the anticipated heat pulse from an exploding nuclear device it had just dropped while dashing away at high Mach. The engineers at North American felt that the added heat pulse from the bomb flash plus the short term heat gain from the dash might be just enough to weaken the airframe elements along the belly of the aircraft through overheating. So the aircraft was painted a nice reflective white.

The contrast between the two aircraft was staggering. One was huge and big and white with great canards on the forward fuselage and painted so white it was hard to look at in the desert sun. The other was small by comparison, sitting low to the ground, sleek and sinister looking, with its inward–canted rudders. And of course painted flat black.

Vice President Hubert Humphrey came to Edwards on a visit to see what was happening at the Flight Test Center. He got the royal treatment and received briefings on every significant program at the Center. After an extensive and detailed briefing on the B–70 he was ushered into a hangar that housed an SR–71 and a YF–12. There he received a full Blackbird dog–and–pony show. He even sat in the cockpit of the YF–12. As he was leaving the closed hangar he turned, looked back through the small personnel door at the YF–12 there on display and asked, "Now, tell me again, is that the B–70?"

Closing on a positive note

People, their dedication, skills, and ideas, are what made the test program as successful as it was. "Wally" Weaver must have watched enough movies of drag chute openings to qualify as the Siskel and Ebert of runway photographic epics. Because he was trying to stop smoking cigars, he would cut a cigar into three pieces and then very methodically chew each end of each piece. The rest of us never understood how he could take a cold soggy chewed–up cigar stump that had been sitting in an ash tray for hours and start to chew on it again. Being associated with wheels, tires, brakes, and drag chutes can do that to a person.

Bill Quasney was a quiet deep thinker with technical smarts not available to the rest of us. Anybody who can visualize what goes on inside a turbojet engine like the J–58 and then conspire with others to create a pile of IBM cards to model portions of the engine's flight envelope has got my vote for creative thinking. Bill and his engine deck made ground simulations of engine flight performance a reality. And he is a graduate of the U.S. Naval Academy to boot.

SAC, the using command, provided experts and people skilled in a multitude of fields. Without their talents and perspective we would have had a little more difficulty in staying true to our course. Guys with worlds of experience like Ray Haupt (U–2, A–12, and SR–71 pilot) flew at The Area, Edwards, and Beale. From straight–wing F–84s with maybe five thousand pounds of thrust on a very good day to managing sixty–eight thousand pounds of thrust on the SR–71 has got to be a giant leap forward. Ray had an intuitive feel for the inlet and its operation during climb and accelerations. He put that talent to good use.

Robert Sowers and Al Hichew brought their own brand of cool professional flying to the test force. Skilled and experienced pilots, both men added that needed sense of operational perspective to assure the

Edwards Test Syndrome did not creep into our efforts. They kept us on the road toward delivering the most thoroughly documented machine we could to the users at Beale.

No aircraft is perfect when it first comes out of the box. A machine designed for performance far beyond anything else always provides opportunities to learn more of its characteristics. When the SR–71 arrived at Beale AFB she had the saddle on and the bit in her teeth. From there on the *Habus* handled her tack and rode her with great pride and skill.

Chapter 12

Security Was Everyone's Business

*"Now you know everything there is
to know about this program."*
Ken Hurley, SR–71 SPO 1964

"The geese fly high in the winter."
Beth Byrnes, Edwards AFB, 1966

To say that black programs have a heightened security shroud would be the understatement of the century. In today's climate of leaks, rumor, and innuendo, it is hard to conceive of a program where everyone kept their mouth closed and nothing leaked. There is little doubt in my mind that it would not be possible for a black program of the magnitude of the A–12, RS–12, YF–12A, SR–71 to exist unblabbed for more than about fifteen minutes. Current rules of governmental and public policy driven by the likes of the ACLU and others, force a contractor and the government to issue security clearances regardless whether the party in question can pass the background checks or the drug screen. Gary Aldrich's book *Unlimited Access, An FBI Agent Inside the Clinton White House,* clearly outlines that problem. At least once a week we see the results of this lack of discipline, inadequate personal character, shoddy moral standards, and the complete absence of individual ethics. The problem permeates the highest levels of our government even to the present.

Not so in the earlier times when people took their security oaths seriously and exercised personal courage in holding the line. At that time security was part of our national identity and jobs where classified information was guarded were considered a personal trust. The Blackbird program and its root programs covered literally thousands of cleared people dealing with every aspect of the project on a daily basis. The people at Area 51, the Skunk Works, the vast network of contractors, subcontractors, and suppliers, all kept it under their hat for years and years. People familiar with the MANHATTAN Project even admitted that their program was not as closely held as the OXCART side of the A–11/SR–71 program.

Extensive black operations are compartmentalized to limit the amount of knowledge any one individual might have of the overall aspects of a particular program. A clearance for any specific part or compartment is called a ticket, in the vernacular of the security–conscious. An entry briefing on the OXCART program took quite a while and the briefee signed several oaths at different times during the course of the briefing. When the briefing was completed to the O–3 level (the third level of the OXCART program; there were other levels) the recipient of the briefing had been walked through nine different levels of clearance above TOP SECRET. Each level represented another ticket. When the briefing was over and all the paperwork signed, the briefer then told the briefee a very standard and very large lie. "Now you know all there is to know about this program."

As a young captain, I received my O–3 briefing from a very seasoned major. He walked me through all nine levels and explained how they built on one another and what the program knowledge limitations were for individuals holding a particular level of clearance or group of tickets. When he finished the briefing he asked me if I had any questions. I asked, "Is it really important that I remember all these levels and what they represent?"

The major frowned, was quiet for a moment and said, "Yes, extremely important. We are going to go through the whole thing again."

When the second briefing was finished I began to understand, then he repeated the lie. "Now you know all there is to know about this program."

It takes the average person about fifteen minutes to discover that he or she is several tickets shy of a full clearance, no matter what the program or project might be. And for good security reasons it should always be that way. I soon found that there were many things going on for which I had no tickets.

My boss explained, "You are quite bright and I am sure with a little effort you can deduce a lot of what is going on around here. It is simply not a wise expenditure of your time, nor is it to your advantage to do so."

Excellent advice, and it was followed to the letter.

It's not easy being more than one person

One of the real traps of serving in a black program is that you are always serving two or more masters. Black programs exist, flourish, and are productive because there are many many normal programs that maintain the technical and procedural infrastructure. Without this parallel, in–the–open world to lean on, black programs would become rather chaotic and in part ineffective. Very few people have the luxury of serving a black program totally. So a person walks back and forth between programs like passing through some kind of Alice–in–Wonderland looking glass. Now mix that problem with an added complexity. Rated aircrew members serving in technical or engineering (desk) jobs throughout the Air Force face a unique dilemma. They serve a third boss with respect to their aircrew duties and proficiency. Now you begin to have a feel for the skitso life of an Air Force engineer, pilot, or navigator, or observer. They are assigned to in–the–open engineering or research programs that cover them for black programs. Separate from those, an aircrew member must maintain his skills and flying currency, being responsive, willing, and ready to travel on short notice to anywhere for any of the three bosses; black program, open program, or flying duties. That was more than a little stressful.

Some cleverness required

Let's add a couple of wrinkles. Some of us flew aircraft based in both the normal and black worlds and dealt with the same contractors in both normal and black capacity. This is living a life jam packed with opportunities for screwups. Now, stir in the fact that your wife and family members must have no clue as to what you are doing in the black world and you begin to have a feel for the really goofy existence led by the average bear in a black program. You must constantly think about who you are talking to, are they in your black or normal world, their clearance level, and what tickets do they hold. This information is not tattooed on everyone's forehead! One of the rules necessary for compartmentalization is that no one reveal what tickets they hold because, as in the case of the OXCART program, even that name was considered TOP SECRET plus. It is still difficult for us, and I am sure it is true for others, to even say that word out loud. Pretty soon you limit your conversations to only a very small circle of people, those you are sure of.

It does not always work out

You tell your kids that you were spending time in Ecuador or Samoa or wherever, anywhere except where you really were. Your wife glares at you when you say stuff like that at the dinner table. The Blackbird wives and kids deserve a great deal of credit for dealing with the problems of never knowing what was going on with their husbands' or fathers' lives. During the early years it seemed like the husband was just passing through long enough to drop off dirty clothes and pick up clean ones, cash a check, eat at least one good meal, and then be gone again for another two or three weeks. One of the original OXCART project pilots living in the San Diego area would be home on one or perhaps two weekends a month. Bill Skliar loved to garden and work in the yard. Because no one ever explained anything to the neighbors—they were always a little suspicious—he was known as "a weekend gardener with privileges."

What a tangled web

When we flew the North Base Cessna 310, we filed the flight clearance in the air after separating ourselves from our departure point when it was a sensitive location. By the same token, we filed for a destination anywhere but where we were going. This created some built–in safety problems. If the aircraft were to go down, no one would have a clue as to where we were or where to start a search. So we always told someone in the group where we were headed and that if they did not hear from us by such and such a time, they were to call a number and tell the person on the other end that the *Canoe* had not arrived.

Some wives were very creative and quick. Late one night, the Cessna 310 services were required. There was no one around with the correct tickets to tell what was going on. I told my wife if I had not called her by 5 A.M., she was to call Dan Andre and tell him that I had not called. She looked puzzled but was used to my unconventional escapades by now, so she sleepily agreed and set the alarm for 5:00. After arriving at my destination safely I called on the Hello Phone (more on that later) to let her know she could forget about the call. When she picked up the phone her first words were "The geese fly high in the winter." After I stopped laughing, I said I was safe and to go back to bed. Our family has used that phrase as a password or code phrase ever since.

We never wore our uniforms on black business. This created another complication when there was limited suitcase room and the trip started at the normal side of the contractor's establishment and then reverted to black business somewhere else in the general area. Once in a while things got screwed up. When I visited the Goodyear plant at Litchfield Park just west of Phoenix on 665A business, I arrived at the front door in my uniform and picked up my badge like everyone else in their right mind. When I went to the Goodyear plant at Litchfield Park on SR–71 business, I wore a suit and tie and usually landed on a dirt strip just north of the plant where there was a cropdusting operation. After tying down the 310, I would make a phone call, and someone from the plant would pick me up in a car and drive me through the back gate. We would proceed direct to the closed off area where the SLR was being produced. This was the worst situation for me because there were people who would recognize me from the other radar program. Except for once, I never left the closed–off area. The one time I did was a Saturday noon. Dressed in T–shirt and jeans I went with Charlie Dotson to an almost deserted company cafeteria for a sandwich. On our return to the black area we met a person from the normal side of my life. Caught completely out of character, my comments and greeting were offhand, casual, and brief, and probably fooled no one, especially my normal–side associate, who knew full well I was blowing smoke in his ear. I learned a serious lesson about being more careful.

New location — same old game

After being transferred to Edwards from Wright Field, some of us went through the process of acquiring separate identifications so we could visit the Skunk Works on a frequent basis. One of the old hands, Capt. James Cooney, took me from Edwards on the drive down to Burbank and introduced me around inside the Works. Because we were all supposed to be civilians working for some commercial enterprise, I was marched over to Kelly's part of the Lockheed security office, fingerprinted, photographed, and given a picture ID card identifying me as an electrical engineer working for the Black Electronics Corporation of Santa Monica, California. A little Kelly humor there, I guess. During the visit it was difficult for me to talk to all these new people who probably knew exactly what my clearance level was. I had no clue as to theirs. So as usual I talked in ever–widening circles of nothingness and fuzzed up the facts from there.

As we left the building to return to Edwards, Jim, who didn't really know me either, said, "It is clear to me that none of those folks will ever have a clue as to what it is that you do. Are you sure you're on the right program?"

Later all those hokey ID cards and papers were reclaimed by Lockheed security. They would have made a great souvenir of the program.

No messing around at the Skunk Works

There were strict procedures for getting into the Skunk Works proper, and here is how the routine went. First of all, none of us ever just dropped in. Our security people always sent a visit notification explaining date and time of arrival, who we would be talking to, the subject of the visit, and the clearance level of the material to be discussed. (This was not the clearance level of the person, but our security folks made sure the tickets held by the person matched the clearance level required.) This was not a trivial job. It required deliberate and careful attention to details.

Arriving at the entrance to Kelly's place, you walked into the lobby, opened your briefcase and placed it on the counter for the guard to inspect. Next you handed him your picture ID—whoever you were supposed to be that day. The guard would make a careful comparison between you and the photo on your ID. He would open a drawer hidden from your side of the counter. The drawer contained slots so that all the badges and IDs arranged in alphabetic order stood facing the guard and he could view them without shuffling them about. He then compared the photo on the Skunk Works badge in his drawer with the ID card you had just presented. Then the guard consulted a list to confirm that you were scheduled to be a visitor on that day at that time. When he was satisfied, he took out your badge and slid it face down across the counter to you. He replaced your ID in the slot just vacated by your badge. You palmed your badge so no one in the lobby could see what it looked like, picked up your briefcase and were buzzed through the door. Once inside, and only then, you put on your badge for all to see. The last step was that you must be escorted to your destination office by one of the secretaries. They were the only official escorts in the place. When it was time to leave, they picked you up at the office you were visiting and took you to the front door and ushered you through, being sure that the lobby guard saw that you had been let out by a proper escort. There were different badges for different areas, but once inside the facility there was less concern about who saw what each person's badge looked like. At my level of tickets, I had no clue as to what the various badge configurations stood for. The process of leaving the plant and recovering your ID card was the same in reverse.

A day's trip to the Sand Pile

Getting to The Area was a little different. I never went except by air, so I don't know what the ground procedures were. My trips to The Area, though frequent, were always in the role of air taxi driver for some of the program's bigger shooters. As before, each visit was documented in a message to the security explaining who was to visit, what for, person to be contacted, clearance levels of discussion, etc. Also included was the time of arrival at an aerial checkpoint or entry point, aircraft call sign, crew and other particulars. The aircraft from Edwards always arrived over the town of Mercury, Nevada. Upon arrival over that location, you switched frequencies, called on the radio giving your call sign, and then were challenged with a code word. It was part of a word–pair game. For each word the ground station gave you, there was a companion word for your response. Once used and responded to, those two words were never used again. Word pairs were changed on a daily–and sometimes hourly–basis. For us in the 310 it was very important to get the words right. Parked on the alert ramp at The Area was a group of F–101 interceptors just waiting for a chance to turn us into space rubble if we proceeded without proper permission. My early years had been spent as an interceptor pilot so I knew how these guys thought. No way I was going to pull their string. This was deadly serious business and we were all dedicated to seeing it get done successfully.

Once granted permission to enter, you headed north past many sunken holes which marked the sites of previous underground nuclear tests. When you reached the north end of the atomic test area you came to a place called the crater. This was a really big hole caused by an underground nuclear blast that inadvertently became an atmospheric event. At the crater we turned and flew east around the north end of a mountain ridge. Once beyond the ridge there was a dry lake bed stretching out to the south. That was Groom Lake, home of Area 51, spawning grounds for the earlier U–2 and now the A–12 and the YF–12s. We did not usually call or talk to the Area tower or anyone during this part of the trip. They knew we were there and were tracking us. No need to be redundant. When we came around the north end of the mountain ridge we would change radio frequencies and turn south. The tower would simply announce our call sign, give traffic information and tell us to call on base with gear down and locked. Departures were not much different except no password was required to be let out. Flying out on moonless nights was a bit unnerving. The radar would guide us low–powered, low–flying, slow–climbing, bug–smashers out to the north and around the mountain so we didn't hit it and mess up their pretty landscape. The nearest light on the ground must have been at least 75 miles away.

Hello, Hello??

The Hello Phone system was invaluable. One of the main concerns of the security managers was to be sure we left as few trails as possible. As you can imagine during the course of managing a complex program like the Blackbird, literally thousands of trips and phone calls were required. Making these as traceless as possible was the goal.

The Hello Phone was an ordinary Ma Bell black beauty hooked to an unsecured line. Every major player involved in the project had one. The unique thing about these phones was that the phone number called to reach that phone was never a number in that phone's city. For example, to reach the Test Force at Edwards you called a number in Los Angeles. And if you wanted to reach somewhere in Phoenix, you called a Tucson number. It was the hard–wired version of call forwarding, all done by the black side of Ma Bell Enterprises. The purpose of these phones was to allow frequent calls here and there without being traceable to the exact locations from which the calls were made. No classified information was passed on these phones and all conversations were recorded, as were all our other phone lines, home, local, and business. From time to time individuals would be taken to task to explain a specific conversation on a particular day. It is quite illuminating to be questioned about those conversations while you are staring at a word–for–word printed transcript of what was said.

What about all the paper and books?

Classified material and information was either hand carried or transmitted on isolated and separate encrypted teletype links. Early Blackbird message traffic was always transmitted and received over systems and units separate from the usual classified message traffic and equipment. The test force had their own vault with its bank of teletype machines and encryption/decryption devices. Because of this complete isolation from the normal world there was considerable literary license exercised by the message originators and some of the traffic contained pretty earthy and direct phraseology.

Printed matter and the control of paper–based material followed a strict set of procedures. Nothing was marked with any classification of the content. All printed matter was considered to be TOP SECRET and every individual was to protect it as such. There were no loose notes and papers. Everything not specifically needed went into the burn barrel. In most offices there were no trash cans or waste baskets. Desk drawers were empty except for a few pencils, a ruler or two and maybe a few cigars. That was it. No paper. There were many safes. Safe maintenance and combination changing was a well–controlled cottage industry. We all learned how to strip a safe and change combinations. In areas where there might be upward of 35 five–drawer safes, everyone got plenty of practice.

What happens if you screw up the combination?

I had always been fascinated by the thought of how one might break into one of these safes. Right on the front of the safe drawer with the combination lock there was a sign that stated, "This container will provide twenty minutes protection from covert manipulation and only five minutes protection from overt attack." As you might suspect there were times when things went awry with the combinations and some safes got locked up and no one could reconstruct the combination. There are several ways to go about this but when all those fail, it is time to call in the heavyweights.

On a particular occasion one of the safes refused to open and after a couple of days of everyone trying out what they thought the combination might have been set to, we put out a call to the cavalry. The safe expert from Los Angeles arrived with two metal–filled canvas–sided suitcases looking and sounding much like the anvil salesman from *The Music Man*. We all stood around to watch this guy open the safe in five minutes using the overt full frontal assault method. The documentation in the safe was one–of–a–kind material. (One does not go around making a lot of backup copies of TS material.) This ruled out all the fun methods like explosives, cutting torches, and shooting the lock dead. The safe guy attached a bunch of brackets to the safe, and commenced to measure and mark the front of the drawer around the combination dial where he would drill out the offending cross bars. Right away the special drill mounted in the special driller broke off and jammed in the hole. There was no way that process was ever going to work. The remainder of the day was spent with sledge hammer, cold chisel, and sweat, accompanied by lots of Anglo–Saxon verbiage and other irreverent comments about the safe's heritage. Late that afternoon the safe was breached. The expert literally beat it to pieces. So much for five–minute entry.

The fix—and we all knew it would happen again—was to place a couple of batts of thick Blackbird insulation inside the safe drawer behind the combination locking mechanism. In the future the ultimate fix would be to torch one's way into the safe. The insulation would protect the documents and the time for opening would be shortened significantly. To my knowledge we never had another grand opening party like that first one.

Sometimes it is just the little things

One of my most prized souvenirs from that period in the Blackbird program, and there are precious few things remaining from the mid–sixties, is a Cross pen and pencil set with an enameled shield mounted on the clip. The shield displays a blue question mark on a field of white.

As contractor field reps at the time were wont to do, Clyde Barnett, ex–Air Force guy and field rep for the camera company ITEK, arrived one day at our hangar with a fist full of Cross pen sets. These were nice looking, silver. Mounted on the clip of each writing implement was a small shield with the word ITEK. We eagerly accepted the gifts and pinned them in our pockets. Then Clyde dropped by Ken Hurley's office and offered him a pen/pencil set. That is where the good times came to an end. Ken refreshed Clyde's memory on security procedures and that this was a breach of several of the rules. With his usual flair, Clyde collected all the pens and pencils he had distributed and disappeared. Within a week he was back and this time there was no arguing with him. Now, the ITEK Cross pens and mechanical pencils all bore a shield on the clip but on that shield there was a large blue question mark. Problem solved, and a wonderful artifact of the Cat II program was created.

Let's look at a serious example

The situation described below took place during the early RS–12 days. We have recounted this story to illustrate how seriously every person took their security responsibilities and how carefully everyone examined even the slightest chance of a leak.

An Air Force C–118 was returning from the west coast with several passengers and a full crew. One of the passengers was a major player on the Air Force side of the RS–12/oxcart/U–2 program office. Putting his briefcase between his feet he dozed off for a nap. Prior to landing the man awoke to find his briefcase open. He made a careful search of the case but could not confirm that nothing was gone or changed. He walked to the flight deck and told the aircrew that he suspected a major security problem had occurred while in flight and instructed them what to do.

When the aircraft landed at Patterson AFB, it taxied to an isolated location, was surrounded by security of every stripe and no one was allowed to deplane. Each passenger was interviewed by the OSI and others, and their baggage and their persons thoroughly searched. No one left that aircraft. Then with everyone still aboard, the security technicians began to examine every nook and cranny of the aircraft interior, even down to stripping out the insulation. They found lots of things but no sign of any material secreted away for later retrieval. After several hours of searching and questioning, the passengers and crew were allowed to leave the aircraft and go home. Allowed to leave only after each of their personal histories and security backgrounds had been meticulously reviewed in detail by FBI and OSI people all across the country.

In the end nothing was found to be amiss and it was concluded by those in the know that the briefcase had been loosely snapped shut and the aircraft vibrations had caused it to open. The handling of this incident clearly illustrates how dedicated everyone was to keeping the security curtains drawn shut.

No visiting firemen allowed

One afternoon at Edwards, a T–39 Sabreliner, the Air Force equivalent of an executive transport, arrived on the ramp outside our hangar, Building 1881, and a very pushy general officer stepped out. He was met by one of the guards who asked what his business was. The general identified himself and told the guard that he was from headquarters and demanded a complete briefing on the Blackbird program.

By this time Lt.Col Dan Andre, our security wizard, had been notified and came out to speak to the visitor. After saluting smartly, Dan asked the general to join him in his office inside the hangar. Once they arrived, Dan dialed a Washington, D.C. number on the Hello Phone, spoke a few words into the phone and then offered the handpiece to the general. After announcing his name and rank into the phone, the visitor listened for a long time without saying a word. After a while the general said, "Yes, Sir," and hung up the phone. Without another word he turned on his heels, marched out the door, got into his marvelous executive jet, and departed. We never saw him again.

It was situations like those that provided a measure of reward to the black program people for all the unrecognized time and effort put in behind the scenes. For not being able to toot your own horn or fly about the country in your own executive jet and demand others knuckle under simply because of your rank or position. How sweet it was!!!

Now and then it's just plain strange

Because there were lots of players in the Blackbird program and only a few knew all the links, off–site meetings were required from time to time. There were periodic meetings between big shooters and other spooks at a place near Sacramento, California, called The Nut Tree. While I was never privy to what went on in the meetings, I did fly the 310 full of passengers up there many times. It was a neat little place. They had a 2,500 foot runway, and all aircraft parking was nestled away in the trees. Once parked, each passenger was issued a ticket and that ticket was used as fare for a ride on the miniature train to the Nut Tree Restaurant and Winery. As the designated pilot, and because we didn't stay overnight, I never sampled the wines.

One hot August afternoon I was sleeping under the wing when the little train arrived with my passengers ready for departure. There was a slight wind from the south but takeoff was going to be tight as there was a significant hill just off the south end of the runway. We taxied out and into the overrun at the north end, trying to take advantage of as much runway as we could get. I ran the engines to full power, released the brakes and began to roll south. At 90 mph I dumped fifteen degrees of flaps and shortly thereafter rotated the nose. We were going to make it after all. Just as we began to lift off, the co–pilot's seat, occupied by Sam Ursini (a back–seater from the YF–12 program), slid toward the rear of the aircraft. Instinctively he reached up and grabbed the glare shield, a plastic shell over the top of the instrument panel, to stop his drift to the rear. I noticed he was disappearing from my peripheral vision but was busy concentrating on our lack of sterling climb performance, and the rapidly approaching hill complete with a huge billboard. Sam's grasp of the glare shield was stronger than its mountings, so the glare shield quickly disappeared toward the rear of the aircraft along with Sam. About now we were just passing over the departure end of the runway at almost no altitude. Suddenly, Dan Andre, sitting in the back seat, began beating me about the head and shoulders with some kind of heavy magazine or book. Still determined not to hit the hill or the sign now directly in front of us, I sucked up the landing gear, banked to the left, and started milking up the flaps. At the same time I inquired in very loud Anglo–Saxon terms, what in the world was going on back there. With a positive rate of climb established and engines set for climb power, I turned to view my surroundings. Sam and his seat were jammed against the rear seat passenger's knees. The glare shield lay on the floor of the cabin. Directly behind me, Andre had a magazine rolled up like a club, still looking like he was going to use it. He spoke two words and I instantly understood. "Bumble bee."

When Sam ripped off the top of the instrument panel, he dislodged a very large and very angry bee. Nothing that happened after that had done anything to calm the bee. It was now crawling along the back of my seat doing its final death dance. One more whack and it was all over.

Once again we returned the aircraft to our long–suffering crew chief at North Base, with most of the aircraft the way it was when he loaned it to us earlier that day.

Doing it with style and grace

There are no adequate words to describe the trust placed in individuals involved in deeply black programs. And equally there is no adequate praise for those who kept the faith for all those long years, for those who meticulously followed the rules which at times added many hours to already long days, for those who protected and babysat materials when there was no one around to help. It is difficult to describe the awesome responsibility one feels when trusted with some of their nation's highest secrets. The oxcart and Blackbird people were true to that trust. They kept their cards close to the chest and thus ensured the success of a very elaborate program of hardware, people, and operations. Ken and I are exceedingly proud to have been members of this group.

Chapter 13

Inlets, Unstarts and High Speed Air

"Controlling the shock off the inlet spike was just a geometry drill. You move the spike so the primary shock wave comes very close to or intersects the inlet lip."
Fred Rall, telephone interview, 1999

"Kelly and Ben Rich designed the inlet with slide rules and calculators. They deliberately made it oversized and then cut down the inlet duct throat area internally with mice."
Ken Hurley, 1998

Whenever guys get together on the street corner or at their favorite watering hole, the conversation does not immediately go to SR–71 inlets, but if it did, the first words to fly out of their mouths would probably be "unstarts." Starting by describing one of the most violent and spectacular failure modes of the inlet would be like talking about your car engine exploding without first mentioning how it was supposed to work normally. After all, the Blackbird inlets ran perfectly more than 99 percent of the time. As the aircraft became operational and matured, the issue of unstarts dwindled.

First some important principles

There are no turbojet engines that can accommodate supersonic flow at the face of the rotating machinery. All jet engines powering supersonic aircraft operate in a subsonic environment, that is, air reaching the front face of the engine (entering the compressor) must be traveling at speeds significantly below Mach 1.

Engines pushing air vehicles at speeds above Mach 1 have an inlet designed to slow the air to subsonic speeds before it enters the engine.

183

The quantity of air an engine inlet can handle (pounds per second) is limited to a fairly narrow range for efficient operation. Too much air or too little air causes the engine to stall or surge.

Sitting on the ground at high thrust, i.e., takeoff, the air supply characteristics are very dissimilar to the air supply when cruising at Mach 3+. It is the job of the inlet to make the air supply at the engine face subsonic for all flight conditions without losing pressure. (The higher the pressure, the greater the density, and thus the more pounds per second of air supplied. The more air available to mix with fuel, the greater the thrust.)

Basic inlet facts

At vehicle speeds up to about Mach 2 an inlet can be designed to slow the air down largely outside the entrance to the inlet, or in terms of the trade, operated in external compression mode without encountering unacceptable losses in efficiency. At speeds above Mach 2, in order to avoid the high drag associated with external compression, supersonic air must be brought inside the inlet and slowed down to subsonic speeds before it reaches the engine face. The inlet must operate in internal compression mode. The higher the speed of the vehicle, the more complex the solution. At Mach 3+ cruise it is equivalent to getting a drink from a fire hose. There is much too much water moving too fast to swallow. You have to take a little in your mouth, let some slop out, and slow the rest down before you can drink. That in a nutshell is what the inlet does for the engine.

One serious complication. The inlet must handle all airspeeds up to the design cruise Mach. Therefore, it cannot be a point design, but must be flexible enough to operate throughout the envelope from the end of the runway to the highest cruise speed and altitude. In the case of the SR, the inlet was optimized for Mach 3.2 and was less than optimum at other speeds.

SR–71 inlet primer and definition of terms

The SR–71 employed a convergent—divergent inlet duct with a translating center body called the spike and two sets of bypass doors to control the air speed at the engine face. There were several other systems involved, such as the center body bleed system, the shock trap bleed system, and others. However, to simplify this discussion, only the major components will be covered.

Oblique Shock Waves. Oblique shock waves, if you could see them, would be oriented at something greater than 90 degrees to the direction of travel of the object making the shock wave. An oblique shock wave has supersonic air on both sides of the wave, but there is a drop in pressure from front to back and a matching reduction in Mach number of the air.

Normal Shock Waves. The normal shock wave, as used in this discussion, is the last shock wave in the inlet where there is supersonic flow on the upstream side and subsonic flow on the downstream side. To help in visualizing this normal shock wave, picture a disk of air stretched across the inlet just in front of the engine face and just behind the inlet throat. On the engine side of this shock wave is subsonic air being fed to the engine.

Inlet. The inlet is the sum total of assembled hardware ahead of the engine that manipulates the incoming air, at whatever speed, and feeds it to the engine in a uniform stream as free of turbulence and distortion as possible.

Spike. The spike is the translating cone, with point forward, used to control the position of the initial, external shock wave. The spike is shaped like a huge bullet and when translated fore or aft, it changes the cross sectional area of the air path. This fore or aft movement not only places the primary shock at the design location, it adjusts both the convergent (compression) and the divergent (decompression) areas within the inlet.

Inlet Lip. The inlet lip is the very front edge of the outer rim of the inlet. On the Blackbird these lips were quite sharp to reduce drag at cruise Mach numbers. This sharpness caused turbulence and boundary layer separation at very low airplane speeds, such as when parked or during taxiing. At these speeds the velocity of the air being sucked into the inlet was much greater than the speed of the aircraft. As the air tried to turn a corner around the inlet lip it became turbulent and in the extreme, sometimes resulted in engine surging due to aggravated pressure distribution across the face of the compressor.

Inlet Throat.   The inlet throat is the narrowest internal portion of the inlet. The normal shock resides just aft of the throat during supersonic cruise. This is an area behind the spike and behind the struts that support the spike. The throat area contains pressure–sensing ports that help the inlet control system determine normal shock location and to adjust its position by manipulating the air bypass doors. In the SR–71 inlet there were two sets of doors, forward and aft.

Engine Face.   This area is where the inlet ends and the engine starts, and immediately before the first stage of fan/compressor blades.

Boundary Layers.   Within the inlet these are areas of airflow immediately next to the skin on the inside of the inlet and on the outside of the spike. Great attention was paid to boundary layer control during design of inlet surface contours and the external shape of the spike. Abrupt changes in surface contour on either the spike or the inlet present an opportunity for separating air flow from the surface. This creates turbulent flow and may produce unacceptable distortion in the air column reaching the engine face.

Turbulence/Distortion.   Just as one sees burbles and turbulence in the water flow in a stream, the same can and does happen in the air stream traveling through the inlet. While some engines are more tolerant of airflow distortion, the real issue is a matter of efficiency and smoothness of operation.

The primary job of any inlet

An inlet provides high rates of subsonic airflow to the engine face. To do that, the position of the normal shock must be accurately and responsively controlled. All the things done upstream support this one objective—proper positioning of the normal shock wave. Corrections made to keep the normal shock in the proper position must be almost instantaneous. The consequences of the normal shock wave getting out of position are immediate and violent for the aircraft, the crew, and the engine itself. In the extreme, the normal shock gets completely out of the inlet. This is called an unstart. The airflow through the inlet to the engine is reduced dramatically, the engine stalls, and thrust is reduced to almost nothing. None of these results were in the least bit helpful to the crew in keeping the SR–71 under control.

Let's talk to an inlet expert

Here's how the SR–71 inlets worked. To be sure we got the right words from the right guy, we contacted someone who knows his onions on inlets, Fredrick T. Rall Jr. Fred is an MIT graduate, a well–known aerodynamicist, a managing engineer of significant stature, and last, but not least, the Air Force's SR–71 inlet consultant during the early Blackbird development days.

We asked Fred for a simple and brief (if there is such a thing) explanation of how an inlet works in general and how the SR inlet worked in specific. Sifting through the facts and paraphrasing Fred's explanation, here is the SR inlet in its simplest form.

"Let me give you a simple–minded explanation and see if this answers your questions. Ideally, air entering an engine should be as high in pressure and as uniform in density as possible. Simply put," as Fred likes to say, "you want to reduce the speed of the supersonic air outside the inlet to a subsonic speed at the face of the engine. An ideal inlet would produce a very large number of oblique shock waves and finally one normal shock wave where the airflow would then drop to subsonic with no loss of pressure. The theory being that the pressure drop across each oblique shock would be so small as to be almost unnoticed. At the end of the inlet you would have all this high–pressure air available to feed the engine. The higher the air pressure and the greater its density, the more fuel one can introduce into the mixture. The more fuel and air through the engine, the higher the thrust.

"The flow at the engine face—at the rotating engine face—is subsonic.

"So if you want dense air, there are two ways of doing that. Either lower the temperature, which takes a radiator and that is not practical, or get the pressure as high as possible. The way you get the highest pressure is to slow that supersonic air down efficiently. Now if you take the worst possible way to slow that air down, that is a normal shock wave. All the way from Mach 3 down to Mach 0.4, that is one great pressure loss. You can do much better by slowing the air down in small increments. If you put a cone out there you can slow it down from

Mach 3 to Mach 2.8 and a little ramp on the cone to generate another shock to 2.6 and then to 2.4, and so on. You keep on going and you get a whole bunch of little shock waves, each of which is pretty small, and when you integrate their effect you lose very little in the way of pressure.

"In fact, you could theoretically make all those shock waves so small, so tiny, that what you get is an isentropic compression. Isentropic is a fancy word for no pressure loss. What you are doing 'in the limit' (now this is all theoretical, of course) is getting each of those little oblique shock waves to be so small that there is no pressure loss across them. That's the theory. In practice you can't do that because life isn't that easy. You understand what I'm saying?"

"What about the primary shock wave, the Mach 3 shock?" I asked.

"That shock falls right at the inlet lip. You want it to intercept the inlet lip at the design Mach number; otherwise you get what is called spillage drag. That is the price you pay for slowing air down that is not going into the inlet, air you are not using. Put that shock wave right on the inlet lip at Mach 3 by moving the spike back and forth. That is just a geometry drill. You know the Mach number, you know what the geometry is, so move the spike until the shock wave comes very close to, or intersects, the inlet lip. You don't want it inside, for a series of reasons. You would like it right on that lip. That is how the inlet really works with the first shock. The real guts of the issue, however, is controlling the internal shock wave. The normal shock wave.

"But, moving the spike changes the whole interior geometry of the inlet. You could make up for that by having an expandable spike inside, but the mechanism to do that is difficult. So you find some other way of controlling where the normal shock wave occurs. And the way you do that is by spilling air through bypass doors that direct excess air either outside of the engine nacelle[1] or pass it back to an ejector nozzle or use it for engine cooling air. You've paid the price to slow it down, don't just throw it away.

"If you don't do that right and the normal shock wave moves forward of the throat, you get an inlet unstart. That's when the normal shock

---

[1] The term engine nacelle refers to the hole-like structure within which the engine is mounted and enclosed. Webster says: a streamlined enclosure on an aircraft, for an engine.

wave gets out in front of the inlet. Not good. That changes the whole flow over the wing and causes major stability and control problems. The trick of keeping that normal shock wave at the right position is through internal bleeding of excess air through bypass doors.

"To determine where the normal shock is located within the inlet, a set of sensors measure pressure drop across the normal shock. The inlet control system uses this pressure–sensing information to modulate air bypass doors. By controlling the amount of dumped air, it holds the shock in the desired location. This system has to have a fast response. This is not a part of physics where you have twenty–five minutes to figure things out. To complicate things, there are huge forces to overcome in the manipulation of spikes and doors."

Ken describes normal inlet operations

Let's start with a normal day, a normal inlet, a normal climbout, and talk about what actually happened as a Blackbird inlet progressed through its daily routine of feeding the engine the kind of air needed to keep aircraft accelerating and scooting along at cruise. Ken Hurley rode on many test missions in the SR–71. Here is how he describes the sequence of starting the inlet/engine combination from takeoff, to steady state cruise, and then what happens during an unstart.

"For takeoff and out to near Mach 2 at about 55,000 feet, the spike was full forward and bypass doors were open. Just prior to reaching Mach 2 the spike was unlocked by the inlet control system and began to translate rearward as a function of Mach number. Since the inlet diameter reduced toward the throat, the spike moving rearward restricted the amount of air going through the throat, however, under all flight conditions except the design cruise Mach number, the amount of air going through the throat was still more than the engine needed.

"To deal with excess air, two sets of bypass doors were provided aft of the throat area which dumped excess air outside the inlet. The primary doors, called forward doors, were controlled by an electromechanical control system, except that the pilot could override the system to full open. The secondary doors, called aft doors, were smaller and were controlled directly by the pilot. The purpose of these secondary doors was to fine–tune inlet airflow so the forward doors would be fully closed at cruise. The forward doors dumped excess air into the outer nacelle, an inefficient use of high energy air. The air bypassed by the aft doors was used more efficiently.

"The forward doors were mechanized to be extremely fast in response to the control system inputs. The primary control input was the Mach 1 shock sensor located just aft of the throat. This sensor told the control system where the normal shock was located and supplied signals to the forward doors to keep the shock properly positioned. This ensures that the engine sees only subsonic air.

"As the spike is programmed further aft, the forward doors continue to close down, until, at cruise, they should be completely closed and the spike should be fully aft. The aft doors may still be slightly open, but the pilot can look at the forward door position and tune the aft doors to assure forward door closure. When everything is set up, the inlet is said to be started."

There is reference above to fine–tuning the aft doors to keep the forward doors closed. The Category II test airplanes did not have forward door position indicators and the aft door control had only two positions, A and B. Changes were made to operational airplanes allowing more effective bypass door management and more cruise range efficiency.

How things went south

When some perturbation occurred and air arriving at the engine could no longer be consumed, the whole air column between the engine face and the inlet front became overpressured. (The air coming in fills up the inlet and there is nowhere for it to go except back out the front and spill over.) When that Mach 1 shock so carefully positioned just aft of the inlet throat was suddenly and explosively ejected out the front of the inlet, you got instant unstart. It happened in a fraction of a second. The inlet, only a moment ago, was ingesting all the air coming in. Now it is eating almost no air. Air spills around the nacelle and over the wing surfaces, both upper and lower. The nacelle becomes a blunt object being shoved through the air at Mach 3+. The net effect is a head–knocking yaw into the unstarted inlet and a roll toward the wing whose air flow has been drastically upset. These events certainly captured the crew's attention. It was like dragging the unstarted side of the aircraft through a sky of molasses. Unstarts in straight and level flight were certainly dramatic, but during a turn, they were downright dangerous. Dramatic incidents of unstarts during turns are described elsewhere in this book.

With the loss of thrust combined with increased drag on the unstarted side, the aircraft yaw was significant. The only solution was to restart the inlet. In later years, after tons of experience, the real solution was to go into restart on the good side at the same time the original unstarted inlet was commanded to restart, and thus avoid all the asymmetrical aerodynamics while trying to get the bad engine back on line.

In addition to exterior unstart dynamics, the inlet no longer supplied air to the engine causing an immediate loss of thrust. The throttle, still advanced, continued to supply fuel to the engine. Hot section temperatures rose rapidly. Engines did not usually flame out but had to be shut down manually to prevent serious over temperature.

A bit of history from Ken

Not many people, even those close to the program, know that the SR–71 inlet was oversized. Kelly Johnson often made the point that the SR was designed with slide rules and calculators, long before computers were available. When he and Ben Rich were calculating inlet area, they feared erring on the short side and the inlet throat would turn out too small. The program was highly concurrent, production airplanes were being built at the same time as test airplanes. Dealing with the cost and schedule fallouts of a mid–program inlet redesign would have killed the program, in Kelly's view.

"Kelly and Ben decided to oversize the basic inlet throat diameter and then provide something to shrink the area to match their calculations. That something was mice. Mice were small aerodynamic lumps used to reduce the cross–sectional area of early jet engine tailpipes and in this case inlets. In all Blackbird inlets there are bumps about halfway back to the throat. These bumps spaced around the inside inlet wall, though never removed, were not a total loss because they provided some flow straightening. But the real reason was if the inlet turned out to be too small, the mice could be removed one at a time until the designers got the match they wanted. Their calculations were dead on so the supersonic mice rode along for the life of the program.

The early airplanes had quite a bit of trouble with unstarts and crews gained much unwanted experience. Inlet controls improved as time went on but unstarts never went away. The original control system was hydromechanical. It never had the heat tolerance or necessary response times to completely eliminate unstarts. Later a redesigned all–electric system brought a significant reduction in unstarts.

Based upon Category II testing experience a system was recommended to provide sympathetic restart capability. That way, if one inlet unstarted, both inlets would be automatically commanded to restart. This significantly reduced wilder dynamics by increasing symmetry and added additional safety margin. This sympathetic system was developed and installed on operational Blackbirds, but the Category II airplanes were never retrofitted. The test force also recommended installation of forward door position indicators to give the pilot a better picture of what the inlet was doing so he could adjust the aft doors more appropriately. Those changes were reserved for the operational aircraft and the Cat II'ers were left to struggle along with asymmetric dynamics and the old unstart–prone control system.

Kelly Johnson and Ben Rich had a vision of how the inlets were supposed to work. They realized the key to an efficient cruise at Mach 3.2 was the engine inlet. Their creativity and intuitive design made it possible for the U.S. to step out in front with an airbreathing supersonic cruising machine that has yet to meet an equal.

Chapter 14

Cat II Camera Testing

"You can't imagine how long it takes for the smell of burning mylar to fade from your kitchen and leave the oven."
Donn A. Byrnes, Edwards AFB, 1967

"Look at that! It's a golf ball. The resolution of this camera must be at least one inch."
Warren Shaw, HYCON Program Manager, 1967

Initially there were many details to be sorted out before the testing could begin. The camera test program was envisioned as a two–way street. The cameras and their imagery would produce data that supported testing of the navigation system, the radar, and the aircraft view sight. In addition to the cameras, there was a large thirty–two trailer processing center parked on the ramp that processed film, evaluated ELINT data, reduced maintenance data collected in flight, and provided areas for film viewing and evaluation. This trailer city was called the MPC, which stood for mobile processing center. It was about as mobile as the Empire State Building! As they say, "Just putting handles on a 65–inch television set does not make it portable." The full–up MPC consisted of fifty–plus trailers. The test force would only use a portion of that to evaluate and to support testing.

A little background on the SR–71's camera suite

First some acronyms and definitions:

TROC. The Terrain Objective Camera was made by the Fairchild Camera Company, had a six–inch focal length lens, used nine–inch wide film, and was mounted on the center line of the aircraft just forward of the nose wheel well. The camera looked directly down out of the aircraft.

OOC. The Operational Objective Camera was made by ITEK. This was a panoramic camera with a thirteen–inch focal length lens. The SR initially carried one mounted on either side of the centerline. These cameras used 70mm–wide film and lay horizontally in their bay looking down through a mirror.

TEOC. The Technical Objective Camera, manufactured by HYCON, had a 48–inch focal length lens and used nine inch wide film. Like the OOC, it was mounted horizontally and used a mirror made of beryllium to view the world below. The TEOC was the only camera capable of being pointed at different angles. The SR could carry two of these cameras, one mounted on either side of the aircraft centerline.

IMC. Image Motion Compensation refers to the adjustments made within the camera to correct for image movement due to aircraft motion along track during exposure of the image.

V/H. Velocity/Height is a ratio derived to provide a signal to a camera's IMC mechanism to permit compensation for the image motion during the time the shutter is open. The term is usually spoken of in milliradians per second. A nominal value for the SR–71 is on the order of forty milliradians per second, while the U–2 values are usually less than ten milliradians per second. This ratio and its application to image motion is appropriate only in vertical photography.

V/R. Velocity/Radial distance ratio is another value used to drive the camera's motion compensation mechanism based on the actual distance to the target to be photographed. When the TEOC was looking out at an angle of 45 degrees or so, the distance to the target was significantly more than the altitude above the ground. The V/R was also used for doing photography while the SR–71 was in a turn. This technique was used in Vietnam to peer into caves and such. It worked quite well. The V/H (or V/R) signal could be set manually by the reconnaissance systems operator (RSO) but the preferred method was for the astro–inertial navigation system to derive the number and supply the correct value to the cameras.

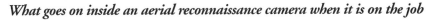

What goes on inside an aerial reconnaissance camera when it is on the job

To appreciate what was accomplished during the SR–71 Category II program it is necessary to have at least a conceptual understanding of the activities going on inside large and delicate cameras of the types and sizes used in the SR–71 or other photo reconnaissance systems.

The film magazine, the film transport, and the platen. During a photo leg, when the camera is cycling, the film gets manhandled in a very careful way. First it is drawn across the platen and stopped in just the right spot. Next a vacuum is applied to suck the film down onto the platen to hold it in the correct shape and hold it still during the exposure. During the exposure sequence many things happen in a short period of time. First the data block is flashed to record information in the borders of the film frame. Other information like a picture of a clock, a frame counter, bubble levels, and other information may be exposed onto the border of the frame. Next, the shutter opens to expose the film. During exposure the IMC system must either move the camera, the platen, or some other part of the camera, so that the image projected by the lens on the film does not move while the shutter is open.

When exposure is complete and the shutter closed, the film must be released from the platen. Sometimes just releasing the vacuum is sufficient and in other cameras the film is lightly blown off the platen by a breath of air. Next, that frame must be whisked out of the way and another rolled into its place. Remember here that the film transport must unroll film from one spool filled with maybe 1,000 feet of nine–inch–wide film and then roll it onto the takeup spool. You can't start and stop the supply and takeup spool instantly, so there must be slack loops on each end to permit these spools to turn almost constantly while the camera is cycling. The film is getting jerked around by this repetitive starting and stopping at the platen for an exposure while a smooth, even motion must be maintained by the supply and takeup spools. If the entire supply of film were started and stopped in synchronization with the frame on the platen this would result in jerking the camera around and smearing the image across the film during the exposure. For large–format cameras with significant footages of film on the takeup and supply spools, the inertial considerations of transporting film without shaking or jarring the camera represent a challenging design problem. Also, one must consider the camera weight distribution as large amounts of film are transferred from one spool to another. The camera's center of gravity has a great bearing on how the stabilization system functions.

For cameras with high cyclic rates, the problem of static electricity generation and discharge within the magazine and along the film path is a chronic problem and must be prevented.

Holding the camera still

During exposure and film transport, the camera stabilization system must be working. One way to look at this is to imagine that the camera holds perfectly still in pitch and roll while the airframe moves around it. The stabilization system uses the inertia of the camera to help it keep the camera steady and avoid movements in roll and pitch while the exposure sequence is underway. Usually the stabilization system works all the time the aircraft is in flight, however, during takeoff and landing the cameras are put into a vibration isolation mode to keep them from hitting the stops and damaging delicate parts. The TEOC and the OOC cameras weighed about 300 pounds each. The TROC camera did not have a stabilization system for reasons explained later.

Maintaining a predictable temperature. Cameras work best when they are maintained at the design temperature, so they must be heated or cooled depending on the circumstances at the moment. In the SR program the issue at cruise was always cooling. There were times, however, during subsonic flight when the cameras could become cold–soaked. To maintain thermal stability so important to proper camera functioning, each camera had to have both the capability for heating and cooling critical components and a sensing system to monitor camera and camera bay conditions to know which was required.

Telling the camera what to do. Cameras need to know when to turn on and turn off, the correct exposure settings, where to look, and what mode to operate in. In the SR this information was supplied either automatically by the mission tape in the ANS or manually by the RSO.

A description of capabilities and operating modes

Camera capabilities are generally described in a couple of ways, depending upon the intended chore assigned. The SR–71 carried three types of cameras. Each had a specific role.

The TROC. The terrain objective camera's job was to photograph the ground directly below the aircraft and provide a set of pictures that overlapped by 55 percent. This allowed everything below the aircraft to appear on at least two frames and the included angle between frames provided for stereo viewing to give the interpreter a three–dimensional view of objects in the photograph. The camera also had a ten percent overlap mode when the intended mission was long and the area to be photographed extensive. Loaded with a 700 foot roll of film it could photograph a strip 7,800 nautical miles long at 55 percent overlap between frames. Ready for flight, the camera and film weighed 135 pounds. The primary purpose of the TROC was to record a photographic image which reproduced the exact relationships of the objects pictured on the ground with great fidelity and geometric accuracy. This term, geometric fidelity, refers to how accurately ground dimensions can be reconstructed from measurements made on the processed negative. How this is done is discussed later.

The OOC. The operational objective camera's aim in life was to photograph from beneath the aircraft out to a 45 degree angle. The SR carried a pair of OOCs, one to photograph each side of the flight path. The camera pictures overlapped by three degrees below the aircraft. Once on the take leg, these cameras operated continuously to produce a series of panoramic photos with a 55 percent overlap. The reason for the overlap was the same as for the TROC or any other camera. In the 55 percent overlap mode a pair of OOCs could photograph a strip of ground beneath the aircraft out to 45 degrees on either side for a distance of 4,000 miles. Each OOC could carry 3,300 feet of 70mm–wide film. A mission–ready, fully loaded OOC weighed 300 pounds.

The TEOC. The technical objective camera had the longest focal length lens, 48 inches, and could pick out the smallest targets. The initial goal was to be able to see a six–inch object from cruise altitude. To describe the resolving power of this camera we often said that if you were to photograph an ordinary office desk from 78,000 feet, you would be able to see a telephone sitting on the desk. To put it in perspective, that is being able to see a standard Ma Bell black beauty telephone from thirteen nautical miles away. More later. The TEOC had several modes and was intended to be pointed at a specific target anywhere from directly below the aircraft out to about 45 degrees. The SR carried two TEOCs, and could photograph points of interest on either side of the aircraft. The cameras were commanded and pointed by the mission program stored in the ANS computer. The nominal area being photographed on the ground was about 2.5 by 2.5 miles square. The requirement for accurate navigation, accurate pointing, and exposure timing becomes obvious when one considers the speed of the aircraft and the distances involved.

The TEOC had four modes.

Burst Mode took a burst of ten photos at a rate of about one per second. The idea here was to capture as many pictures of the object of interest as possible while charging along at one half mile per second. Usually the camera caught the target at least five times and in some cases it imaged the target on six frames.

The Stepping Mode slewed the camera head back and forth (across track) first four degrees to one side and then four degrees to the other side of a commanded look angle. This mode provided wider coverage when the exact location of the area to be photographed was not well known or when the area of interest might be wider than the normal frame width.

A 55 percent overlap mode was that of a normal camera where the exposures were timed to provide a 55 percent overlap from frame to frame.

A ten percent overlap mode provided a strip of photographs with only a ten percent overlap between frames. This mode was used only to photograph long strips of ground or where many targets were intended to be photographed on a single mission. The TEOC carried enough nine–inch–wide film to provide 1,800 useable frames per flight. The normal roll length was about 1,500 feet. One TEOC pointed down on each side of the aircraft centerline, would provide coverage of approximately 22,500 square miles of ground with great detail. That is 6¼ square miles per frame directly below the aircraft multiplied by 3,600 frames.

What do you do with miles and miles of Top Secret film?

Dealing with a single mission's output of film was another part of the camera test program. This activity included processing, reviewing, assessing take results, evaluating camera performance and, though seemingly mundane, getting rid of all this TOP SECRET material. Some of the most interesting aspects of the program dealt with the latter problem.

Consider a full load on a test mission, 700 feet of nine–inch film for the TROC, 6,600 feet of 70mm film for the two OOCs, another 3,000 feet of nine–inch film for the two TEOCs, and then add in a mere 100 feet of 70mm film for the IR system. Finally throw in about 1,000 feet of five–inch radar data film and 100 feet of ground–produced SLR map film and you have a major mountain of mylar film to deal with after a completed mission. It does not take long to fill a storage vault with all this film. When we started casting about to see how to dispose of this material, we went to the people at Edwards to ask how they got rid of their film. Their answer was simple. They did not expose or use or store TOP SECRET film. But, they had this new handy dandy shredder/pulper. They would be glad to demonstrate how well this new machine could destroy our film.

Bruce Hartman went down to the shredder place with a blank nine–inch wide, 100–foot roll of 2½ mil (.0025 of an inch) thick mylar film to give it a test. We had high hopes because, even with the test program in its early stages, we had well over 50,000 feet of film to be destroyed. The Edwards AFB handy dandy shredder/pulper did about three feet of Bruce's sample nine–inch film before the machine ground to a halt and refused to shred or pulp any more. So much for that neat idea. At that point we decided the only way of destroying this stuff was to burn it.

Burning mylar is not a simple or effortless task. Sgt. Wong, the test force welding, tube bending, and general metal genius (and I mean that sincerely) said he would build us a state of the art mylar melting machine. Two weeks later it was delivered. It was an old 500–gallon propane tank mounted on legs to stand vertically. On the top was a great round tube for a chimney and, in front, this huge Flying Tiger mouth with teeth, where you loaded the film. Above the mouth were large glaring eyes. It seemed to say, "I can eat anything." There were also various levers and doors for draft control and cleanout. It was parked outside the fence for all the base to see. Here is how it worked.

Once a fire was going inside (started with paper and wood and diesel fuel because mylar is not readily flammable) the film could be fed in. But it was not like just throwing another log on the fire. First the film had to be removed from the metal reel for ease of handling, then it was rewound on a stick. We tried to just unroll it into an unruly ball–tangle–mess–birdnest thing and then stuff that mess into the mouth of the furnace. It was a terrible failure, as the film would melt and put out the fire before it burned. The ultimate solution was to hold a roll of film under one arm and slowly feed it like a long stick, out from the center of the roll and into the mouth of the furnace.

Because one was destroying classified matter, more than one person needed to be present to identify what was being destroyed, to verify the destruction, and sign the certificates. There was no Air Force job description for film burner, so everyone took their turn at film–burning/classified–destruction duty. In the summer this was a bear of a job because the temperature was usually about one hundred and ten in the shade, and there you were feeding that silly film into a sillier looking furnace face, and the heat coming off the outside of the furnace just added to the discomfort. If you fed the film in too slowly the fire went out. If you fed the film in too fast then some of the mylar melted and dripped out the bottom of the furnace, flowing over the ground and spreading fire everywhere. There were seven zillion ways to do this burning thing and we tried them all. Based on Murphy's law, the most ridiculous looking, hottest, most time–consuming, and least comfortable way to burn the film was the only one that worked. It was a lousy job and everyone had to do it.

Some of the more frequent burners formed the 2904th Burning and Recreational Society (Composite) to soften the blow of this socially unredeeming task.

Another method of film destruction was attempted. It was reasoned that if mylar melts and drips out of the bottom of the furnace, it can be poured. It could be cast into molds and some sort of program souvenirs could be made, thus not just letting this valuable material simply go up in smoke, so to speak. I took home several blank rolls of processed 70mm waste film. The idea was to heat the film in the oven and let it drip into a mold directly below, thus casting our way out of the destruction problem. The result of this experiment produced only unwanted and unexpected side effects. The smell of molten, burning, smoking mylar hung around in our kitchen for several months. It was damn near impossible to remove from the oven. Easy–Off was ineffective. The children living in the home learned to live with the lingering taste of mylarburgers. And one's wife remained an unhappy camper long after the smell and memories had faded into the dim distant past.

Evaluating geometric fidelity

Without the help of the US Navy and the dedicated people at the Pacific Missile Range facilities located at Pt. Mugu, throughout California, and offshore, the precision and speed with which the SR–71 and YF–12A flight test programs were accomplished would never have happened. The Navy provided radar tracking, range space for missile firing, and accomplished an incredible amount of data reduction to exacting levels of detail. The latter efforts, conducted at the Pt. Mugu facilities, were quite labor intensive and involved the evaluation of literally thousands of frames of TROC imagery. They plotted actual ground tracks and then constructed a backfit track comparison to establish a common algorithm to allow adjustments to radar tracking site coordinates. This combined both photo–established ground tracks and multiple–site radar tracks to calibrate the overall tracking system. The objective was to establish accurate ground tracks over long distances (2,500 nautical miles) for evaluation of the navigation system's ability to guide the bird along a preplanned route with predictable accuracy.

But before using the TROC to establish exact ground positions, the TROC imagery had to be validated itself. The personnel at PMR and the Fairchild Camera Co. both performed an independent analysis of selected frames and were able to verify each other's findings. Once one of the elemental tools had been validated, progress could be made toward the next step. The process of laying out the range and verifying aircraft tracks is discussed in detail in Chapter 18, *The 2,500–Mile Micrometer.*

Since the TROC was used to provide the foundational single points for initial range calibration, it was imperative that the evaluation of the TROC be rigorous. The following describes the construction of the camera and how that information was used to develop exact locations from TROC imagery.

The Stainless Steel Brownie

Though some might consider that nickname to be derogatory, it really was an affectionate term used by the test force engineers to describe a piece of hardware that quietly did its job each and every time, each and every day. It was the first camera flown in the Cat I and the Cat II program and it performed well at every assigned task.

In the early days of the tests at Edwards we had no film processing capability, so we relied on Lockheed facilities at Burbank. After one of the early flights we were very eager to see the results of the TROC's first efforts. The Fairchild rep took the film down to Burbank to have it developed and promised to bring it back to the desert on Saturday. Friday night I was called and told that the Fairchild rep would meet me at the main intersection in Mojave at noon on Saturday. Arriving early, I parked and thought I recognized the Fairchild rep's car parked across the street in a used car lot but was not too sure. I waited. At precisely high noon, straight from the script of a B–movie, the rep got out of his car among the used vehicles for sale and walked across the road. Without a word he passed a large black can containing a 700 foot roll of nine–inch film through the driver's window, turned and walked away.

Back to the Brownie

Faithful reproduction of the ground in a film image, was the key to success, as was knowing the exact relationship between a perfect lens and the lens in the camera. In other words, if the real lens distorted the geometric relationships between objects on the ground and the image of those same objects as they were projected on the platen/film in the camera. (All have some distortion. None are perfect in the real world.)

When the film is held on the platen at the focal plane of the lens and exposed it is one shape. When it is then wound onto the take–up spool in the camera's magazine it is another shape. When that same exposure is processed and dried and rewound or copied it is another shape. These changes in shape are anticipated and there are devices built into the camera to allow these errors to be zeroed out.

When the images of the objects photographed are later measured by the interpreters or evaluators there are issues of the accuracy of the measurements to be considered.

Because the aircraft is not always perfectly level or, the plane of the film is not always exactly perpendicular to the true vertical, so compensation must be made for this distortion. The task is to correct for the kind of distortion you might see when a projector is not aligned exactly with the screen and the projected image appears somewhat trapezoidal. The question of exactly where the centerline of the camera was pointing at the time of exposure became critical, and that is why the TROC was not a stabilized camera. Vibration–isolated yes, but the camera body was not allowed to move to compensate for aircraft motion as the other cameras were. The camera was fixed in a known relationship to the aircraft keel line and water line. Information taken from aircraft systems at the exact time of exposure allowed interpreters to assess the cameras deviation from true vertical in both the along–track and cross–track directions.

What was the evaluation process? Information was recorded in the data area between each frame of TROC film needed to evaluate the images produced by the camera.

The serial number of the lens

Each lens had been mapped to document exactly where and how much it distorted the image it projected. This was a distortion based on the image a perfect lens would project.

The identifying information about the camera body and the configuration of the platen. The TROC platen contains a one–inch grid of Reseau dots. These are holes in the platen that at the time of exposure allow a small light to be flashed through each hole. This exposes a very tiny donut–like circle on the film. These are essentially invisible to the naked eye. Armed with the specific identity of the platen and the exact measurements between each dot for that platen, the evaluator can, through geometric calculation, reconstruct the exact shape and size of the film at the exact time of exposure.

The film frame data also contained a clock and a data block describing the aircraft attitude, altitude, and speed at the time of exposure. This block also contained information from the navigation system providing the latitude and longitude at the time of exposure.

With this information it was then possible to reconstruct the aircraft/camera/earth relationship at the time of exposure. Having done that, it was then possible, knowing how the lens distorted the projected image, to calculate the precise relationships between objects in the photograph. Additionally one could define the spot in the photo and on the ground, representing the exact geographical position of the aircraft at the time of exposure.

But there was more

In 1965 there was no data available to define, with sufficient accuracy, the relationships of various places on the ground within even small localized areas. This was a time before ECHO I and ECHO II satellites, and long before the Global Positioning System (GPS) was invented. The U.S. Army came to the rescue and provided a Class 1 survey[1] in certain areas along intended SR–71 flight test routes. The areas surveyed by the Army were a strip between Pahrump, Nevada, and Edwards AFB, California, and a street–corner–by–street–corner survey of the area of downtown Phoenix. No small task, but the priority of the test program, and the SR–71 program in general, was sufficient to warrant the expenditure of effort by all concerned. These surveys provided the last piece of the puzzle in the evaluation equation for determining the geometric fidelity of the TROC. A comparison between what the camera saw and how the ground really was let the evaluators determine the accuracy and quality of the camera's capability.

---

[1] A Class 1 survey defines the relationships between designated geographical points within the area bounded by the survey to within less than a one-foot error.

During the course of the evaluation program and the photo reduction effort to establish aircraft ground tracks, PMR reduced 4,495 TROC photographs and ACIC, Aeronautical Chart and Information Center in St. Louis, Missouri, reduced 358 photographs for vehicle position using the three–point method. On several occasions over the Edwards test range, where multiple–site radar tracking was available for exact positioning, these evaluations of TROC photography were able to establish the aircraft position to a probable error of five feet, and determined the altitude of the aircraft to a probable error of one foot. The Stainless Steel Brownie was a success at its primary task.

Some unintended results

In a surprise move the TROC also did a great job at intelligence gathering. During one period Ken Hurley advised Bruce and me that we were not to go up to North Base under any circumstances until further notice. These rules were complied with and, since our U–3 support aircraft were stationed at North Base, we had to use the Edwards, AFB, support aircraft instead. One afternoon after a test mission Bruce came over from the processing trailers with a roll of film from the TROC. He and I went into the evaluation room and started to run it across the light table to see how the resolution targets looked. As we spooled the film past the images of North Base we noticed a pair of U–2s parked on the ramp. Not anything unusual most of the time, but this time the two aircraft were of different sizes. The TROC had just divulged the reason we were not allowed to visit North Base. There was a new aircraft there and we later found out it was called the TR–1. Much to Ken's consternation, we happily presented this photo to our boss and explained that we now understood our exclusion from North Base.

Evaluating resolution

The term photographic resolution is usually referred to in terms of lines per millimeter (l/mm). For comparison, the TROC had an advertised resolution of about 35 l/mm, the OOC had a design specification of about 100 l/mm, and the TEOC was also specified at 100 l/mm. The resolving capability of the lens, when adjusted by the focal length of the lens and height above the target, gives an estimated size of the smallest ground object one might expect to see. In the following examples the assumed altitude of the aircraft/camera is 80,000 feet. In the case of the 13–inch focal length of the OOC, 100 l/mm results in a ground resolution of about twenty-seven inches. The same lens resolution specification for the TEOC, 100 l/mm, with its 48–inch focal length lens, gives approximately six–inch ground resolution.

The military has a specification for doing everything and the specification governing resolution measurement was Mil Standard 150A. Photo targets used for measuring resolution are called three–bar targets, three white bars with black spaces in between. The contrast ratio between the white bars and the black spaces should be at least 90:1 to qualify as high–contrast targets. The width and length of the bars and spaces varied from just a few inches, all the way to great numbers of feet. The ratio of width–to–length, however, always remained the same.

Data collection legs or flight passes were laid out so that in each size group one set of bars lay parallel to the flight path and one set of bars with the same size and spacing was oriented perpendicular to the flight path. This not only allowed for troubleshooting of the camera's lens capabilities based upon the along track and across track resolution, but it also gave the evaluator the ability to see whether the camera was consistently getting bad stabilization information or bad V/H information. If the cross–track bars were smeared, then something could be wrong with the image motion compensation system.

To put this issue in perspective, look at the camera that was trying to resolve the smallest objects. Assume for a moment that we have selected an exposure time of 1,000th of a second for the TEOC. In that brief period the aircraft traveling 3,000 feet per second will advance three feet. If one wants to see a six–inch object, that object will be smeared unless some compensation is made to keep the image from moving on the film while that part of the exposure is made. The TEOC compensated for image motion by moving the mirror in the camera head just slightly so that even though the aircraft was moving, the image on the film remained still during exposure. Classically, image motion problems show up in cross–track target bars. While the along–track bar targets would be equally smeared in this example, the problem does not come to light because the bars are still resolvable when viewed through the evaluator's microscope.

Where does one find such bar target arrays?

Good question. When the test force engineers started arriving at Edwards, one of the first things we sought was a listing of where all the photo arrays were in the local area and those throughout the rest of the U.S. There were almost none. There was one major array located at Pahrump, Nevada. This target was actually on private property and had been constructed years before. A camera engineer and photographic guru at Wright Field named Lenny Crouch supervised the contract that maintained the target arrays. When there were no ongoing camera development programs the contracts were allowed to lapse. The farmer at Pahrump, having not had his contract renewed for quite some time, figured the good deal was over so he began parking his farm equipment and other vehicles on the concrete pad painted with the bar targets. With the help of Larry Redmond at the SR–71 Program Office at Wright Field, we set up a contract with a company called Calspan. Calspan not only installed, painted, measured, and maintained new photo resolution targets, it also restored ones that had deteriorated. The farmer got paid his lease money for the array at Pahrump, and Calspan resurfaced and painted new bars on that parking pad. The farmer had to find other places to park his tractors.

An additional bonus was that Calspan maintained a traveling road show that could place large photo resolution arrays almost anywhere in the free world on very short notice. This company also had field targets for measuring the sensitivity of IR systems by putting out bar targets that had thermal contrast rather than optical contrast. Finally, all the arrangements fell into place and permanent photo resolution targets were installed or refurbished at Pahrump, and at Edwards proper, and Calspan portable targets were available on–call at Edwards South Base, Yuma, Arizona, Dallas, Texas, and Memphis, Tennessee.

On many of the sensor runs the flight paths were set up so that the aircraft could complete one pass at speed and altitude, decelerate/descend to refuel, then accelerate to make another pass down the line with the resolution targets. During the Cat II camera test program we collected only a handful of TROC photo frames to evaluate the resolution of 35 l/mm. That specification value was well within the camera's capabilities.

What about the OOC?

During the OOC test program we collected several thousand frames of imagery but only 1,168 were collected under conditions allowing a fair evaluation of the camera's resolution capabilities. The resulting distribution of resolution samples varied from 50 l/mm to a few at the far end of 125 l/mm. The curve peaked at the majority of samples being collected at the 80 l/mm value. As a reference, 80 l/mm resolution is equivalent to a ground resolution of about 35 inches from 80,000 feet. This is a fairly non–emotional number, but when looking at some exceptional images taken over the San Francisco area, one of them showed three men walking across the street in the down town area. One man was wearing a hat, one had a nice head of hair, and the third was bald. Not bad information considering it was collected from a thirteen–inch focal length lens on 70mm film from a vertical distance of thirteen nautical miles straight up. Obviously this kind of detailed information could not be collected on every single frame or every flight, but it gives an indication of the capability of the camera, the film emulsion, and the skilled SAC photo processing personnel who processed all the Cat II test film in the trailer city next to the hangar called the MPC.

Saving the best for last, the TEOC

While the TEOC did not complete the Cat II testing for many reasons (the Cat II testing was halted in December of 1966) there were thousands of frames of resolution targets evaluated by the test force. The entire flight test program for the TEOC at Edwards generated 66,944 in–flight frames of photography. A total of 814 frames of photo resolution targets were evaluated and, while the conglomerate l/mm numbers were disappointing, there were individual frames that produced some incredible results. Because of its focal length, the TEOC was the most affected by aircraft motion, stabilization errors, internal camera vibrations, and V/H anomalies. In general, the least little thing tended to degrade the photos produced by this cranky but talented optical instrument. A couple of the good points showed up about half way through the test program. High over Los Angeles, California, on a nice balmy afternoon, the TEOC snapped a frame showing a foursome of golfers on a green. One of the players was putting. On the photo you could see the flag, the hole, and as incredible as it may seem, you could also see the golf ball. Not bad for traveling at 3.2 Mach and 78,500 feet. Obviously the sun angle and the contrast levels were major players in this one exceptional frame, but none the less, you could see a golf ball from thirteen miles away. On another occasion, while photographing some office parking lot in the Burbank area it was easy to pick out the painted stripes marking off the parking spaces. The stripes were only about four inches wide (yes we measured them) but were very long and had great contrast to the black asphalt parking lot which accounts for their showing up so clearly. These short windows into the performance of the TEOC were just teasing glimpses of what was to come as the bugs of its installation were worked out.

There are many factors to consider

One last comment on measuring camera performance. To properly evaluate the resolution capabilities of a camera, you have to be sure you have given it the proper environment promised to the engineers when the camera was being designed. Next the exposure settings must be correct for the day of the photo run. And, the film emulsion selected for that particular flight and target conditions must be proper. Finally and certainly not the smallest task, the film had to be processed correctly. Only then can one start looking at the photo bar targets through the microscope and get a real feel for the resolution capabilities of the camera being tested. We spent a lot of time staring through a microscope. Each photo was evaluated by two people and the individual evaluator's results written down independently. When all of that batch of targets had been read, the results were compared. Where there was a disagreement, those photos were revisited and the differences reconciled. All the film target reading was done about 3 A.M. when there were no interruptions and the tables and floor mounted equipment were not subject to vibration from engine runs or passing aircraft.

Doing it in the trailers

A discussion of camera testing at Edwards would not be complete without mentioning the MPC, the personnel who worked there, and how the processing was done. These pros lived in a blue–box mouse maze with connecting tunnels, miles of wire to supply power from the four megasaurus Caterpillar diesel generators, a nightmare of tubing and pipes to transport the photo chemicals from the mixing trailers to the photo processing trailers. There were photo interpretation trailers, ELINT processing trailers, maintenance data processing trailers, and last, but certainly not least, there were trailers with maintenance shops inside to take care of the other trailers.

The MPC trailers began arriving early in the Edwards test program. First came the generator trailers, then the maintenance trailers, and on and on until the partial complex was connected and ready to support testing. The integrating contractor for the MPC was Fairchild Industries, the parent company of Fairchild Camera. The trailers would usually arrive at night. This was not a deliberate attempt to deceive but simply a reflection of the time for loading a C–124 transport and flying it from the East Coast to California. Like magic, every morning there would be another trailer parked on the grid laid out on the ramp. There were many questions from onlookers and, of course, we were not supposed to say anything about what these things were or even that they might be connected to our program. Our security chief, Lt.Col. Dan Andre, suggested jokingly that several of us dress up in white coats and operating room attire. Then at random times of the day and night, we could wheel other members of the test force around on gurneys from trailer to trailer. Our cover story then could be that the MPC was in truth a multi–unit portable field hospital. Fortunately this suggestion never went anywhere.

There was a multitude of emulsions used for individual sensors. To add interest, there were varieties introduced from time to time. Processing for every emulsion was tailored to what that sensor was attempting to bring out on that particular film. Without the dedication and creative thinking of the guys who worked the MPC it would have been impossible to salvage some of the data collected. Just as when you take your film to the processor to be developed you can ask the processor to push the film to make it seem a little faster than it really was, or you can tell the processor that because of conditions, you believe the film is under or overexposed by how many stops, etc. Just as you do that with your commercial processor, we did that with the people in the MPC and they would doctor the processing to match our requests. Sometimes the film from one camera of a pair would be processed first to see how it turned out before the second camera's take was processed. This allowed for adjustments, if necessary.

Keep in mind that we are not speaking of flopping a few negatives in a tray to see what develops (a tasteless pun I admit). Processing activities were accomplished using huge stainless steel machines that looked like the world's biggest ice cream makers. These machines exceeded twenty feet in length and on later versions the length of leader to thread the processors could exceed 300 feet. The manufacturer of these film processors was a company named Houston–Fearless. They made the processors we used in our dedicated lab for Program 665A as well. They worked well and lasted a long time.

The problem of disposing of expended photochemical solutions was not as difficult as it would be under the same conditions today. The base civil engineers made a two–and–a–half acre holding pond out on the dry lake bed. Base CE bulldozed a rim of dirt all the way around. We ran a large drainpipe from the trailer city to the holding pond and let'er drip. The government then sold the mining rights for the silver that would be eventually deposited within that holding lagoon to an enterprising fellow in Lancaster, California. A simple but true solution. (oops, another shameless pun).

Last looks at the camera program

The SR–71 camera test program was as thorough and exacting as possible, always keeping in mind that the object was not to invent new camera performance and not to bad–mouth the machines under test, our task was to define for the operational outfit at Beale, the capabilities of the hardware. We identified exactly what the systems were capable of when the cameras were operated by the manuals when using the support hardware and materials provided. It was not a small or easy job, but it sure had its rewards.

Chapter 15

Supplies, Spares, and Consumables

"Now let me get this straight—you want a four inch
hex socket with a quarter inch drive?"
Billy Shipley, Supply wizard, Edwards AFB, 1964

"Next time wipe your footprints off the desktop"
Charlie Dotson, Goodyear Aerospace, 1967

O ne of the greatest fears of any field commander is that he will not be able to keep his troops supplied with the materials they need. Any military historian will quickly make the point that no operation can be successful without well–planned logistics and supply. During World War II the U.S. out–produced the enemy and provided sufficient quality of hardware to do the job. But the real success was our ability to supply the type and quantities of items needed to the right place at the right time. The SR–71 was no exception. In the test environment as well as in an operational setting the machine was dead in the water without a smooth running and responsive supply system.

The Category II test program was the halfway point in transitioning the SR–71 supply support system from one primarily dependent on contractors to one operated by the Air Force. Going into the Cat II program the contractors supplied parts and repairs for their specific equipment and acted as their own prime repair depot. A major objective of the Cat II program was to gear up the normal (relatively speaking) Air Force commands to handle their job of supporting this operational weapon system. In the latter phase of testing, the system was operated and maintained using the approved manuals and the designated supply lines, relying on the Air Force logistics network as well as the family of contractors. The equipment contractors provided major repairs and modifications through a system of Special Repair Activities (SRAs) under Air Force control. This was a fancy way of saying, "Send the equipment back to the guy who built it to get it repaired."

Getting it together

The Cat II test program was the time to transfer responsibility for equipment care and feeding from contractors doing all the heavy lifting to a designated Air Force maintenance and supply team. It was a bear of a job. This transformation was equivalent to leaving home for the first time, moving into your own home, with your own job, and solving your own problems. One of the most daunting tasks was to make such an adjustment. The struggle of contractors, vendors, and suppliers to regularize the logistics side of their support was monumental. From the test force's point of view, it was similar to a heroin junkie trying to quit cold turkey. Nothing is easier than just calling the contractor and saying, "I need _____, (fill in the blank) by noon tomorrow. Can you make that happen?" True to a fault, any one of the contractors would say, "It will be there." And it was.

The test force maintenance people, equipment operators, and engineers and aircrews got hooked on this heady kind of support. In a high–priority program it is strictly "ask and you shall receive." The Edwards AFB end of that supply string was managed by an Air Force major named Billy Shipley. Without his knowledge and ability to make whatever we asked for appear overnight, we would not have gotten far. Some of the supply kinks in the Blackbird were enough to make anyone pull their hair out. Billy and his staff of supply experts did the job along with an equally energetic and skillful staff at the depot. The Air Force Logistics Command depot at Norton AFB, San Bernardino, California, served as the big supply daddy rabbit for the SR–71 from the beginning. Nothing was too tough for these guys and gals. Everything from five–drawer safes, to boxes of C–clamps, to liquid helium on demand, they delivered it all.

Film? Just say what size, how long, what emulsion, and how many rolls. It was delivered. Need 100 gallons of liquid nitrogen by tomorrow morning? It arrived on time. Have to have a truckload of photo chemicals before the weekend? The next thing you knew, someone was asking, "Where do you want us to stack these boxes?" The most striking part of all this was that early on the operations team was busy getting the job done while Billy Shipley's supply people took on the task of managing the paperwork. You simply expressed the need. The rest was done by this group of supply pros who knew where to go and what to do. Lockheed's long history of black program support contributed significantly to the ease with which many of the chores were done. It was tough to return to the real world after being spoiled like that.

Taking one problem at a time

Examples of peculiar requirements were not hard to find, and one that comes to mind immediately is the necessity to have only certain things come in direct contact with the titanium parts of the airplane. In the beginning Lockheed launched an extensive testing program using small squares of sheet titanium. Pairs of these small squares were spot–welded together and then contaminated with various common support items or standard chemicals. The welded pairs were heat soaked or cycled and then the spot welds were tested for strength. Using the results of these tests, Lockheed compiled a list of compatible and noncompatible items. Ordinary things like common lead pencils were forbidden. Cadmium–plated hand tools were another. Only one brand of masking tape was acceptable. Any products containing even minute amounts of chlorine, such as soap were a no–no. The list went on and on. The rules associated with keeping the area clean of undesirable items were strict and unforgiving. An Air Force maintenance sergeant could lose his stripes for having a cad–plated tool in his toolbox. Everything was tightly controlled. The need for individualizing down to the piece part level would drive a normal supply system crazy. In the standard supply world of crowbars, flashlights, toilet seats, and land mines, masking tape was masking tape and hand tools were hand tools. The people at the Blackbird depot and test force supply rose above this need for sameness and assigned special numbers to items peculiar to the SR where there could be no substitute. Working as the tiny tail, they wagged a willing but cumbersome worldwide supply system. It was not easily accomplished. Everyone on the logistic side of the house deserves a giant gold star for making these seemingly impossible issues come true.

We made several C–118 trips between Edwards AFB and McClellan AFB at Sacramento, California, simply hauling cad–plated tools (because those were the only ones in the Air Force system at the time) to be stripped of their cadmium plating in huge acid baths. The stripped tools were neutralized, cleaned up, and then flown back to the maintenance operation at Edwards.

Another more complex example popped up in the aircraft itself. Air Force aircraft usually carried the same kind of instruments for airspeed, attitude reference, navigation, and approach. These instruments came from the Air Force logistics system. Those in the SR–71 soon became different and it was not due to speed. It was a problem with instrument lighting. When the test force started flying at night doing night rendezvous and aerial refueling, aircrews complained about instrument lighting. Not all instruments were illuminated at the same brightness. Also, some appeared in slightly different shades of white. So we tested cockpit lighting. The aircrews sat in the SR cockpits while the aircraft was parked in the hangar, canopies closed and a thick mattress affair placed on top to eliminate outside light. First they would park themselves in there for thirty minutes so their eyes would become dark–adapted. Then they would start talking to the rest of us on the outside and telling us what it looked like. They would adjust the light levels of the entire instrument panel, up and down, trying to find the right setting. Bottom line was, it was not possible to reach an acceptable setting where the brightness from all instruments was the same. When the brightest instruments were adjusted to a comfortable level, the dimmer ones would be unreadable.

This was not a trivial issue. With a single lighting control, in order to see some of the dimmer instruments, the control was turned up, which made the bright ones cause reflections within the cockpit. Worse than that, some of the same instruments in different cockpits displayed different shades of white. It took a while to find the root of the problem. The Air Force supply system furnished many of these instruments to

Lockheed for installation in the aircraft. The variation from instrument to instrument of the same kind was due to age. The bulbs sealed within certain instruments were affected by the inerting gas held within that instrument. That gas was helium. Helium atoms are very tiny and eventually migrated through the bulbs' glass envelope, drawn in by the vacuum. This turned the bulb's light output a bit yellow–white and decreased the amount of light output for a particular voltage applied to the bulb. Because the instruments were sealed and inerted with the bulbs already inside, the problem could not be solved at the local level.

How do you fix that?

The solution took two actions. Lockheed installed a rheostat panel to allow individual instrument adjustments on aircraft going through final acceptance testing. Someone would sit in the blacked–out cockpit and make adjustments to the supply voltage for each instrument. Once done, these settings could not be changed by the crew. The goal of these adjustments was to have all instruments at the same relative brightness when the single lighting control was adjusted up and down. The other half of the solution was that certain instruments intended for the SR–71 were inerted with a gas other than helium and had a slightly different stock number assigned. That resulted in two varieties of the same Air Force instruments made by the same manufacturer, but with different federal stock numbers. Different because the inerting gas inside one was not the same as inside the other. Except for that the instruments were identical. The supply system and the people that made the system work kept many items just like these separate. Without individual care, meticulous attention to details, and long hours of dedication, careful changes to make the aircraft operationally better could never have been managed. There were literally thousands of unique items within the supply system that varied from standard Air Force issue. The jet fuel, the hydraulic fluid, the engine oil, all the way down to the standard–sized drill bits that had to be ground with a little different angle and cutting edge relief to accommodate titanium. Nothing was standard or simple.

Sometimes "better" is not the right answer

Early on, a young crew chief who was extremely proud of the Blackbird entrusted to him decided to make his machine look better.

Clean off the dust, spiff it up a bit. Not unlike the U–2 crew chief who painted whitewalls on the tires of his aircraft. But this time the results were much more serious. On his own hook, he went out and bought some cleaning supplies to wash and clean his aircraft. Sometime later, routine inspections revealed cracks in the upper wing panel spot welds on both wings. These cracks compromised the structural integrity of the wings, so the panels had to be replaced. Initially it was not understood what caused the cracking and there was widespread apprehension that some very basic design flaw existed. A full investigation was launched. Multiple analyses were completed and for a brief time it was thought that perhaps the smog in Burbank was the culprit with its excessive levels of H_2SO_3, (sulfurous acid vapors in the air) As soon as the crew chief understood the severity of the problem he stepped forward and described what he had done. The chlorine in the soap this young man had purchased was the culprit. He was found innocent of any conscious wrongdoing and no disciplinary action was taken. Another non–compatible item was added to the list and an intensive training program was launched.

The supply impact of this happening was significant. There were no spare upper wing panels just stacked about to be brought forth at a moment's notice, but they appeared when needed to keep the program on schedule. Somewhere behind the scenes there were logistics experts, Lockheed production planners, and sheet metal suppliers who lost a lot of sleep before things recovered from this reshuffling. But it got done without a bunch of arm–waving and shouting, and we marched on.

A nasty job but someone has to do it

When you meet and talk to logisticians from the early days, and those supporting specialized programs today, you become infected with the energy and dedication they apply to their job. Many times it was truly a difficult and paper–filled boring daily activity, but these people carried the load when it was needed. Parts to Edwards AFB, Beale AFB, to England, to Okinawa, Thailand, or wherever, the system spit them out at the right place and the right time. The system got the items there but it was then, and is today, the people and their dedication that make it work.

With such highly specialized hardware and equipment in such limited quantities, from the word go there were supply people involved,

involved because there were issues bigger than any one contractor could handle. Think about it for a minute. Titanium was available only in very limited quantities. The titanium sponge used to produce the titanium sheet and forgings in the A–12, YF–12, and the SR–71 came from Russia by a very obscure route. This one instance alone highlights the fact that many piece parts and developmental components came from unknowing vendors or suppliers. Once manufactured, the parts would disappear into the supply system to who knows where. A part needing repairs would magically resurface at the manufacturer's plant for upgrade or refurbishing. When the repairs were done, the part was off to the black world again. The logistics and supply entities engaged in furnishing parts, components, and consumable supplies to the Blackbird programs represented a major security curtain. What might have been one of the largest security holes actually turned out to be parts laundering at its finest. The supply system represented a great place to lose a grip on security. In the Blackbird programs this never happened.

People make or break the system

No system is perfect. There were times when conflict within a contractor's plant would rise to the surface and sometimes the local solution, while getting the job done, was not exactly by the book. As the program began to mature, the contractor's responsibilities became more diverse. On the one hand they were manufacturing and supporting test hardware and making changes driven by field results. On the other, and based upon a different government contract, they were producing production systems for operational birds and the necessary spares for those systems. These assets had to be kept separate and accounted for separately because the government was, and still is, very picky about using materials paid for under one contract for application to another contract's deliverables. And with a black program both contractor and Air Force people held themselves to a much higher standard of performance. Everyone had a license to steal, but no one ever did!

The production assets were always stored and accounted for in a system and location called bonded stores. This assured that money intended for one contract's hardware was spent on that hardware and its spares. Sometimes there were conflicts, test systems broke or pieces got fried or overtaken by events, and something closer to the production configuration was needed to support flight testing. Sometimes assets needed to fulfill test needs did not exist. Humans focused on the goal are sometimes tough to keep within the appropriate accounting box when it comes to getting the job done. One contractor's factory expediter, we will call him Mr. Goal–oriented, received a call at home one night from Edwards. The field rep told him they needed part such–and–such for tomorrow's flight.

The factory guy said, "But we don't have any of those right now."

The field rep begged, "We really need that board to get the test done tomorrow."

So at 2 A.M., Mr. Goal–oriented went to the plant to see if he might scare up one of the parts from test program assets. He found none. But, right there on the other side of the wire mesh enclosure, one of the production parts sat quietly in its bin. Our hero, or villain if you prefer, climbed over the chain link enclosure wall, let himself down onto a nearby desktop, made his way to the bin and got the needed part. To make his get away, it was back onto the desk and over the wire. He sped to the airport and dropped the part off with a courier service.

When Goal–oriented arrived at the plant at seven that morning, the entire place was abuzz about the breakin at the bonded stores enclosure. Mr. Goal–oriented stayed cool until the company's internal security personnel lifted his feet and checked his shoe soles. The footprints left on the desktop at the breakin site matched his shoe prints perfectly. Our over–achiever received a strong warning and a long talking–to about the sanctity of bonded stores and the reason they were isolated from the rest of the plant. However when he returned to his work station in the test support area he received a great pat on the back for getting the job done.

The part arrived on time at Edwards, and later that day a successful test flight was made. Once the flight was completed the part was returned and replaced in the bonded stores enclosure, this time through the door, not over the fence and onto the desk. By then test support techs had assembled a production configuration board out of leftover pieces and everyone was back on an even keel. Nice recovery from doing things a little differently.

Henry Pedrosa, we love you wherever you are!

They all turned the crank

People made the supply system work. There were literally thousands of individuals involved. No one leaked a secret. Everyone turned to. They pushed pieces, parts, and supplies to where they were needed, when they needed to be there. An incredible logistical success. And almost nobody knew their names.

Chapter 16

SLR Flight Test
at Edwards

*"Charlie, I'm telling you right now, with the high potential
for leakage of chemicals into the rear cockpit of the SR,
there is no way we are going to call this thing the ICP."*
Ken Hurley, Wright Field, 1962

"We're carrying a secret government cargo."
Don Beckerleg, Blythe, California, 1964

T he GA–531 side looking radar could map a swath width ten miles wide or twenty miles wide. The distance from the flight path could be varied from twenty miles all the way out to eighty miles. The system could look either side of the aircraft but could not map both sides at the same time. Eventually the term synthetic aperture radar (SAR) became the radar's designation.

Radar testing at Edwards was filled with the same heartburn, enthusiasm, and accomplishment experienced by other systems and their contractors. But certain things stood out from the rest. And these were not necessarily technical, but human issues.

Let's test that subsystem

Ken Hurley always wanted to know what was going on with all the systems controlled from the RSO's cockpit. Part of knowing was to have small panels that presented each system's status to the rear seat operator. In the case of the radar this was a small panel with a few colored lights and a switch or two. One of the switches was covered with a big red guard and was called the Dammit Switch. Every designer and test engineer puts in selected fault protection devices in their systems to prevent that particular box or system from killing itself on purpose or by accident. The SLR was no exception. If a shortage or over temperature cooling air or some other form of circumstance should suddenly threaten the life and well–being of the radar, it would just shut itself off.

Ken, being a veteran of some serious World War II B–29 combat missions said, "If I arrive in the target area, and my job is to collect radar data, no damn system is gonna tell me it doesn't want to turn on." Ergo the Dammit Switch. He concluded that, after all the risk of getting to the target, there was really no choice of whether to operate the radar and fry the transmitter or whatever. After all, the warning or self protection device might just be a false alarm. The maintenance guys could deal with the results after the mission was completed.

There was a system for the maintenance guys as well

Every line replaceable unit (LRU) of the SLR system had a small indicator on the outside. The purpose of this indicator was to tell the ground crew whether the unit considered itself in good health and functionally correct. This was part of an overall concept called BIT or built–in–test. Each LRU had a circuit card or a portion of a circuit card dedicated to checking the health and welfare of its internal functions, and then sending information to an indicator on the outside of the box as well as to the display panel in the RSO compartment. These circuits were called BITE, or built–in–test equipment. This system was a great tool for doing quick and dirty go or no–go testing and major component replacement in a hurry. However...

Charlie was very proud of the Goodyear BITE design and suggested that Ken come to the plant at Litchfield Park to give the system a test. When Ken walked into the lab, there was a system running on the test bench, cooling air blowing, lights blinking, and other sounds of a healthy electronic system. All the boxes were open to view so one had full access to the circuit cards.

Charlie invited Ken to reach over and remove a card. You know the routine, "Pick a card, any card." He explained that the system would then tattle on itself and display the fault on the RSO's panel and also show the appropriate fault on the box BIT indicator.

Ken reached into one of the open LRUs, undid the latches on the a circuit card, and carefully lifted it out. *Nothing happened.* Much to Charlie's dismay, Ken had unknowingly removed the BITE card itself. The system, though it had failed, had no circuits available to tell on itself. Sometimes it just doesn't pay to invite the customer down to kick the tires on a new machine.

Taking the U–Haul to Burbank

When it came time to transport the first system to the Lockheed Skunk Works, time was short and there was no desire to send a super–secret one–of–a–kind system by UPS. The guys at the Goodyear plant at Litchfield Park, Arizona, decided they would rent a U–Haul truck to take the system to California. They could not use a company truck because no one was supposed to associate the radar, the Skunk Works, and the SR–71 with the Goodyear name.

The shipping containers housing the system black boxes (which in this instance were all painted white) were loaded onto a suitably anonymous rental truck and Don Beckerleg and a fellow employee started for the West Coast. When they arrived at the California border, the Fruit and Vegetable Police stopped their truck at an inspection station just over the border and demanded to search the rear of the truck. Don and friend were ordered to unlock the back of the truck for the inspector. They had been briefed by their security folks that they were not to unlock the back of the truck for anyone, no matter what, until they reached the inner confines of the Skunk Works and could hand the system over to the proper people.

Don, dressed in T–shirt and jeans, replied "Can't do that, we're carrying a secret government cargo."

The agricultural inspector looked at the two for a long time in silence and then to Don's complete relief, he smiled, waved his hand, and said, "Go on through."

A system full of pieces

The SLR was not a simple system. It had several major components besides the basic radar system carried within the nose. All the radar data acquired was recorded on film in a recorder mounted separately from the rest of the system. Then there was the recorder correlator display (RCD) mounted in the Reconnaissance Systems Operators cockpit.

The RCD was an in–flight optical correlator combined with an almost–instant film processor. It took the radar output, recorded phase histories on data film, and processed that film. Then it performed the task of optical correlation and exposed the result on a radar map film. The final task was processing the radar map film and projecting the resulting image for viewing by the RSO. The total delay between the time the SR passed abreast of a particular point until that point was projected on the RSO's viewer was about thirty seconds.

The RCD optics and other innards were a nightmare to assemble and calibrate. This subsystem required considerable hand tuning and skilled care. At one point the units reaching the final test and checkout area were suffering from multiple fingerprints on some of the lenses. Charlie, being the ever constant problem–solver, published a printed announcement indicating the problem and reminding employees that the company had everyone's fingerprints on file. But solutions to problems are not always straightforward. Immediately the fingerprint problem disappeared, but was replaced by another more severe problem. Now the lenses appeared scratched where some clever soul had removed their fingerprints with Bon Ami.

Shipped in a bag

RCD chemicals were not only an in–flight concern but were an issue in the supply chain and storage. Here were all these chemicals that could cause who–knows–what, intended for shipment to who–knows–where and they had to be packaged, ready for use, in just the correct quantity and strength. On one trip, Charlie showed Ken and me the company solution to the packaging and shipping problem. He hauled out a bunch of very pliable plastic bags with screw caps on the top. Ken and I were both horrified that anyone would even consider shipping this stuff around in plastic bags.

Before we could voice the words, "What happens if one of these is dropped?" Charlie raised a full bag high above his head and with a devilish smile let it fall to the floor. Plop! No splash. No burst. No fountain of ghastly chemicals. "I could tell what you two were thinking before you even said it," Charlie replied. "We even dropped full bags from a ten–foot stepladder and they still didn't break."

Drop test complete!!

The main portion of the radar imagery recorded in flight was on a five–inch–wide data film which was returned to the ground–based mobile processing center for processing. The data film was then optically correlated and a radar map film exposed and processed by the MPC. When that was done the results were available for viewing in one of the photo interpretation trailers within the MPC.

Early on there seemed to be a problem with the radar map every time the aircraft tried to settle out after a turn or when some slight course corrections were made. The problem was chronic and no easy answers came to mind.

The great interface rain dance of 1966

There were some questions as to the content and accuracy of interface signals shared between the cameras, the radar, and the astro–inertial navigation system. One of the basic issues was the validity of the ANS signals sent to the radar to assist in antenna stabilization, and pointing. To explore this area, Bruce and I approached Ken for permission to conduct a test on the ground. Because it involved two or more days of dedicated airplane time in the hangar and we needed Lockheed's analysis of the effects on the main landing gear when the nose of the aircraft was lifted to an attitude of seven and one–half degrees nose up, this was not one of those instant experiments we could charge off and do on our own. The concept was to block the main landing gear and then raise the nose gear with a pair of huge forklifts until the aircraft assumed a normal seven and one half degrees nose up flight attitude. We would trick the ANS into thinking it was flying and making some turns and slight in–flight course corrections and then view the results on the sensors using various optical and mechanical measurements. We needed to steal time from all contractors to support this effort. After

227

considerable discussion on what we might discover or prove and what we could do if we found a problem, Ken finally agreed to allow the test.

I flew back to W–PAFB, and "borrowed" three theodolites that were stored as part of the old QUICK CHECK and 665A assets. Bruce and Nortronics worked out the mechanics of getting the ANS system up and running and thinking it was flying while the aircraft was actually just sitting with its nose up in the hangar. The maintenance guys were a great help even though they were not particularly in love with the idiot exercise two of the engineers from the second floor had dreamed up. In the end the test was a success and the results were published in a hundred–plus pages containing electronic readings and calculations, pages of geometry and trig, and several pages of drawings, diagrams, and raw data.

Three really neat things happened as a result. We discovered that the polarity was reversed on some of the signals provided to the SLR by the ANS. This accounted for the radar mapping problems following course corrections or turns. We proved that radar noses could be changed without going through any elaborate boresight or calibration activity. And when it was suggested to Lockheed that they ought to do a similar test on each production aircraft to verify all signals, Lockheed surprised us by figuring out a way to do the whole thing in fifteen minutes. The aircraft did not have to have its nose jacked up. Instead they used a stretched wire for a centerline, a couple of plum bobs, and a ruler. A very clever solution to a difficult interface documentation and verification.

There were specifications to meet

Besides mission readiness that paid the contractor a bonus for meeting the criteria, there were resolution measurements to be verified. Once again we had to hitch up our technical tractor and plow some new ground. At the time, radar resolution was substantiated by viewing arrays of reflectors spaced geometrically to provide measurable results in range and azimuth. Resolution in range is a function of pulse width, timing, and received signal processing. Resolution in azimuth is dominated by the qualities of the system's beam width and antenna characteristics.

There was only one radar resolution range near by and that was located on a dry lake bed near Wilcox, Arizona. It was called Wilcox

Playa. There were a few problems with this range. The reflectors were aimed the wrong way, they were cut for the wrong frequency, and they were not arrayed at the proper distances to allow the SR's system to demonstrate that it met its requirements.

Phil Simpson and Sgt. Ayres take a canoe trip

Capt. Phil Simpson, a SAC maintenance guy assigned to the test force, loved to do things with a flair. One day he dropped by to see what added tasks he could perform. I explained that we needed to do some radar resolution measurements and were stuck at the moment. Because of the classification we could not call Wilcox Playa and tell them to change the size of their reflectors, nor could we ask them to turn theirs around to face a direction we could use. Phil suggested that some of his troops in the sheetmetal shop could make the reflectors and we could put them up somewhere. Charlie Dotson of Goodyear provided the measurements and specs on orientation and placement. Phil had about 75 reflectors made.

We needed a space of dry lake or clear level ground about a half mile wide and a mile long. While there were plenty of dry lakes in the southwestern U.S., most were used for either, local glider flying, X–15 emergency landing strips, or night bombing ranges for the F–4s out of George AFB. As far as our nearby Rosamond Dry Lake was concerned, it was used by hundreds of local radio control airplane aficionados on the weekends, and during the week that area was used by the southern California film industry to make automobile and other commercials and to film the TV series *Rat Patrol*. So we started a snipe hunt, looking for a more out of the way place to put up our reflectors.

One morning we jumped in our U–3 in search of such a place. The search ended over the southern portion of Silver Lake, a dry lake bed located on a line between Edwards and Las Vegas, Nevada. We made several passes up and down the lake, even touched our wheels, but the surface didn't seem solid enough for a landing that day.

Silver Lake was isolated, had no apparent human activity, and it was easily accessible by someone with a four–wheel–drive pickup, plenty of water, and a good map. The final good news was that it would be possible to view this array of reflectors from test flight routes already planned and being flown for other purposes. Two days later Phil, Sgt. Ayres, and two others left Edwards before dawn in an Air Force pickup truck loaded with transits, measuring tapes, and a truckbed stacked with radar reflectors. When they returned that evening there was a brand–new radar resolution range located on the southern portion of Silver Lake, and no one was the wiser.

Sometimes things just don't work out

Much as I would like to say it was success and the little clandestine range was a great help, such was not the case. We managed to map the reflectors on a few missions but the little radar reflector range did not provide the kind of data we had hoped for. I flew by there on the way to and from other locations to see whether the reflectors were still there, and they were. But they just didn't provide the resolution measuring tool we had hoped for. We never went back to pick up the reflectors. Maybe one or more modern–day dune buggy drivers have run across that strange geometric garden of equilateral, metal pyramids on metal stakes and decided tiny green men really have visited this planet.

Hey, what time is it?

One of the items present on the data block area of all the SR–71 sensor films was an image of a clock. This clock was used to show what time the particular frame was exposed. All the clocks were set and checked prior to the mission, so that there was a direct correlation between individual frames or images. The decision was made to acquire the absolute finest in timepieces that would fit within the small spaces required. Every sensor was equipped with a Bulova Accutron watch. These wristwatches were the ultimate in earthbound portable timekeeping and cost well over a hundred bucks. The Accutron used a small tuning fork as the primary reference and based the passage of time on the cycles of the tuning fork. Early on the missions were flown at lower speeds and altitudes and the watches worked out well, but when the test missions began to reach operational speeds and altitudes, something funny happened to the watches.

Without warning the Accutrons would go to a ten–times faster speed and would indicate the passage of hours when only minutes of time had elapsed. This was especially troubling to the radar people as there was a significant time interval between exposure of the clock face on the film. Sometimes on a three–hour mission, the Accutrons would show elapsed times of six to eight hours. On some of the camera frames, the second hand was moving so quickly it was blurred on the exposure.

Distressed by this fault in time keeping, the Goodyear crews went out and bought a fist full of Timex ("Takes a licking and keeps on ticking.") watches at the local drugstore for about ten bucks a pop. They selected a model which had a particularly large imprint of Timex on the face. Installed for several test missions at speed and altitude, they kept great time. And there was the word Timex on every piece of radar film for all to see. They made their point.

In defense of Bulova, the watches were very well designed and kept excellent time where they were intended for use. The company had no idea these watches were being used at 80,000 feet and at 3,000 feet per second. Lockheed conducted some environmental tests and determined that the tuning fork was affected by the altitude and the vibrational spectrum of the SR–71 when at its cruise Mach number. All the sensors at Edwards had their uptown Bulovas replaced by the very plebeian Timex watches.

To the victor belongs the spoils

Because each sensor contractor bought the watches on their own directly from Bulova, each contractor had a supply of altitude– and speed–deficient Accutrons. Both Charlie and Don have one of the Bulovas left over from that enterprise. Why is it that the contractors always get to keep the good things?

Life and times of an RCD

Life on the cutting edge was sometimes difficult. The concept of having near real time radar displayed in the rear seat of the SR was a mouth–watering challenge to all of us technical weenies but I'm not so sure the operational crews or the maintenance people cared all that much about it. This device had all the laws of physics tied up inside except nuclear fusion: electronics, chemistry, optics, mechanical relationships, and a laser. The greatest risk was that of spilling any of the very rude chemicals outside the box and having them drip down onto the dainty titanium interior of the rear cockpit. This led to many snide comments about fluid containment, and resulted in some clown making a diaper to put on the box, and in general caused an elevated case of apprehension among all test personnel and the aircrews. To my knowledge RCD never leaked into the aircraft proper. But it did provide some interesting background stories.

Don't touch that stuff

To process the film and present the data in the shortest time frame, it was necessary to optically correlate the data film and project the map film while each film was still wet. This was done by using a device called a liquid gate. This was nothing more than a narrow chamber which the wet film passed through. This gate had lip seals on both sides so nothing would leak out and windows top and bottom so light could be passed through to project the image of whatever was on the film for the next step in the process. To make the projected image as clean as possible, the liquid in this gate had to have the same index of refraction as the processed film, i.e., the liquid had to bend light rays in the very same manner and amount as the film in the gate. A search was conducted and a suitable photo–compatible chemical found.

Talk about unintended consequences! Almost immediately the Goodyear factory people working with the test and production hardware and testing began having serious diarrhea. At first it was not too obvious what was causing the problem but some careful detective work put a finger on it. This new optically perfect chemical was very easily absorbed by human skin and once that happened it produced a super Ex Lax effect. Talk about "A little dab'll do ya," this stuff was wild. The problem was controlled almost immediately by strict procedures and some educational programs for all handlers.

The system proved itself in the end

The SLR made a good showing in Cat II flight testing. Off to a rough start initially, once the interface issues were ironed out between itself and the ANS, the SLR produced good imagery. Resolution samples were taken and measurements made that showed the system met its requirements more than 85 percent of the time. This covered the straight nose (original configuration) as well as the two degree up–tilt configuration adopted later to accommodate the trim drag and stability issues flowing from the crash of aircraft 952. The system met its alert requirements one hundred percent of the time.

During one mid–Category II flight test sample period there were 45 flights made with an operable SLR on board. During these flights 29,615 nautical miles of ground was radar mapped.

A look at progress

Of all the Blackbird sensors, the SAR has shown the most improvement over the years and has experienced the greatest growth in capability. The advent of electronic processing instead of optical, the change from film to magnetic media, and the maturing of digital techniques over analog, brought this sensor to the forefront of all–weather intelligence gathering and reconnaissance. Operational SAR today far exceeds what was, in 1966, considered to be the phenomenal resolution of thirty feet in azimuth and range. Today's systems consistently produce imagery with demonstrated resolutions of one foot in azimuth and range. Now that's all–weather, through–the–clouds, in–the–dark, in–the–rain, over–your–territory, and in–your–face reconnaissance. Just the way the Blackbird and her *Habus* did their jobs when she was in her prime. She is still capable, and we are foolish not to use her.

Chapter 17

Flight Testing the HRB-454

*"We're not gonna fly that scope until
you test it in the altitude chamber."*
Dick Miller, Lockheed, Edwards AFB, 1966

*"Hey Dutch, just take a whiff of this helium
gas and you can talk like Mickey Mouse."*
Donn Byrnes, Edwards AFB, housing area, 1966

Probably the only sensor system arriving for testing at Edwards that had been out to speed and cooked at the cruise temperatures beforehand was the HRB–454 Infrared (IR) system. Both the X–15 flight tests and the Skunk Works lab experiments on the window had provided a pile of information about how the system would react to the anticipated flight environment. The one issue that was not explored in its final design was the appearance of the window seams seen by the scanner. The material for the window IRTRAN IV was not all that easy to manufacture and, because of that, it came in only small pieces. This necessitated the assembly of several pieces into a single window. There was no way to cement or bond the pieces together into a homogeneous single piece, so the individual segments were polished and fitted together. These seams showed up on the early IR imagery as lines running down the map as it progressed. (The epoxy bonding between window segments used in the initial windows had already been removed before Cat II flight testing began.) Because the scanner mirror rotational speed and the mirror geometry with respect to the window did not change during flight, the window seams showed up as a constant frequency and could be electronically filtered out.

You want to put what in the backseat?

While experimenting with different filtering frequencies and looking at the potential for degrading the IR image, Jerry Hogan and Bill Engle decided it would be a good idea to have the RSO look at what was happening to the IR system in flight. If Lockheed would just put this little oscilloscope on the floor of the rear station then the backseater could observe various signals direct from the scanner amplifier to see how the system was performing. There were a couple of options set up so the RSO could make changes to scope inputs during flight. There were several commercial scopes available but none were SR–71 flight qualified.

Dick Miller was adamant that nothing was going to be bolted into the backseat of one of his airplanes without first being declared "safe."

"Just run that baby through an explosive decompression to 80,000 feet and I'll let it fly," were Miller's words.

After a few phone calls and some begging, our next stop was the altitude chamber at Edwards with hats in hand and one small oscilloscope under our arms. Dick made it clear that this little box should operate safely at normal cabin cruise altitude and would not come unglued if it were up and operating when suddenly taken to the aircraft's actual cruise altitude due to loss of cockpit pressure.

The chamber techs, like always, were great about accommodating the Blackbirders and their goofy requests. They ran enough of us up and down in their machines to check for trapped air under tooth fillings and to be sure the aircrews did not suffer jaw or sinus pain after new dental work had been done. One afternoon, after the day's other chamber rides were finished, Jerry and Bill installed their modified oscilloscope in the small test chamber, got it operating, and sealed the power wires and signal lines where they led to the outside. The chamber was evacuated to an altitude of about 27,000 feet and the Little Scope That Could continued to operate. This was no surprise because we had checked out similar scopes for use in the 665A aircraft should it lose cabin pressure during one of the missions.

After enough time to convince everyone the scope was stabilized and operating, a larger chamber was pumped down to a much higher altitude. When an X–ray film membrane between the larger chamber and the test chamber was intentionally ruptured, the scope suddenly found itself operating at 80,000 feet. An altitude sensitive safety switch attached to the box shut off power, and there it sat, safe, in one piece, no glass or other items scattered around the test chamber. We all watched for about ten minutes to be sure no delayed explosions might occur. The Little Scope That Could turned out to be the Timex of Test Equipment.

One flight with this instrumentation verified the results the designers had hoped for. With the implementation of this final fix all the design problems associated with the window had been put to bed with the available technology.

What happened during the flight test program?

The IR system carried one hundred feet of 70mm film. This was sufficient to image a strip 12,000 miles long and 45 degrees either side of the aircraft flight path. The first Cat II flight was flown on 3 May 1966. The system angular resolution was specified to be 1.0 milliradian. Test results demonstrated that value to be 1.02 milliradians. There were a grand total of forty–nine official Cat II IR flights. Total film exposed was 1,122 feet. When adjusted for an average altitude of 75,000 feet, that comes out to an along–track coverage of 175,000 nautical miles. Based on cross–track coverage at that altitude, Cat II flights mapped a total of 4.45 million square miles of ground during that part of the test program. The test systems operated for a total of 778 hours in flight and on the ground with only eleven failures.

Are you ready to go?

One of the elements of the performance contracts with all the sensor manufacturers was the flight readiness alert requirement and the incentives associated with meeting the goals. The contract required an alert be declared seventy–two hours before a designated mission. In the real life of the test environment these alerts seldom exceeded twelve hours notice. In all, the IR system was alerted twenty times (the number required by the contract) and all twenty were met. Each takeoff time was made with an operational system.

Where do you get all that liquid helium?

One of the great joys of being around the edges of a flight test program, and especially the SR–71 flight test program, was the variety of support equipment, systems, and all the strange and exotic materials. Liquid helium, at –269°C, was one of the most interesting. When you look at it in the liquid state, it is blue. Not because it is so cold, but because that is the way it reflects light. Getting something that is roughly four degrees above absolute zero (–273.16°C) to hang around in the desert when the outside temperature is near 110°F is a chore. Recognizing an operational and test force recurring need for a ready supply of liquid helium, and not wanting to advertise what was going on at the test force, Ken Hurley decided, while he was still assigned to the System Program Office at W–PAFB, to purchase a small liquid helium plant. This plant arrived at Edwards in time to support flight testing. There was a small block building behind the Cat II hangar and that is where the liquid helium machine was assembled. That machine and its care and feeding provided great opportunities for some of us engineers to share the wonders of science and physics with our fellow test force members and our families.

The machine, a device purchased from Air Products, arrived in a large box, and several smaller crates. Some assembly required. Jerry Hogan, the HRB tech rep, drew the short straw, so he was elected to assemble this device. If there was ever a case of silver solder torch in one hand and assembly manual in the other, this was it. After Jerry finished the assembly Andre arranged for a pair of fifty–gallon dewars filled with liquid nitrogen. The supply guys obtained many high pressure bottles of pure helium gas, as well as several large cylinders of pure nitrogen gas. We were ready to give it a shot. The first run made some super cold liquid nitrogen because we had the bottles plumbed in wrong. Several later tries produced no liquid helium. Even after pumping the system down to the lowest vacuum we could obtain, our efforts were still unsuccessful.

Finally an Air Products rep, who had by now been cleared for the program, came to the rescue. He blessed the assembly as being absolutely correct and physically sound and suggested that maybe there was some form of contamination in the work engine. This was a mechanical portion of the system that forced the chilled helium gas to do work so it could give up more of its residual heat, be chilled further, and eventually transition to its liquid state.

The cleaning facility for the work engine was a large flat pan of acetone set on a nearby table. Once the parts were cleaned and reassembled, the Air Products person picked up his end of the pan and I picked up mine. Long wide shallow pans filled with liquid are a hazard because two people just cannot coordinate their movements. Inevitably, the liquid began to slosh back and forth. As we carried the pan through the doorway a standing wave developed, the acetone leapt from his end of the pan, drenched his polyester slacks, and filled his shoes. The slacks became some new form of solid material after being soaked in acetone. The days of bending at the knees were over for those pants. Later, dressed in one of my spare flying suits, he helped us make the first successful run and generate our very first batch of liquid helium.

Do you just pour it into the dewar?

The short answer is *No!* The process of getting liquid helium into anything is not simple or easy. None of this turning on the spigot and filling a jug. First the detector/dewar had to be pre–chilled with liquid nitrogen and then the liquid helium was fed down a special tube that had also been pre–chilled, into the detector/dewar for the IR system. With all the extra supplies and equipment lying around there was an opportunity to take some leftovers home. I could not resist sharing this technology with my family. So I took a thermos of liquid nitrogen one afternoon and the kids and I, much to my wife's disgust, froze small pieces of everything we could find, including some very nice looking fresh strawberries. Once frozen we threw them against the side of the garage and watched as the strawberries shattered.

M–I–C–K–E–Y M–O–U–S–E

The closing act of technology transfer to the Byrnes household occurred during an evening get–together with another member of the test force. Air Force Captain Dutch Duschame was a SAC photo processing expert and ex photo interpreter. He was really the man to see at the MPC when you wanted to have special processing done with any of the films. We worked closely together and, since he was a bachelor, he had a standing invitation to our home for dinner.

Some of the helium cylinders were due to be refilled, and as we never used them down to zero pressure, there was always some helium left in each returned cylinder. Why not take a little home in one of my diving tanks and blow up balloons for the kids? With an adapter made in the garage, I managed to pump a good bit of this lighter–than–air gas into one of my tanks and took it home. Dutch was there as usual and as we filled balloons for the kids, and they floated all over the ceiling of the living room. We let a few go to scoot around the room like little misguided rockets and were having a generally good time. Then I took a whiff of the helium and my voice sounded just like a Disney character. The kids loved it. Beth, my ever patient wife, was not pleased with this turn of events. Soon Dutch had monopolized the diving tank exhaust and was delighting everyone with his funny voice. He forgot to breathe in oxygen between Mickey Mouse voices and passed out cold right there on the living room rug. The kids thought he was fooling, my wife thought we were sick, and that was the end of magic voices. Beth grabbed the diving tank, walked to the back door, opened the tank valve, and heaved the hissing thing into the backyard. Dutch recovered in about thirty seconds (it seemed like a lifetime) and dinner was served. The meat *du jour* was cold shoulder.

What a bunch of memories

The Cat II flight test program for the HRB–454 infrared system was another step in the progressive development of IR technology. That system was the only one made by HRB–Singer to ever have a detector cooled with liquid helium, and the only sensor system to ever have flown so high and fast on an earthbound aircraft, the X–15. It is our understanding that in later years the SR–71 no longer carried an infrared reconnaissance system. Perhaps the trade–off between scanning spot size and thermal resolution could never be suitably resolved. Perhaps it was scale factor, or maybe the mission did not demand collection of information in that part of the electromagnetic spectrum. Whatever it was, the system was not dropped because it failed to meet its design specifications or because it was not reliable.

From the HRB Reconofax 4 and 6 systems that were flown on the B–58, QUICK CHECK, to the system flown on 665A, to the SR–71's IR eyes, there was steady progress made under a number of flight environmental conditions toward refinement of IR mapping scanners. Ken and I value the people we worked with through all those programs. You couldn't ask for a better bunch of associates and friends.

Chapter 18

The 2,500 Mile Micrometer

"Now if you just imagine a one foot square piece of plywood with this fifteen mile long dowel perpendicular to its center, you'll have a picture of the problem."
Bruce Hartman, Edwards AFB, 1965

"There is just no way we can get all this stuff done on time."
Nobody ever said that! 1962 – 1970

How does one measure something that keeps flying off the end of the ruler? How do you track and record the performance of a machine that leaves states and small countries behind like coins through a hole in your pocket? As soon as planning started for Blackbird Category II flying, it was obvious—a brand new problem was facing the test force. There had never been a weapon system before whose performance parameters were critical all along the path of flight. In most missiles and attack aircraft, the departure location and delivery point were the places of prime interest. How you got there was not as critical. With the SR–71, from the first acceleration to Mach 3+, to the exact planned course, to the hot–leg targets, to deceleration and rendezvous with the waiting tanker, everything depended on knowing exactly where you were and where everything else was with respect to the bird's flight path.

In the classic flight test program of the 1960s it went like this. The contractor conducted the Category I flight test program. The objectives of the program were to first establish that the aircraft was safe to fly within a major portion of the envelope and then collect enough flight test data to demonstrate initial handling qualities. While doing that, begin writing the flight, and maintenance manuals, establish emergency procedures, and show that the aircraft and its systems meet or exceed the design characteristics specified in the contract. This is a very simplified representation of the contractor's task. There are literally thousands of system and subsystem aspects to these initial tests.

One small example

To illustrate the types of tradeoffs, consider the aircraft system designed to deliver cooling air to the crew station and to all the electronic and photographic equipment on the aircraft. In the early design, every item or black box was assigned a heat output value. The box was to perform its function while only generating so many BTUs per unit of time. Each box had to be maintained within a certain internal temperature range to assure all its components would operate without going into heat exhaustion or getting frostbite. The flow rate through the box was also allocated so that there was no hurricane whipping along through the printed circuit boards causing them to shake or vibrate excessively and fling off their little electronic arms and legs or break loose solder joints. Lastly, air delivered to each box had to meet moisture limitations so components did not drown and short out. The box also had to offer only a specified resistance to the passage of cooling air. A given ratio of the pressure at the input to the pressure at the outlet needed to be maintained. Other boxes downstream of the first box depended upon their cooling air from the exhaust of the first box. It was a delicate balance.

Consider a whole system of boxes of different sizes, shapes, internal contents and heat–generating capacity spread throughout the fuselage of the aircraft. A radar transmitter, for instance, took much more cooling air and flow than an ELINT receiver. Some circuitry was more heat tolerant than others. Every piece of equipment in the aircraft requiring cooling air got its supply from an elaborate system of pipes, tubes, orifices, heat exchangers, flapper valves, flow–control butterfly valves, blowdown turbines, and water separators. In the harsh thermal environment of the Blackbird, everything needed cooling air.

One of Lockheed's early tasks was to produce an environmental control system that satisfied the black box requirements so all systems would perform and stay healthy. The Category I flight test program was the proof of the pudding for the ECS system. If some component of the stability augmentation system, for instance, overheated and died during a critical period, catastrophic loss of the aircraft was a direct possibility. Supplying cooling air was complicated by how it was obtained.

Where does all this cold air come from?

Cooling air was generated by a device called a blowdown turbine, a turbine driven by very hot air bled from the last stages of the engine compressor. High–pressure air was diverted to a device that makes the air do work, thereby reducing its temperature and at the same time causing the air to expand greatly. The result was very cold moisture–laden air. Typically the input air from the engine compressor is above 300 degrees. This small turbine idles at about 35,000 rpm but for the most part is a non–complex device. Because of the way the cycle works, the cold air produced was much colder than could be tolerated by any of the aircraft systems, so more hot air was taken from the engine compressor and mixed with the newly generated cold air to get the right temperature for feeding the ECS system. This same system also cooled and pressurized the cockpits. In the Blackbird the ECS also furnished a flow of cooling air to the aircrew's pressure suits.

It should come as no surprise that engine performance was adversely affected by how much of this precious last–stage–of–compression air was drawn off. The engine had done all the work to compress this air in anticipation of getting good results by burning it with fuel and producing thrust. Now at the last minute, some pirate called the ECS hijacked this valuable air so the engine had to produce whatever thrust it could with the air that remained. In the final analysis this was a small percentage of the compressor output, but when pushing something at Mach 3, every little bit helps. This air theft adversely affected fuel consumption. Fuel burned to compress air that did nothing to move the aircraft forward. An analogy would be the air conditioner in your car. You can go a lot farther on a gallon of gas when you leave it off. But on the other hand, that was not an option for the aircraft. Your car will not crash if you shut off its ECS and roll down the windows.

Added to the tug–of–war between the avionics designers and the propulsion people was the simple fact of life that all the black boxes or components were not ready at the same time. Those missing had to be represented by a simple orifice or a butterfly valve adjustment to simulate the cooling air the missing box would use if it were actually attached and getting cooling air. This does not even address the fact that many boxes come in over budget on their heat–producing requirement and thus need more cooling air than originally planned. This is one, if not the greatest sources of heartburn and stress among design and test people.

At one design interface meeting during a heated discussion over cooling air budgets, one avionicker complained bitterly about the quality and temperature of air being delivered to his box. He had instrumented the box and was raving on and on about internal temperatures during various segments of the flight. He allowed as how at some point the input air temperature was above the melting point of his solder joints. A problem, he said, could result in molten solder collecting inside the box's circuitry. The propulsion man, already in difficulty with respect to thrust and fuel specifics, was unwilling to give up any more of the engine's high–priced air and said, "If that seems to be a problem with your particular equipment you had just better install some solder drains." These problems continue throughout the life of all major aircraft test programs and on into the early operational phases. By the time Cat II flying ended for the Blackbird, most of the lumps had been ironed out.

The ECS system is only one aircraft system that must be balanced with the needs of the other systems. Every aircraft system interacts with others and all are compromised somewhat to reach a series of operating points that allow the aircraft, its aircrew, the sensors, and other equipment to get the assigned job done. Demonstrating that this symphony of individual mechanical and electrical nightmares all plays from the same sheet of music was one of the Category I contractor's most daunting tasks. This tapestry of engineering system relationships hangs behind and is usually upstaged by flashy aircraft aerodynamic performances and record–setting splashes in the headlines. An appreciation for this necessary and complex background was usually absent for all but the seasoned and experienced aircraft system designers, test engineers, test pilots, and maintenance people.

Mix in all the other tradeoff design issues associated with a flying machine and you have the background issues present in everyone's mind at the beginning of a flight test program. The equivalent of accomplishing a successful system test flight in the early days of the SR program would be to stack seventy–five Gerber baby food jars end on end, then stand on them and hold that position for about an hour. We started stacking our baby food containers as soon as the Cat II test force arrived at Edwards in July 1964. Perfect system test flights were indeed rare, but as Kelly Johnson used to say, "We usually learn much or more from test failures than from completely successful test flights."

The starting setup

Classic flight test activities such as envelope expansion, demonstrating stability and control, developing takeoff and landing data, determining crosswind landing limits, flutter speeds, single–engine performance, in–flight refueling envelopes, night flying characteristics, point–by–point engine performance, and instantaneous fuel specifics (mpg), can all be done in a relatively small geographic area. As some experts say, these are activities that generate charts with lots of spots and dots. For the Blackbird, "small" was larger than most aircraft needed and included the Edwards area, most of southern California, a good part of Nevada, and a significant chunk of the Pacific Ocean along the California coast, not to mention pieces of Arizona, Colorado, Utah and Wyoming. But—and this was significant—a major portion of the area was covered by overlapping data–collection radar systems that had long since been back–fitted with respect to each other in the tracking of an airborne target. This network of radars produced time, space, position information (TSPI) data anchored to a common reference coordinate system. In this local area the tracking data from the Pacific Missile Range (PMR), and a well–spread network of Edwards Air Force Flight Test Center and China Lake Naval Weapons Center radars, were able to continuously monitor the flight position, altitude, and velocity of test aircraft. This tracking network was supporting the flights of the X–15 at the time. The Blackbirds were tracked and controlled by FAA radars while beyond the range of test data collection radars. These traffic control systems could not provide TSPI data. The availability of TSPI data was limited to the areas around Edwards. This had always been sufficient for previous aircraft tests, again because those programs had been data–point or end–point driven.

A look at the real issue

Enter now the Blackbird whose performance was more like a missile and whose legs were longer than anything ever tested at the Edwards Test Range before or since. This machine was designed as a straight–line flyer. Minimal turns were employed operationally to avoid hostile or high risk areas or to align with the next collection leg for more radar, photo, ELINT or whatever additional data was needed. Flight path planning was one of the keys to extended range flying. Turns took energy; the gentler they were and the fewer made, the longer the range. A fully loaded aircraft screeching along at 3,000 feet per second represents a large amount of momentum and Newton's laws still applied at 80,000 feet. Once headed in one direction and at speed, it took significant energy to change direction. Blackbird flight planning was a delicate dance between the departure base, hot–legs, tanker rendezvous, area avoidance, intelligence collection, fuel management, and getting home.

Within the continental limits we were not allowed to accelerate or decelerate over towns or cities especially around Mach 1.2 as the sonic boom produced at that speed was horrendous. More than once the plate glass of some unfortunate casino in Las Vegas bit the dust, but it could easily be blamed on the F–105s flying out of Nellis AFB, Nevada.

Where we started

The Blackbird Category II program charter was to demonstrate and document for the SR–71 SPO and the user (SAC in this case) exactly what the SR–71 could do toward satisfying the performance requirements. This included speed, range, altitude, endurance, aerodynamic envelope for flight conditions, navigational system capabilities, and of course, sensor system performance. The test force needed test missions to mirror as closely as possible the operational implementation. The airframe and the engines took the system to cruise speed and altitude, but where it went, how well it worked, and the quality of the information and data collected was pretty much the sole responsibility of the astro–inertial navigation system.

Given the complexity of navigation at a nautical mile every two seconds, determining the location of targets to be sensed from fifteen miles up and flight path management and rendezvous planning, nothing but the most rudimentary operational sortie could have been accomplished without a fully functional and reliable ANS.

The ability of the navigation system to know exactly where it was at all times, to know where the anticipated targets were from the aircraft, to point and operate the cameras and SLR over the appropriate area, to gently correct the flight path to avoid flying into a surface to air missile (SAM) nest, were all critical. Because the worst–case operational "take leg" was anticipated at the time to be about 2,500 miles, the task was to establish a ground–based radar tracking capability so that the aircraft's position, altitude, attitude, and velocity could be continuously recorded throughout the test leg. The ANS kept careful track of where it was or where it thought it was and what the aircraft velocity and attitude were.

Unlike the A–12 aircraft with its pure inertial navigation system, the SR's ANS possessed the capability for very long–term navigational accuracy by incorporating an astro–tracker that provided frequent star fixes to update its inertial position. There were requirements that the ANS demonstrate no more than a one–nautical–mile per hour drift in the pure inertial. This gave the planners a ballpark figure of performance so they could place a tolerance band on either side of the intended flight path. For a successful mission the bird has to spend most of its time in the middle of the road and not visit the shoulder very often. The astro–tracker's chore was to update the ANS system for genetic pure inertial errors and lapses in accuracy due to oscillation and drift of the inertial platform.

A fully functional ANS would keep the SR smoking down the middle of the road, pointing and clicking the cameras and sweeping the radar across preplanned targets. At the same time it would assist the aircrew by displaying accurate deceleration start points (a normal "decel" takes twenty plus minutes and covers hundreds of miles) in anticipation of rendezvous with the tanker. A small miscalculation in determining the initial deceleration start point from cruise speed and altitude could result in a major problem in arriving at the tanker.

Setting up the range

The 2,500–mile leg would be the basis for defining a multi–functional test range. Throughout the length of this leg there would be precision tracking radars to verify ANS performance. The flight path should include multiple photo resolution targets and radar resolution targets. Emergency landing bases needed to be available all along the test leg.

Captain, later Major, William (Bruce) Hartman was a guy who grabbed a problem and hung on until it was solved or everyone was dead. A seasoned and operationally experienced Air Force navigator with plenty of test experience gained at Eglin AFB, Florida, Bruce was a self–starter. You never had to explain how to do anything, just suggest what result must be obtained and then back out of the way. He was a cranky sort of guy, opinionated and forthright, but he could flat get the job done. He was a terrible golfer. The task of building the 2,500 mile mostly straight–line micrometer fell on Bruce. First, we all sat around and tried to establish a track that would provide frequent Air Force bases for emergency landings should a problem occur. After all, this was a test program and things did not always go as planned. We avoided places where residents were distressed by the soft boom of a high flyer. Next, was to line up as many existing facilities with FPS–16 radars along a fairly straight path. Good, precision trackers, the FPS–16s were the best available at the time. Most of the existing FPS–16 stations were located across the southern U.S. When linked they would provide a transcontinental test range. Then we mapped out overlaps in radar coverage so at least two radars would simultaneously track the aircraft for sufficient time to develop a common database of geographic coordinates and altitude references.

In the early and mid–1960s there was no such thing as a functional global positioning system (GPS), and the ECHO satellites had just been launched. Bruce soon documented what he already knew. While there existed several national datums, and a handful of scholarly documents describing various versions of the shape of the entire planet Earth, the cruel facts of the matter were that no one could tell you exactly where the center of Fort Worth was with respect to the center of Dallas, Texas. There was absolutely no way to tie a street corner in Los Angeles, to another street corner in Phoenix, or anywhere else in these United States within the accuracy needed to measure the performance of the Blackbird's nav system over the long haul. While this was the modern high tech 1960s, we were actually dealing with data that had not been updated since the 1920s. One might ask, "Hey, if things were so loosey–goosey in the geographic coordinate department, how could we expect to hit targets in the Soviet Union with our missiles?" The answer was, "If you are using a bunch of megaton hydrogen warheads all targeted against the same place, who's gonna notice a few miles here or there?" The first test missiles fired out of Vandenburg AFB, California toward the island of Eniwetok missed by a large margin. While it is hard to survey ocean, once the errors were ironed out, the old data was off by five miles. On the Eastern Test Range out of Patrick AFB, Florida, it was discovered that Ascension Island's location on the charts was eight miles removed from its actual location The Blackbird needed more accurate information than was currently in the national database.

The solution was painfully clear: the Blackbird would have to use its sensors and its nav system to measure itself. At the same time the aircraft would become a common reference point between radars to allow linking geographic data between them. Piece by piece, the system would bootstrap itself across the country, adding one radar site or system at a time. We needed a lot of help. And it came from other Air Force units, the Army, the Navy, the U.S. Geological Survey, Air Charting and Information Center, and a contractor called Calspan. By hook or crook, Bruce got teams sent out with precision star–tracking equipment and laser measuring devices to resurvey every location where there was an operating FPS–16 radar along the Blackbird's intended test flight path. The service that did most of the heavy lifting was the U.S. Navy. Many participated knowingly, some without a clue as to their contribution, but all turned to and carried their part of the load willingly. The test leg started about 800 miles off the west coast of California where the aircraft could accelerate and attain cruise speed by the time it reached the 300–mile limit of the shore based FPS–16 tracking radars. Flight continued from there to Phoenix, past Dallas, to near Memphis, and then the trail turned south to a refueling track off the west coast of southern Florida. Once refueled, the aircraft accelerated to cruise speed and altitude and retraced its steps exactly (at least that was the intent) ending up back out over the Pacific Ocean three or so hours after the start. The bird then decelerated and returned to Edwards. Once the kinks were ironed out, the worst the Blackbird ever did was to have the return track across a carefully surveyed area in Phoenix be 1,200 feet north of the outbound track. This bird could walk right down a razor's edge and do it any day of the week.

Making a silk purse from a sow's ear

Here is how Bruce sewed it together, wrote some very clever equations, and how the rest of us contributed.

The SR had a vertical camera mounted on the centerline just forward of the nose wheel bay. This camera, labeled the TROC, for terrain objective camera, was a very sophisticated relative stemming from a long line of Fairchild vertical mapping cameras. The T–11 was its nearest relative with zillions of miles and frames under its belt. The film was nine inches wide and the camera lens had a focal length of six inches. The TROC on the SR, affectionately labeled The Stainless Steel Brownie, was intended to take photographs of the ground directly below the aircraft at a frequency that would allow a 55 percent overlap from frame to frame. The Fairchild camera could reproduce the ground's geometry directly below the aircraft by compensating for all the hardware imperfections introduced by the camera and the film processing. Another element needed was the aircraft's exact altitude above that piece of ground. The aircraft's pitch (nose up or down angle) and roll (leaning right or left) and yaw (alignment of the aircraft's keel axis with the flight path) had to be recorded at exactly the time of exposure. Imagine a nine–inch square piece of plywood with a fifteen–mile long piece of dowel rod sticking out from the middle moving along at a one half mile a second with the far end of the dowel just skimming along the surface of the earth. The slightest wiggle of the plywood and the other end of the dowel moves a large distance. To know exactly where the other end of the dowel was by measuring the tiny movements of the plywood square was what Bruce and the rest of us were trying to do. It is a little game the engineers call "very small differences between extremely large numbers."

If the interpreters or analysts could integrate these factors and thus adjust out the measurable errors by reducing the information in the photograph, an exact determination could be made as to the precise piece of real estate directly below the aircraft when the picture was taken. (After it was determined where the end of the dowel was when the picture was taken).

The mechanics of photo reduction

To properly position the SR along its flight path at any instant there needed to be some very careful analysis of each TROC photo. The Navy volunteered to carry the ball. This analysis was done by people at the Pacific Missile Range, Point Mugu, California, in temperature–controlled rooms using microscopes on optical comparison devices called Mann Comparators.

To determine the location of a particular ground feature in the photo, the distance of that feature from the nearest Reseau dot had to be measured (for more on this see the Camera chapter). Going from feature to feature and dot to dot, the interpreters reconstructed exactly (within a few feet) how big or how small or how far something was from something else on the ground. Adjust all that by the birth certificate data of the platen (the backing–plate behind the film during exposure) and the lens used, and they would calculate, using the aircraft's pitch, roll, yaw, and altitude data, the exact spot directly below the aircraft. At that instant the exact position in space was known for the aircraft—if and only if—you knew the exact geographic location of that spot on the ground with respect to the rest of the surrounding geography. Before all the planning and dogwork, no one knew where anything was. After Bruce and many others finished their magic we knew the precise locations of all the FPS–16s along the route, the photo resolution targets, the radar targets, and other geographic points with respect to a common reference. Not bad for a guy who had a really sorry golf swing.

Bruce Hartman orchestrated efforts that made it possible to tie all the individual parts together. The U.S. Coast and Geodetic Survey field experts were called in under the auspices of the U.S. Army, to do Class 1 surveys of several areas and tie them to other known areas so we could build geographic stepping stones along the intended flight path. The tracking radars from more than one location would simultaneously track the Blackbird as it crossed and photographed one of these stepping stones. This allowed, beginning with the Edwards and PMR radars, both systems to look at the Blackbird when it was above a known geographic location. Later PMR would reduce each radar's mission tapes for altitude, latitude and longitude, flight path direction and velocity. Using that information, they were able to tweak each site's computational information and the assumed geographic location of their radar antenna. After several flights following this procedure over known locations, the errors began to smooth out and soon both tracking radars agreed that the aircraft was in the same place at the same time. Then the procedure would be repeated a little farther down the line until all tracking radars assigned to this task could be related to the PMR coordinate system. This effort was carried on as a constant background activity while the test Blackbirds flew all sorts of other missions collecting other data and completing other tests.

The ANS recorded its data on the Mission Recorder System (MRS). The MRS had two tape decks, the A deck, which recorded aircraft systems and sensor system parameters, and the B deck, which recorded all the navigational system information. Because of program classification, no data was telemetered from the test aircraft. All test information was recorded onboard and brought home for analysis. That presented a data transportation problem. All this material was TOP SECRET, kill–you–if–you–lose–it kind of data and there was absolutely no way to pump it around through normal security channels. (See the chapter on Security) First, none of it was marked, and second, none of it existed as far as the real world knew. Moving the data from the B deck and the TROC films, along with the tracking output tapes from the radars turned into a big job. During the initial phases of the test program everything had to be handcarried to its destination and the reduced results handcarried back. We had an ace in the hole.

Nestled away at North Base on Edwards, just off the northwest corner of Rogers Dry Lake in among the U–2 support aircraft and other spooky things, was our own Cessna 310. The 310 belonged to the SR/YF test force and we used it to travel to contractors' locations, travel to the Skunk Works, up to the Sand Pile (Area 51), and trip after trip to Point Mugu delivering and collecting data. We made regular flights to Beale for coordination and technical assistance. Throughout the test program I spent a zillion hours in the pilot's seat of the 310 from nowhere.

It was an Air Force aircraft and was painted the standard dark–blue and white Air Force colors. The USAF designated these 310s as U–3 aircraft. The adopted nickname was *The Blue Canoe*. Ours was simply called *The Canoe*.

One of the necessary tasks was to travel to other testing centers like the Army's facilities at Yuma, Fort Huachuca, and White Sands, to first brief high–level personnel on portions of the program and then whip out our priority and plead for their assistance in our tracking support. While Bruce did all the brain work and Ken Hurley stayed home to keep the test program train on track, Lt.Col. Daniel Andre and I did all the traveling, briefing, and associated dogwork. As the test program progressed, the traffic in film and data between PMR and the test force intensified. When the *Canoe* was occupied elsewhere the data was transported in other aircraft or by car, when the weather demanded.

Low–tech trips and tribulations

Late one afternoon we departed for Point Mugu to pick up one of the PMR experts, then were to fly to Fort Huachuca so we could conduct briefings the following morning. I had called ahead to the Army Air Field at Fort Huachuca to confirm they would be open when we arrived which would be well after midnight. They said they were a twenty–four hour a day operation so come ahead. After an uneventful flight from southern California to central Arizona, we turned south over Tucson. Shortly thereafter I began trying to raise Fort Huachuca on the radio. No luck. We arrived in the local area and descended to pattern altitude but there were no runway lights and no taxiways lit up. We put down the landing gear, turned on our landing lights and began circling. At least the rotating beacon on their water tower was working. As always in situations like this, there was no moon and in case you have never been to Fort Huachuca after midnight, there are no local lights. Finally a very sleepy voice answered our calls and confirmed that we were indeed circling the correct air field. He said we could land any time we felt like it as there was no other traffic. I asked for wind information and which runway was active, the normal Air Force stuff.

The reply came back, "Can't really tell, I'm down here in the basement talking on this radio."

"Do you suppose you could turn on a few runway lights and some taxiway lights so we could see what the choices might be?" I asked.

"I'll see if I can find the switches," was the reply.

We continued to circle the water tower and were mentally calculating the amount of fuel needed to get us back to Davis–Monthan AFB at Tucson. We would have to decide soon. Then the blue lights of the taxiways lit up and we could see something at last. We waited for the runway lights to come on. None did.

"I've got the taxiway lights in sight, could you hit the runway lights please?"

"I'm afraid that's all the switches I can find," came the reply. "Actually the runways pretty much run right along beside the taxiways. Can you make them out?"

We slogged around a little more and finally lined up on a taxiway, made a low pass, and the PMR expert in the back seat said, "I see the runway, it's over to the left."

"Fort Huachuca, we have the runway in sight and are going to land."

"Go ahead," came the reply.

Once we had rolled to a stop we asked for taxi instructions to the operations building and a place to park for the night.

"Can you see the flashing lights?"

All three of us looked around and finally saw the interior lights of some building flashing on and off.

"Got the flashing lights, now what?"

"Just head for that building and park anywhere you want. I'll call the motor pool for transportation."

The remainder of the visit was comparatively uneventful. The briefings were conducted as planned and we were ready to depart by mid–afternoon. The PMR expert was not impressed by either my flying

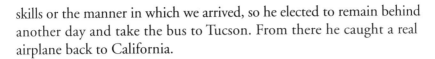

skills or the manner in which we arrived, so he elected to remain behind another day and take the bus to Tucson. From there he caught a real airplane back to California.

We could not have done it without the Navy

There is no way to adequately describe the value of support services supplied by the U.S. Navy in general, and the people at PMR in specific. Their creative expertise, range leadership, and dedicated dogwork made the 2,500 mile micrometer an effective and accurate measuring device for the SR–71's ANS. The key to this success was the PMR's agreement to become the lead range and act as overall operations manager for this transcontinental test range. It put the day–to–day functions into the hands of experts who could do that job effectively and it also provided a buffer organization in the security fence that surrounded the SR–71 flight test operations. Thank you!

A wrap–up

This test range arrangement performed well and effectively. The SR–71 received the most precise and complete testing of any aircraft up to that time. The superb performance of the SR–71 in operations all over the world was in no small measure due to the 2,500 mile micrometer and the people who did the measuring.

When the Cat II flight test program was winding down it was repeatedly suggested to the Pentagon and other DOD agencies that they might want to use this range for upcoming aircraft. There was no interest expressed. The range died. This is a backhanded way to illustrate the fact that this country does not have anything like the Blackbird in operation nor is it producing a similarly responsive air breathing system. No need to measure things you don't plan to build.

Chapter 19

The SR-71 Had Big Ears

*"We're not going to talk about that until
I'm sure it's been declassified."*
Donald P. Rhude, Col. USAF(Ret), 1999

Reconstructing the life and times of the SR–71's electronic snooping gear is not as easy as one might think. For one thing, issues that drove the design and collection criteria are not all dead yet, even in 1999. Second, people in electronic warfare professions are not given to lots of idle chit chat. Mix this with the fact that the specific officer and engineer assigned these tasks at Edwards AFB during the testing of the SR–71 systems is a closed–mouth New Englander, and you have a picture of the problem. Major Donald P. Rhude did an incredible amount of work during his stay with the SR test force. He tackled the test program for aircraft radios and navigational electronics as well as the Mission Recorder System, but ELINT and electronic warfare (EW) were the main course on his plate.

To further appreciate ELINT and EW systems design and testing, one needs to know that this sort of science and black magic is almost totally reactive. You can't go out and listen to some enemy's signals on a particular frequency until you find that he is transmitting on that frequency. There's no way to build and test a jammer designed to jam signals not yet received and recorded. The electronics countermeasures business and signal collection activity are intimately interrelated making each activity co–dependent on the other. It is hard to establish a single set of design parameters and then create hardware. In short, the design, development, and flight test of a fixed and stable EW suite is quite unlikely. System flexibility and adaptability require design improvements be made on the fly. The conduct of a well organized and carefully documented EW flight test program is a tough cookie to bake. Don Rhude had several chefs to help him in the baking process during the Category I and II flight testing of the SR–71. It all came out just fine, except for one thing, Purple Plague.

Silly as it sounds for a dry desert climate, some form of purple fungus or virus or whatever that purple fuzzy stuff was, began to attack certain chips made by Texas Instruments that were incorporated within the ELINT boxes. The electronic impact of this growth was not clearly definable but it did add just a dash of color to the interior circuit cards of the system. This problem was never resolved during Category II testing. Later Texas Instruments discovered the cause and replaced the chips with a Purple Plague–proof version.

The operational scenario in the mid 1960s was driven by the Southeast Asia model, which said there were two threats to aircraft, AAA and SA–2s. With the Blackbird's mission altitude well above the 27,000–foot limit of anti–aircraft cannon, the designers focused primarily on the SA–2 threat.

The use of simulators and evaluation facilities throughout the design and test program was imperative. Both the Air Force engineers and the EW designers leaned heavily on the expertise available at General Dynamics (GD), Fort Worth. There was a little known operation at the GD plant called the Air Force Electronic Warfare Simulator (AFEWS) managed by Maj. Larry Grayson at Wright–Patterson AFB. The GD manager of this facility was a man named Henry J. McDonald. Henry was always ready and willing to assist and support no matter what the chore was. Everybody in the EW business knew and respected Henry.

The ELINT and EW system flight testing during the Cat I and II programs covered several areas.

Electronic intelligence gathering

The SR–71's ELINT system built by Airborne Instrument Laboratories (AIL) was essentially an airborne electromagnetic vacuum sweeper. It sucked up and recorded every signal in the air as it whipped by. The system was so sensitive that during early integration testing at the Skunk Works in Burbank it could only be baselined for certain frequencies in the wee hours of the morning. And that was when the system was already inside the electronic isolation provided by a screen room. Later, to accommodate the system's sensitivity, Lockheed replaced the screen with solid copper walls in an effort to further isolate the system from outside electronic noise.

All received electronic information was stored on tape. The only tape recorder with the bandwidth and data density available at the time was one made by RCA for recording color television programs. This recorder used two–inch wide tape. The information was written back and forth across the tape as it was moved from reel to reel. The RCA recorder was adapted for use, and proved to be quite successful. An additional tape recorder was incorporated within the system which used one half–inch tape. This smaller tape recorder gave the test people plenty of grief because the oxide coating on the tape kept coming off and clogging the heads. The problem was later solved by purchasing polished tape late in the flight test program.

Don did his homework

A baseline was needed to establish what emitters were out there and who was transmitting what kind of signal and when. Don went to all agencies that operated or controlled emitters along and for several hundred miles on either side of the test flight routes. He developed a catalog listing each signal of interest and its characteristics. These characteristics included power output, basic frequency, pulse repetition rate, pulse shape and frequency content, phase relationships, and polarization (vertical, horizontal, or circular). It is not too difficult to imagine how many agencies and emitters were listed and cataloged along a 2,500 mile flight path. With that information in hand, he would query every agency after every ELINT system test flight and collect the exact status of listed emitters in the catalog along the route of flight for the time period of that flight. In addition, each agency had to confirm that their emitters were operating within the parameters provided earlier and if not, identify what the parameters were on that particular date and time. It had to be done to establish a record of what was along the flight route and operating at the time the SR passed by. That was a bugger of a job.

This information was provided to the test evaluation team at Edwards who compared the reported data against what was collected. This was done on site in the MPC trailers located just across the ramp from the Cat II hangar. One of the trailers had a CDC 3200 computer installed where the data was reduced and the results processed. This same ground information and flight data were provided to the AFEWS at Fort Worth for incorporation in their database and for further analysis.

The Electronic Warfare Suite

There were several other components in the SR's electronic suit of clothes. There was an air–to–air warning system, comparable to the tail warning systems of today, that alerted the crew when they were being painted by an airborne threat such as an interceptor. This system was made by International Telephone & Telegraph (ITT).

The Blackbird also carried a very clever deception jammer made by Sanders. This system received a tracking radar's pulse, fiddled with it a bit, and then returned it. The returned pulse from the deceiver was just a little stronger than a normal reflected pulse would have been, so the tracking system processed the modified pulse in preference to the one that was normally reflected back. This allowed the deception system to create a false location for the aircraft in the ground system's computer.

All deception systems that manipulate received pulses and return them have a receiver and a transmitter. The receive and transmit antennas for the deceiver must be separated electronically by a significant isolation factor or the bad news is that the system begins to talk to itself, it's called ring around. When this happens, instead of misleading the ground radar as to where the aircraft really is, the system becomes a beacon for the ground to track and shoot at. It screams, "Shoot me, shoot me!!!" Deception systems, when they are good they are very very good but when they are bad you're in big trouble.

Here's what happened on a good day

Near Walker Lake, Nevada, is a small town named Hawthorne. There were a couple of claims to fame for this area. One was the Naval Ordnance plant near the southern end of Walker Lake where, at the time, they were turning out 500–pound general purpose bombs for the Vietnam war like they were going out of style. The second big attraction was SAC radar site used for operational crews to practice against. A site operated and maintained by a clever bunch of Air Force GIs. When a test of the Sanders jammer was scheduled we would hop in the *Canoe* and proceed up the Owens Valley to Hawthorne, land at the local airport, and then be on the ground as witnesses when the Blackbird sang by and spoofed the site.

There had been considerable concern about earlier SR flights in this area because the Navy's bomb makers were understandably jumpy about hearing booms in the area around a bomb factory. So, after a masterful application of inter–service statesmanship by Dan Andre, we finally received permission to fly our missions during the local noon hour when the bomb–fillers were brown bagging it.

I know it's irrational but I always had a mental picture of little old gray–haired ladies dressed in dust bonnets and checked aprons walking down endless rows of tail–sitting 500 pounders. With a soup kettle in one hand filled with RDX or the current explosive, and a ladle in the other, each lady would pour just the right amount into the top hole of each bomb as they went from one to another. When the SR's sonic boom would rattle the factory, the ladies would takeoff for the exits sloshing RDX from their kettles as they ran.

The Hawthorne site had the capability to track aircraft using characteristic ground–launched missile system tracking frequencies, and also an X–band tracker which could follow a Navy/PMR–supplied X–band beacon mounted on the test aircraft. This beacon track was used to establish and record the actual flight path of the aircraft. The X–band tracking operation was separate from the defensive missile portion of the site and its Air Force operators. The generic ground–to–air missile system had three active operators when tracking a target and preparing to launch a missile. (Not a real missile, just a computer simulation.) One operator tracked the target in range, one tracked the target in elevation, and the third operator was responsible for azimuth tracking.

263

On this particular run they picked up the target SR from a search radar handoff and began tracking immediately. These guys were good. The shadowy blip from the SR stayed centered in the tracking gates of each operator and, like pros, they followed the weak radar return until the command was given to launch three missiles. Then they were doubly careful about their tracking because their missile that day was a beam rider and was guided by signals from the ground radar and not from a self–contained guidance system. At the point of projected intercept they all yelled out their success as it looked like a clear kill.

But that was not the case. After the sonic boom had faded, the little old ladies got a grip on their RDX buckets, and the test aircraft was well on its way, we all went to the computer room. There we viewed the plotted X–band track showing the real flight path and then overlaid that on the path that the generic missile and its operators had been following. They were not the same!!! It was easy to see how the deception jammer had drawn the trackers away from the real aircraft. The tracks slowly (relatively speaking of course, because the whole experiment lasted only a few seconds) curved away from each other. When the computer missiles had been fired, the SR–71 was far away from that point in space where the site was aiming. The Sanders' system was really slick.

Testing the other EW systems

One of the very best places in the world, other than actual enemy territory, to test electronic warfare systems was at Eglin AFB, Florida. The entire Gulf Coast is ringed with every domestic and foreign threat radar known to man. There are systems from everywhere, some bought, some stolen, some reverse–engineered from pieces. The Beach, as it was called, represented an electronic environment containing every possible form of pulse polarization, frequency manipulation, signal sorcery, and transmitting trickery imaginable at the time.

Lockheed's test pilot Darrel Greenameyer took a fully equipped electronic Category I SR–71 to Eglin to fly against this array of emitters. The aircraft carried, among other things, a brute force jammer powered by traveling wave tubes. This system was made by Hallicrafters. The plan was that Darrel would fly out of Eglin for a quite a few missions while the folks on The Beach recorded their results and the aircraft recorded the internal goings on of its systems. The idea was to collect a significant sample size from both the air and the ground. This data was shared by the electronics contractors, Lockheed, and the Air Force. In addition, the data from both ground and air was furnished to the AFEWS at Fort Worth for their data base and further study.

There were some scheduling conflicts

Because of program priority and an urgent schedule, the SR–71 SPO at Wright Field took the position that they needed prime time on the Eglin Range. Lt.Col. Fred Trost, Test Director at the SPO went to Eglin Range Scheduling and requested daylight morning range time. The range responded by assigning a daily block of time from 2 A.M. to 5 A.M. Fred Trost countered with the comment that they could not fly in the dark because the SR–71 was a test aircraft and could only be operated in daylight hours. The Range allowed as how it started getting light about 5 A.M. so maybe 5 A.M. to 8 A.M. would be just fine. Because the timeline for an SR launch started many hours before takeoff, the SR–71 SPO got the last word.

About 3 A.M. Lockheed troops would roll the bird out of King Hangar at Eglin, point the back end at the housing area and do engine trim runs for about thirty minutes in preparation for that morning's flight. In no time after all the complaints about the noise from sleeping residents, the SR–71 range time was changed to the 9 A.M. to 1 P.M. time slot.

The test results were welcomed elsewhere

The data collected during these flights was used not only to evaluate the Blackbird systems but to assess responses from the systems on The Beach. This information was combined with other data at the AFEWS to develop EW scenarios for Southeast Asia, Europe, and other areas of the world. The ongoing evaluation process led directly to developments and techniques used later in the F–15 aircraft Tactical Electronic Warfare System (TEWS) definition and specifications. Don Rhude was a major player in this effort.

Chapter 20

Jim Zwayer and Number Three Died the Same Day

"Even though these machines are made on a production line, each individual airframe is handmade, each is just a little different from the others"
Kelly Johnson, Skunk Works, 1965

"Screaming along at 79,000 feet and looking up to see Crater Lake does nothing for your sense of aerodynamic security."
Ken Hurley, Edwards AFB, 1965

Each aircraft in a production run has its own characteristics and its own personality. Modern–day aircraft are quite complex and contain thousands of piece parts, all of which have their individual tolerance bands. A stacking of tolerances can result in significant differences from airframe to airframe. One of the early Blackbirds was actually an inch and a half longer than its companions. Combine the physical size issues with the possibilities of differences within the hydraulic plumbing, the fuel tankage and delivery piping, control surfaces and how they relate to their mountings, and one begins to realize that these machines are not cookie cutter replicas of one another. They may all look alike and be the same external shape and color, but as every pilot, aircrew member, and aircraft mechanic knows, they are all just a little different under the skin. Some fly faster on a given power setting, some rumble in the turns just a little, some seem to always be just a little askew with the relative wind or show a tendency to drift off heading more than others. In extreme cases there are certain airframes, like certain people, that are never exactly right. always sitting around because they don't meet the standards for flight. These machines are usually referred to as hangar queens. Every squadron has one or two. Some get the label "Old Yeller" because aerospace ground equipment (AGE) is painted yellow and, of course, never flies. The longer an aircraft sits and doesn't fly, the more likely it is to continue sitting on the ground.

Test airplanes have even greater extremes of personality. Not only do they have the normal variations but there are also new engines, new control systems, experimental stability augmentation system authorities, and CG limits associated with various airspeeds and altitudes. When you mix the unknowns of a new aircraft, the estimated performance of the nominal version of the bird, and the personality traits of each individual test aircraft, test pilots and flight test engineers must deal with a variety of test issues. They have to understand and recognize individual traits of a specific tail–numbered machine. Separating the normal from the quirky is not so easy to do. Here is where the test aircrews and the ground–based test engineers really earn their money.

Not just another test mission

In November 1965 Fox Stephens and Ken Hurley were taxiing out in Number Three, tail number 952, their intended flight path was called the Northern Route. As they moved along the taxiway Ken handled all the radio conversation. Fox liked to concentrate on the aircraft and its systems. Like many experimental test pilots he was able to get the feel of the machine as they rolled slowly toward the takeoff end of the runway and did not like to have his thoughts interrupted by the demands of tower calls and other radio conversation. Ken and Fox were the only Air Force aircrew to fly the Lockheed Category I aircraft at this early point in the program. Both men were extremely knowledgeable and experienced. Their intercom conversations were almost nil as they had flown together so many times each was aware of their individual jobs as well as their obligations to the other.

After takeoff they accelerated north along the east side of the Sierras and about twenty–five minutes later were making a slow turn to the west around Klamath Falls, Oregon. The mission called for them to return south toward Bakersfield, California, decelerate and then land at Edwards. Up until now everything in the flight had been quite normal and peaceful. About the midway through the turn with a bank angle of 40 degrees, the left inlet (the lower inlet in this case) unstarted. Their bank angle increased immediately which was to be expected under these circumstances, but the aircraft continued an uncontrolled roll to the left. Fox was busy in the front seat evaluating and responding to the conditions of the aircraft; in the back, Ken had the distinct feeling they would not get this thing under control. He felt that whatever he wrote in his notes might be found later, hopefully giving someone a clue to what happened. Because of program security, both were prohibited from broadcasting the circumstances on the radio. He wrote furiously in his logbook trying to explain everything that was happening from his point of view in the rear station. At the same time he was trying to quickly tidy up his cockpit in preparation for ejection. His lap–board (his writing desk in this case) was made of cardboard for just this reason. He could use it until the last minute and if the time came to eject he could blow right through the cardboard without a problem. The aircraft continued its slow roll progress toward the left and Ken looked out of his side windows to determine what their roll angle was at the time. Out the left side he was looking straight down at Crater Lake and knew that their bank angle was 90 degrees or better at this point. They were very close to getting upside down at 80,000 feet and Mach 3.1. Ken still has a very clear view of looking out the top of an SR–71 and seeing Crater Lake. Gradually the roll rate ceased, they hung there at that extreme bank angle and then slowly the aircraft began to roll back to the right until it reached wings level.

Fox spoke to Ken (nothing had passed between them until this point), "If the roll had not stopped where it did, I had already made up my mind to continue the roll all the way around to the left."

No one knows how that might have worked and fortunately they didn't have to find out. The application of control surfaces that had finally been successful was something the stability and control people said should not have been done under the circumstances. Fox had applied full roll and full rudder control at the same time. The experts thought at Mach 3 or better, such extreme control surface movement might cause the aircraft to break up. Fortunately for Fox and Ken it did not occur that time. (In–flight data recorded showed the bank angle exceeded 98 degrees!)

Dodging a second bullet

Fox Stephens restarted the inlet and engine, they accelerated back to cruise speed, and all seemed to be in good shape. Reaching Bakersfield, he pulled the throttles back, cutting off the afterburners and began the long deceleration toward Edwards. Without warning the left engine began to complain bitterly as it popped and shook the aircraft. Steve pulled the left throttle back to idle but did not shut the offending engine down. (An idling engine still provides electrical power, cooling air, and hydraulic power to control and utility systems. If you can keep it turning without burning, that's a good plan.) After landing, the aircraft was pulled into the hangar and the left wing lifted to get at the engine for an examination.

For those of you who don't know, the J–58 engine has six stainless steel tubes spaced around the exterior of the engine. Each of these tubes is about six inches in diameter and carries high temperature bypass air from the fourth stage of the compressor to the afterburner. The temperature of this air at cruise is about 1,200 degrees F.

As soon as the outer left wing had been lifted they saw that three of these stainless tubes were split wide open for a distance of about five and a half feet. The 1,200–degree air had turned the titanium of the outer wing panels blue. The metal had been seriously weakened. The aircraft had returned and landed without unnecessary G–loading, otherwise they would have lost the wing then and there.

Another day, another flight, same airplane

Number Three was repaired and placed back in service. Now she was scheduled for another test mission. This one would be flown along an east/west route we called "The Light Bulb," because on the map the flight path looked like a light bulb at the turn around point over east central Texas. All the photo resolution targets and other physical structures to be photographed as well as the radar points of interest were concentrated along this route.

It was a quiet January day in the desert as the early morning sun pushed through the first shimmering heat waves off the surface of Rogers Dry Lake. Bill Weaver carefully guided tail number 952 into the takeoff position on the Edwards runway. While the number painted on the tail identified the aircraft for all to see, she was really known by her Lockheed handlers and Air Force test engineers as simply Number Three. It was common practice among aircraft test and development people to name their test birds by birth order, seldom referring to them by the numbers on the tail.

Number Three was the Lockheed systems bird. She was the first to carry all the cameras, radar, IR, ELINT, jammers and other parts of the full–up sensor suite destined for the production Blackbirds to come along later.

Jim Zwayer, RSO, read through the pre–takeoff checklist and the two talked back and forth over the intercom about the test card for this day's mission. Today's flight was to test sensor performance, to evaluate the navigation system as an integrated sensor and aircraft management controller, and to examine cruise specifics (equivalent to mpg) as a function of CG position.

Bill Weaver released the brakes and lit the afterburners; 68,000 pounds of thrust pushed the crew and a fully fueled Number Three into the air and on their way. They climbed and accelerated to Mach 3 and cruise–climbed to about 80,000 feet. Approaching a planned turning point over New Mexico, they entered a right turn with a programmed bank angle of forty degrees. Just like the earlier flight with Fox and Ken, the lower engine, this time the right, experienced a violent unstart causing the aircraft to roll uncontrollably to the right but at the same time pitching up. The aircraft turned plan–view against the oncoming airflow. Today there was no time for thought or action. It was beyond human control. Everything happened at once. From the unstart on, what followed was driven by aerodynamics, relative wind, dynamic pressure, inertial coupling, structural mechanics, and the laws of physics. The fuselage broke apart at station 720, the point where the forward fuselage was joined to the delta portion of the wing. The forces in command caused this forward section of the fuselage to turn backwards with the pilot and RSO compartments now at the rear of the tumbling structure. The airflow stripped all the skin off this forward piece of the aircraft. Both crewmembers and their seats were ripped from the structure by the incredible forces of this disintegration. Jim died at that moment.

Bill Weaver was thrown through his seat belt. If his seat belt had functioned as designed, he would be dead as well. The belt should not have broken. There was a small knurled roller on the standard GI seat belt, a part of the take–up assembly. This small knurled roller cut the belt releasing him from the seat. Bill's parachute functioned correctly after that. After landing he found himself staring out at a small herd of antelope grazing nearby. The grass was green and there was no sound save the hiss of oxygen entering his helmet. He knew he was in Heaven. The sound of a small helicopter brought him back to earth. A New Mexico cattle rancher picked Bill up and flew him to a Tucumcari hospital. Most of the aircraft debris and Bill and Jim had landed on the Mitchell Ranch. Bill Weaver was essentially unhurt, with the only injuries being a bruise across his middle from being thrown through his seat belt and a cut across the bridge of his nose. To hear Bill tell it later, he was more fearful of the bumping and jolting of the rancher's small chopper than anything else as they raced to the hospital.

Jim Zwayer's parachute opened, and like Bill, he reached the ground in the same area. But he did not survive the departure from the disintegrating forward fuselage section. It is believed he died instantly of a broken neck before he ever became separated from the aircraft structure.

Others saw what happened

During the development of the SR–71 we had been given the authority to confiscate voice and radar tapes from various traffic control centers around the country if the SR was involved in something unusual or revealing. We also spent a significant time briefing the various controllers and supervisors to be noncommittal about anything they might hear about the SR or the flight paths they observed on their radar. The following is a paraphrased recounting from one of the voice tapes recovered from the Albuquerque Center after the crash of Number Three. (The airline flight numbers have been lost to a poor memory so those below are not those on the tape and were simply inserted for convenience.)

There were normal aircraft traffic control conversations on the tape at first and then suddenly —

"Albuquerque Center! Albuquerque Center! This is American Flight 20. There has been a huge explosion out here at an altitude way above us."

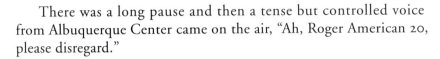

There was a long pause and then a tense but controlled voice from Albuquerque Center came on the air, "Ah, Roger American 20, please disregard."

At this point the American pilot sounded more urgent and agitated. "Albuquerque Center, you don't understand. It's a big explosion and there are parachutes and debris falling."

Another long pause and the controller finally responded, "Ah, Roger American 20, please disregard."

"Albuquerque, there is something bad happening and you better get someone out here immediately."

Another long pause and, "Ah, Roger American 20, this is Albuquerque Center, please disregard."

This last announcement was followed by an extended period of silence on the tape, then finally a different voice, "Albuquerque Center, this is United Flight 1035, we didn't see it, too."

Picking up the pieces

Almost immediately security people from Clovis AFB and military aircraft began to pour into the little Tucumcari airport. Swarms of accident investigators streamed out to the Mitchell Ranch. The Edwards contingent arrived within hours. There were three main objectives. Keep prying eyes out, recover as many of the aircraft pieces and systems as possible, and initiate an intense investigation into the circumstances surrounding the loss of the aircraft and Jim Zwayer's life.

The hospitality afforded by the Mitchells to the investigating and recovery crews was above and beyond anything that could have been expected. Mrs. Mitchell and her cooking crews fed and housed as many as possible. Mr. Mitchell put himself and his small chopper at the disposal of the search crews, salt of the earth people, filling in where they were needed and where they could help. Neighboring ranchers and their hands came with extra horses to assist.

Pieces of Number Three were scattered over vast areas and the Mitchell Ranch was a huge place, so it took lots of mounted searchers.

Silly little things that happen

From the beginning the people who designed and cared for the HYCON cameras, the technical objective cameras had told us the camera had a very delicate lens. It was big, had nine optical elements, and was mounted in a great long titanium barrel. Like anything designed to be at the outer edge of its performance range, these lenses proved to be both effective and temperamental. There was a rumor passed around implying this lens was so delicate that if turned on end, some of the elements would shatter from their own weight. True or not, we believed it. At first we nearly carried these things around on pillows to be sure they were not bumped. Number Three was carrying two of these cameras and lenses when she broke up over New Mexico near 80,000 feet. One of the items recovered was a complete and essentially undamaged lens barrel from one of the TEOCs. How about that!

As an aside—later after an SR–71 aircraft crash off the Philippines when the main fuselage section was raised from the ocean bottom, there, clearly visible, was a seemingly undamaged lens barrel section from one of the TEOCs.

Andre and I make a parts pickup

For a period of several months after the crash and the main cleanup effort, pieces of aircraft skin, structure, magnetic tape, and other artifacts were continually being found by the cowboys on the Mitchell Ranch and surrounding ranches. For the most part, these individuals would bring parts to the headquarters of the Mitchell where they were stored in the pumphouse until someone would show up to collect them. When the pumphouse got a little crowded, the rancher would call Dan Andre and tell him there was another load of bird droppings to collect. If there was a large pile Dan would send a C–130 with an Air Force station wagon tied down in the back. They would land at the Tucumcari airport and unload the station wagon. The station wagon would drive out to the ranch, load up the pieces, return to the airport, drive up the rear ramp into the C–130 and off they went, back to Edwards. Other times when the load was small or there was something found that demanded some careful attention Dan and I would fly directly to the ranch, land and pick up the parts right there.

One day in April 1966, Lt.Col. Andre strolled into my cubicle and announced the need for a *Canoe* trip to Tucumcari. At 5 A.M. the next morning we were airborne from North Base headed for New Mexico. The aircraft was full of fuel and the rear seat had been removed to accommodate the anticipated load of sheet metal and some electronic pieces. By mid–morning we were turning north over Tucumcari airport headed for the Mitchell Ranch. This would be my first visit to the Mitchell ranch by air.

"Are you sure you know where we are going?" I asked, as I checked the fuel.

"Of course I do. And if you have any other silly questions, just hesitate."

I continued to look out over the deserted landscape as we cruised along about a thousand feet above the terrain. I was unsure how much needed to be picked up, so the game plan was to land with only enough fuel remaining for a return trip to Kirtland AFB in Albuquerque. This way when we were ready for takeoff with a full load of scraps and the air was hot, we would not be heavy with fuel.

"It's over there," Dan said as he pointed his cigar dead ahead.

"Over where?" I asked, expecting to see a well–defined runway of some sort.

"You see that windmill at about twelve thirty?"

"Got it." Sure enough there was a windmill stuck in the dirt out there about 5 miles ahead and next to it were some buildings and a big white Quonset hut. "I see the buildings and trees, where's the runway?"

"It's right there."

"Right where?" We were rapidly approaching the cluster of buildings and the windmill.

"You see those two orange barrels down there by the Quonset hut?"

"Yeah, I got 'em. Where's the runway?"

"It's right there," he shouted as he gestured toward the barrels with his ash–laden cigar. "Just line up between those two barrels and aim toward that other orange barrel way over there toward the west."

His cigar shot past in front of me and deposited hot ashes in my lap. The "runway" as far as I could tell was nothing more than a not–so–flat, sage and tumbleweed covered piece of desert with two orange barrels on the east and about 1,500 feet toward the west was another orange barrel. About 3,000 feet beyond that, in a straight line, stood a very tall windmill. Reality hit! "That's it?"

"That's it."

With gear down, full flaps, and as slow as we could fly, we hit the dirt dead center between the two orange barrels. The landing roll was a series of strut–bottoming sounds, nose gear banging, and dust clouds, interspersed with moderate to severe sagebrush and tumbleweed shredding as the props ate their way down toward the remaining orange barrel. When we finally bumped to a halt, relief swept over me and I turned to look at Dan.

He was smiling and said, "You can turn around right here and taxi back on the runway. It doesn't look too smooth over there."

We taxied our twin engine weed wacker back to the two–barrel end with more dust and weed parts flying. As we stopped and shut off the engines next to the Quonset hut, we were met by Mrs. Mitchell. You could not ask for a more gracious hostess. We were treated to a five star luncheon, and within two hours the pumphouse contents were transferred to the back of our Cessna 310. Our previously empty and clean aircraft was filled to the ceiling with ugly looking titanium pieces, chunks of radar–defeating plastic, several black box corpses, and some camera pieces painted white; the whole mess was topped off with a bird's nest of about 2,000 feet of inch–wide magnetic tape.

We said our goodbyes. Dan stood fire guard while I cranked up the two engines. Once he was back inside with the door closed, we turned between the two barrels and aimed for the windmill. Full power, pop down fifteen degrees of flaps, dodge the westerly orange barrel, rotate a little to get the nose wheel out of the weeds, and we shot straight toward the windmill. Bouncing a couple of times on the main gear, we groaned into the air. One major turn to avoid the windmill and we were on our way. Circling back over the ranch, we waved our wings good–bye.

The weather was beautiful and we arrived at Kirtland AFB with an aircraft covered with dirt, and sagebrush pieces stuck here and there, with just enough fuel remaining to make a safe pattern and landing. When we parked and shut down in front of Base Ops, the transient alert crew approached our aircraft suspiciously.

"Will you be needing fuel and oil, Sir?" the question was asked as the man eyed the pile of pieces through the open door and tried to remain cool.

"Need a full load fuel. We have our own oil." I said. (As a special accommodation to the engines on this bird we carried our own brand of oil in a large plastic Clorox bottle tucked away in the baggage compartment.) While the transient crew refueled, I went around to each engine and added just a little oil from the Clorox bottle. This did nothing to enhance our image.

"Would you like the aircraft washed, Sir?" they asked while still trying to figure out what on earth we had inside.

"It would be nice if you could clean a few of the bugs off the windscreen."

Once the aircraft was serviced I walked into Base Ops and filed a VFR clearance to a totally false destination, usually the dry lake bed near Las Vegas called Silver Lake. Once we passed by the lake we used the radio to close out our flight plan with the nearest Flight Service Station and continued on to our home field at North Base. We arrived well after dark. It had been a long, long, day. Andre and I pulled our dirty canoe into the hangar, rolled the doors shut and locked them. In the early hours of the following morning our ever–faithful crew chief would arrive at this hangar, deal with the results of what we had done, and once again question his judgment for ever letting those two Blackbirders use his wonderful machine.

To this day I cannot believe they actually paid me to do that stuff.

Reading the tea leaves

A brief discussion of Aero 101, Aircraft Stability, and some of the issues associated with this particular accident is in order here. Insufficiently rigorous for the pure aerodynamic scholars and not as detailed as the stability and control expert would like, but it should assist the reader in understanding some of the dynamics leading to the demise of Number Three.

There are all forms of aircraft drag, the resistance shown by the aircraft to the air that passes over it. The higher the combined drag the more force an aircraft's engines must provide to maintain a given airspeed and altitude, and the more fuel they must consume. With lower drag the aircraft travels farther on a gallon of fuel. This figure of merit, called miles per gallon (mpg) for automobiles, is referred to as fuel specifics for aircraft.

It's all one big tradeoff

There is a delicate balance between overall drag and aircraft stability. The road to a compromise solution is littered with the bones of test pilots and aircraft destroyed in the process. A fact of life is that aerodynamically unstable aircraft cannot be flown or controlled for any meaningful period of time by even a skillful pilot without the aid of computers. In the Blackbird this system was called the SAS. But even that system was limited as to the amount of control surface authority available at certain aerodynamic conditions so the system would not overstress the aircraft structure.

When the aircraft CG is located forward of the CP (the CP is generally coincident with the center of lift, or CL) on the wing, the aircraft is said to be statically stable in pitch and we are primarily concerned with the pitch axis here. When the CP and the CG coincide, the aircraft is said to have neutral stability. When the CG moves behind the aircraft CP, the aircraft becomes unstable and, without computer assistance in the control system, tends to become uncontrollable once a disturbance to the delicate aerodynamic balance occurs.

There are some excellent reasons for having a near neutrally stable aircraft and one of them is reduced drag, because all the control surfaces can be aligned with the air stream and therefor create no trim drag. There is a balancing risk here as well. If strict attention is not paid to CG management the aircraft may become unstable. As long as the SAS is working and excursions into the unstable margin are small, the risk to aircraft and crew is minimal. However, any significant disturbance, unexpected system degradation, or sensor/ stability system failure can result in disaster. That is where Number Three went wrong, not because the crew was inattentive to the relationship between the CG and CP or because the pilot was not sufficiently skilled, neither of these was the case. The problem was that the stability margins and acceptable CG excursions for minimizing trim drag were still under investigation as the aircraft's envelope was being expanded during the test program. Subsonically the center of pressure for a delta wing with no tail is about twenty–five percent. When this same wing goes supersonic the CP moves to the rear. The faster the flow, the further to the rear the CP moves. For optimum range and minimum drag at cruise, the aircraft CG should tag along after the CP so near–neutral stability can be maintained.

In the SR, the fuel system started transferring fuel, or sequentially burning it, so that the CG was moved aft automatically to follow the rearward migration of the CP on the wing. This reduced the amount of trim drag and increased the range factor. From the beginning we had trouble with CG control and the mechanics of moving the CG fore and aft to match flight conditions. The CG moved back automatically during acceleration and supersonic cruise, but when it became necessary to decelerate, fuel needed to be transferred forward to move the CG to coincide with the forward movement of the center of pressure on the aircraft's wing and thus retain the static stability margin necessary for subsonic flight. This was a manual operation performed by the pilot. Now if an unstart and resulting engine flameout or other problem occurred at altitude and a deceleration was required, then fuel had to be immediately transferred forward to maintain the static stability. If the problem was then cured and a re–acceleration was performed, the aircraft was stuck with a forward CG condition and the resultant high trim drag. Normal trim in the early days of the program was one and a half to two degrees nose up. That was not particularly fuel efficient but it was safe. Now in the case of a re–acceleration after performing a forward transfer, and with no capability to manually do an aft transfer, one was stuck with much of the fuel in the front and now requiring five to six degrees nose up trim. Lots of drag.

Some changes were made

In spite of this problem, Kelly Johnson did not want the capability for aft transfer into the aircraft. He had continual concerns about getting the CG too far aft. Finally in a meeting at Edwards to discuss the block changes that would be incorporated in the cockpit design of production aircraft Number Seventeen and up, Ken spoke out forcefully about the aft transfer capability. He recommended three things to assure safety of the system:

The cockpit switch had to be spring–loaded so the pilot would have to hold it down to transfer fuel aft. It could never be forgotten and left on.

The aft transfer valve had to be spring–loaded closed, so in the event of any failure, the valve would close and stop aft transfer of fuel.

The aft transfer rate should be half the forward transfer rate.

We never saw a system like that in any of the test birds but later heard pilots complaining about how slow the aft transfer rate was and that they had to hold the switch down to accomplish the transfer. The aft transfer modification gave the operational aircrews real control over their aircraft's CG and allowed them to minimize the trim drag for optimum range.

Bill Weaver, Jim Zwayer, and Number Three did not have the luxury of well defined stability boundaries or the advantage of fine–tuning the aircraft cruising CG on the fly. After the accident investigation was completed, it was determined that their CG had been about 28 percent. That was well behind the neutral point on the SR of 25 percent. The aircraft was statically unstable but the SAS was able to compensate sufficiently to maintain fully controlled flight. Once the right inlet unstarted, causing aircraft movements well beyond the control surface authority of the SAS to correct, the game was lost.

There were aerodynamic modifications to the SR family resulting from this accident as well. After an exhaustive investigation it was decided to cant the nose section upward. A wedge structure was introduced just forward of the pilot's compartment, increasing the upward angle of the radar nose section by two degrees. This rebalanced the aerodynamics, resulted in reduced trim drag, and restored the needed static margin.

Jim Zwayer was buried with proper services and respect. His body was laid to rest in a proper grave. Number Three with most of her innards and engines, was dumped into a huge deep hole just west of the Edwards Air Force Base riding stables. Bulldozers pushed the dirt over her while a few of us watched. She is still there. Desert winds have long since blown away the tracks. Tumbleweeds and sagebrush serve as her only headstone. Neither Jim nor 952 will ever be forgotten.

Chapter 21

Anatomy of a Rendezvous

*"Serving as a Blackbird team member was
the highlight of my Air Force career."*
Chuck Woodward, KC–135Q Navigator

The Lone Ranger always said, "Tonto, I want you to meet me at the edge of town just at sundown, and be sure to bring the…" Tonto would say, "Right, Kimosabe." And that was it. A place and time had been assigned and agreed. Nothing else was necessary. With an SR–71/KC–135Q rendezvous, the basics were the same but the mechanization was a little more sophisticated. Because this act of meeting in the middle of nowhere for an aerial refueling was an absolute operational necessity, techniques were developed and confirmed during Edwards testing.

The Basics

While it sounds terribly casual now, the original aerial meetings and hookups during the flight test programs were pretty much Lone Ranger and Tonto style. The tankers were told to meet the SR or the YF–12s or the A–12s at an assigned location and at a particular altitude. Even those meetings were not a piece of cake because the tankers were nearly always flown from different bases than the Blackbirds. An additional complication initially was the lack of reliable electronic means for the tankers and receivers to locate and approach each other.

In the flight–test environment there was always the assistance of Air Traffic Control (ATC) and ground–based radar. Controllers would tell the receiver just where the tanker was with respect to his position, and vice versa. As the two aircraft approached each other more closely, visual contact was established for the final phase. On a clear day, who could miss something the size of a Boeing 707 floating around in a racetrack pattern at an altitude of a 1,000 feet or so above the approaching receiver? Silly as it sounds, it was not easy. The SR pilot was looking through a faceplate with multiple reflections, which in turn were reflected on a slanted windshield with more reflections of the instrument panel reflecting images of the pilot's silver suit, which reflected the sunlight back into his faceplate, adding more to this symphony of reflected light. Of course, during nighttime there were no sun–made reflections, just the reflections of the lighted instrument panel bouncing off the suit, careening around inside the pilot's faceplate among other things. At night, visually locating the tanker was somewhat less complicated because the KC–135Q was equipped with alternately flashing strobe lights. For the tanker crew the job was a little tougher to see the approaching Blackbird even when it was using anti–collision lights. Their search was the equivalent of trying to see a rapidly approaching, edge–on razor blade. At night the anti–collision beacon, the tanker strobe lights, and navigation lights were of considerable help. In the daylight however they were of little use.

Advanced skill and knowledge required

In the early days the tanker flew its racetrack pattern across the projected flight path of the approaching Blackbird. In that way the KC–135Q spent most of its time broadside to the arriving receiver. These patterns were normally four–minute straight legs with a two–minute, 180–degree turn, at the end of each leg. A full pattern took twelve minutes. The tanker navigator had to be on his toes to be sure that their racetrack pattern did not drift off down wind as it loitered in the sunset waiting at the edge of town. The tanker navigator also was constantly checking relative positions (provided by flight–following ground–based radar) so he could instruct his pilot in adjustments to the racetrack pattern. Ideally the receiver would spot the tanker and broadcast "Set Course." At that time the tanker, depending on where it was in the orbit pattern, would make whatever size and direction of turn necessary to roll out level in front of the approaching

Blackbird at the proper altitude, heading, and airspeed. The receiver would make the final adjustments for the hookup. The Blackbird would snuggle up beneath the tanker, the boomer would fly the boom to the receiver's receptacle, gently make a connection, and then begin transferring fuel. But it wasn't always that simple.

The laws of physics complicate this activity. The tanker can go only so fast and the SR can go only so slow. As the refueling progressed, the SR became heavier as it took on fuel. It was a struggle just to stay in the air. The SR had to increase its speed to accommodate an increased stall speed (actually an ever–increasing single–engine minimum control speed). To make it possible for the receiver to stay on the boom to complete the refueling, the tanker progressively increased its airspeed. Near the end of the refueling activity the tanker was screaming along at its maximum recommended Mach number and the SR was barely staying in the air, hanging onto the tanker's boom by the skin of its aerodynamic lips. The tanker flying along at a pretty much horizontal attitude and the SR hanging on underneath with its serious nose up position demanded skill on the part of the boomer and the aircrews of both aircraft.

Early in the program, in an attempt to reduce this airspeed mismatch between the two, the SR would drop off the boom, light one afterburner, throttle the burner back to minimum, and re–connect with the boom. In some respects this was self defeating, as the receiver's fuel burning rate goes up significantly, and the tanker has to supply more fuel for a longer period of time, thus prolonging the whole experience. While the test force pilots explored this type of refueling procedure and developed and documented this technique, it was seldom used operationally. As experience was gained, test force pilots were able to light one afterburner while connected to the boom and could make the necessary control adjustments without unhooking.

After a successful refueling with the tanker smoking along as best it could, the SR would disconnect, pull off to one side, and light both burners. Then, as the tanker crew watched, it would accelerate and disappear into the upper atmosphere as if the KC–135Q were parked.

Blackbird missions included flying at night, so tests were done to define the procedures for rendezvous, hookup, and refueling in the dark, a chilling concept when all the aspects are considered. The tankers still went down to the edge of town and waited for the Lone Ranger, but now no one could see very well. Night refueling was not anyone's favorite activity. It required great skill on the part of the crews of both aircraft. Those faint of heart need not apply.

Adding some electronic assistance

About the middle of the SR–71 Cat II test program, electronic help arrived for the rendezvous problem in the form of the ARC–50 radio and later, the ARN–90, an airborne TACAN. (TACAN is a navigational system that allows the signal–receiving aircraft to determine both its distance and direction from the TACAN transmitter.)

The ARC–50 provided the approaching pair with secure voice, a ranging capability between the two, and azimuth. With this information both aircraft could fine tune their approach. If someone were listening on that particular frequency, all they would hear was a static–like signal unless they had set in the code for that particular mission. Both the SR–71 and the KC–135Q had to have their radios set to the appropriate encryption code. The two ARC–50s worked in a cooperative manner to provide information to the crews of both aircraft. The airborne TACAN was the equivalent of a ground station mounted in the tanker. With this information available, the approaching Blackbird had clear and unambiguous information as to his course to the tanker and how many miles to go. This, however, was a non–encrypted signal and in the case of operational missions, there were many times when the tanker did not want to advertise its location to the world. They relied on the ARC–50 for secure information.

After the installation of airborne TACAN systems in the Beale KC–135Qs, the rendezvous changed. A modified point parallel orbit was developed. The orbit procedure was similar to that used for the B–52, but the tanker would orbit downstream and parallel to the inbound track of the receiver. The tanker orbit was anchored at a point forty nautical miles down stream from the SR–71's level–off (bottom out) point. Once distance ranging was established using the ARC–50, the tanker navigator, using special charts, would instruct his pilot to modify the orbit. The object was to position the tanker heading toward, but offset from, the approaching SR–71 inbound track, just abeam of the anchor point. (Air Force jargon identified this point as the Air Refueling Control Point (ARCP). The time version of this location was the Air Refueling Control Time (ARCT). The tanker's goal was to be opposite the ARCP five minutes prior to the SR's arrival at the anchor point. When the two aircraft were twenty–seven miles apart the tanker would make a 180–degree turn and proceed down the refueling track.

Planning was the key

In actual practice the rendezvous planning began long before the mission was ever flown. It was just one of the zillion things that had to be considered by the mission planners. Blackbird work was not a "kick the tires and light the fires" kind of operation. The planners would spend many hours laying out the exact course for the mission. Their task was to marry all the requirements for getting to the desired targets, the best headings for the best sun angle, the safest course for avoiding defenses, the optimum approach for remaining undetected for the longest period, the locations and altitudes for both the cold and hot refuelings, and on and on. When the planners were finished, their work was reduced to a nav tape which contained all the information for a particular mission. This mylar tape was a punched tape much like that used in teletype machines of old. This was the way mission planning information and data were transferred from the planners to the ANS computer. Later when there were sensitive operational missions, the tape was made of paper, loaded into the nav system and verified and, once the SR–71 was airborne, the tape was burned. The output of the mission planning cycle was a concerto of well laid out ground tracks, locations, sensor instructions, navigation system commands, maintenance instructions and air crew responsibilities. Tanker support was a part of this planning. The Boston Pops doesn't play any better music with any better timing, coordination, and fortissimo than the Blackbird Team when they were on the job for real.

Operational refuelings ran hot and cold

A cold refueling refers to the initial aerial refueling which takes place almost immediately after the Blackbird becomes airborne for a mission. The idea behind this kind of operation was that lighter weight takeoffs by the SR saved on tires and brakes. Because of shorter takeoff rolls needed, there were less severe safety problems in the case of an aborted takeoff. The Blackbird used much less precious time and fuel hauling a full load up from the ground. They would meet a flying filling station which had already carried all that weight to about 25,000 feet or better. These cold refuelings were pretty well standardized by the fact that they always took place near the SR's initial departure base. In the Cat II days, the Lone Ranger frequently met Tonto at the Beatty refueling track just north of Las Vegas, Nevada. At every Operating Location for the SRs there were similar standard cold refueling locations and altitudes.

A hot refueling on the other hand, required the most painstaking planning and real–time execution. This was an aerial refueling conducted at the end of a high speed, high altitude leg. The Blackbird would descend from its cruising altitude and speed and rendezvous with the waiting tanker or tankers. Here's where the planning got a little tight. What if, for some reason, mechanical or otherwise, the Blackbird could not take on the needed fuel from the tanker? The mission planners were always sensitive to this issue and rendezvous points were selected so that if this happened, the Blackbird would be able to divert to an alternate airfield. Not the kind of thing one wants to do but sometimes it was necessary.

One train leaves Chicago going south at 300 miles per hour and another train leaves Los Angeles going east at 2,000 miles per hour. Calculate when and where they will meet and… Now we have the basic setup for a Blackbird rendezvous and a hot aerial refueling. While the mission planners laid out all the basic parameters it was the two aircrews who had to make the whole thing come true. The SR–71 RSO calculated when the pilot was to pull the power back and start the long descending deceleration toward the tanker rendezvous point. The real name for this point was the ARCP, as explained earlier. This was a place in space where, if all worked out perfectly, the tankers would roll out of their turn, and be exactly in front and 2,000 feet above of the arriving SR. During the turn there would be one very simple radio call. When the approaching SR–71 closed to within three nautical miles the lead tanker would instruct the other tanker "Descend and accelerate." This gave the airborne spare tanker on the leader's wing a little heads–up so they could stay together. The tankers would descend 1,000 feet and accelerate to refueling speed. The receiver would climb 1,000 feet to meet the tankers. The SR–71 never broadcast anything during the rendezvous.

The intent was to drastically limit unnecessary radio transmissions from either the tanker or the approaching receiver. When contact with the refueling boom was made, the two aircraft crews could talk to one another through an intercom link established up and down the boom so no radio transmissions were made during the refueling.

To assure success on every operational aerial refueling mission the tanker side of the house would designate three aircraft. One would be a ground spare, full of JP–7, sitting and waiting to sub–in if either of the two primary tankers had mechanical problems on the ground or aborted once they became airborne. There was a primary airborne aircraft and an airborne spare. The two airborne tankers flew a loose trail formation, chugging around their racetrack pattern at the edge of town. The navigator in the primary airborne tanker worked his fanny off during this time. His job was to continuously update his information with respect to the exact time that the inbound SR would arrive at the designated refueling point. Using this estimate he would direct his pilot to either lengthen or shorten his racetrack legs, so when the Lone Ranger rolled up behind them the tankers would be side by side, just beginning their trek down the refueling leg that lay directly in the path of the oncoming Blackbird. As one might suspect, some clever navigator devised a table of distances between the tanker and approaching receiver to figure out how to adjust the length of race track legs. In the early days, when weather was bad and visibility poor, the tankers would fly within fifty feet of each other so the receiver could drop off of one tanker and pick up the other without ever losing visual contact with either bird. Later this distance was changed to a quarter–mile.

Sometimes one tanker would unload the entire 80,000 pounds of fuel needed and at other times, the two tankers would share the offload. Who did what and unloaded how much to whom was a function of the mission, the surrounding circumstances, and other operational considerations.

Planning for the unexpected

Of course there are times when things don't go as planned, and part of the test program was to determine whether the SR–71's engines could burn the more common JP–4 and on the other hand if the tanker could burn SK–1 (later named JP–7). To determine the J–58 engine's performance using more common Air Force fuel (JP–4), the test force flew several subsonic missions using JP–4. Because JP–4 was considerably more volatile than JP–7, the SR was restricted from flying at supersonic speeds, but the test force did determine that using JP–4 the SR–71 could cover about the same miles per gallon at .9 Mach number as it could using JP–7 at Mach 3.2. The travel time was, of course, much longer at .9. While restricted to subsonic cruise using JP–4, the SR could always use it as a get–me–home kind of fuel.

This then begs the question of could the tanker burn JP–7 if, for some reason, there were a need to do so to get them home safely. The answer was yes. The KC–135Q could, and routinely did, burn JP–7 fuel. Once any of the tanker's engines were shut off or flamed out, however, they could only be restarted using JP–4. There could be no restarting when JP–7 fuel was being used. Within the KC–135 there was an elaborate system of plumbing and valves to ensure that the two fuels were never mixed by accident and that one fuel could not contaminate the other.

There was one other aspect of refueling from a tanker that was a little out of the ordinary. In the early days of the program and in fact throughout the Blackbird program, the aircraft sometimes landed at places where there was no SK–1 available and it was difficult if not impossible to get fuel to the stranded Blackbird. Early on, Lockheed developed a special hose and nozzle system so a KC–135Q could refuel a Blackbird on the ground using the tanker's boom and one of the Blackbird's refueling connectors. The tanker would fly in a load of fuel, park next to the stranded aircraft, the ground crew would connect this hose adapter to the tanker's boom, plug into the Blackbird and on would go the needed fuel.

This mobile ground filling station was especially valuable in the early testing programs because not only did the aircraft sometimes develop unexpected mechanical and electrical problems, it also carried the light weight version of the Air Force standard aerial refueling receptacle. Kelly Johnson was hard–over on keeping aircraft weight down. But from time to time one of these lighter weight devices would get damaged when the refueling did not go as planned. When that happened the

Blackbird would have to land at an alternate airfield because there was insufficient fuel on board to return to Edwards. The tanker adapters were just the thing for getting stranded SRs back home from their unplanned emergency landing locations.

The tradeoff on receptacle weight went something like this. With the heavyweight receptacle (the B–52 version) the receiver could run off with a piece of the boom still in the receptacle without damaging the receiving aircraft. The unit was that sturdy and tough, but it was heavy. In the lighter version, the fighter version, the weak link in the aerial refueling lash–up was the receptacle. It would be damaged before the tanker boom was incapacitated. A very handy concept when refueling a group of fighters. You don't want the tanker damaged when there are several others waiting for a drink. In the end it was decided that the most effective concept was to avoid damage to the Blackbird, so heavyweight refueling receptacles were added to all operational SR–71s.

A tribute to all, past and present

One final thought before we leave the rendezvous issue. Consider the U–2s and how they did it with the earlier models in the 1960s. At lower altitudes their airspeed mismatch with the tanker was just the opposite of that between the SR–71 and the tanker. They were the slowest thing in the sky at the refueling rendezvous point. They would sit and wait for the tanker to find them. Think about puttsing around on a moonless night, painted flat black, waiting for a 350,000–pound fuel–filled elephant to stumble across you in the dark.

Maj. Gen. Pat Halloran, who flew operational missions in both the U–2 and the SR–71 described it this way.

"Imagine being at 20,000 feet out over the Pacific somewhere, flying through a bottle of black ink. At exactly the right time, you look up and see this beautiful flying filling station ghost past, just above you."

Now with the newer U–2R, that is not a problem. These modernized machines have a new engine and a larger internal fuel capacity which gives much longer endurance on internal fuel. The pilot runs out of gas long before the aircraft does. Fourteen–hour missions are not unheard of.

Nobody ever said the Blackbird business was easy. The members of this team: aircrews, ground crews, planners, logistics people, security and intelligence personnel, and contractors, have, over the years, maintained airbreathing surveillance programs which did and still do produce facts and heroes, that generate the legendary reputations they so richly deserve.

Chapter 22

Mission Planning

*"Hooray, hooray, it's the first of May and
mission planning begins today!"*
**Lt.Col. Harold "Pete" Peterson,
Edwards AFB, 1965**

*"Now tell me one more time, you want how
many things printed on the pilot's map?"*
Bruce Hartman, in a meeting at SAC Hq, 1966

Test flight planning, even in the initial phases, involved more than than Scotch tape and a typewriter. Engineers and aircrews tried to jam pack every last data point and test into each flight. We followed Lockheed's lead in using a simple wind'em up scroll–like test card for the pilots. It was typed out on long narrow strips of paper Scotch–taped together. This scroll device was made of brass and had knobs on one side so it was easy for the pilot to move the card along as the flight progressed. Information printed on the card was arranged to follow flight activities. It included radio frequencies, rendezvous data, and flight routes. It was a complete mini–flight plan. The RSO had more room in the back so he was able to carry a much more detailed description of the particular mission tasks, test points and associated information.

With the incredible variety of systems and aircraft behavior to be explored, there was an absolute mountain of information to be collected. Building from test to test and from data point to data point, the engineers' wish lists were overflowing. We had limited aircraft, more limited flight time, and some make–sense restrictions on flying above Mach 3.0. Flights above Mach 3.0 caused the aircraft to leak like a sieve. We had a choice, we could fly at 3.2 and spend most of our lives fixing fuel leaks, or we could hold the majority of flights down to 3.0 and get more hours of semi leak–free flying.

There was one guy who became the master magician of mixing and matching test points and system requirements. Major and later Lt.Col. Don Seehafer, a quiet fellow from the U–2 side of the Blackbird program office at Wright Field, was very clever at putting the pieces together. He created the mother of all matrices. He took navigation system requirements and added camera, ELINT testing, IR system data runs, engine and aircraft performance requirements, antenna pattern flights, and combined them with a million and one other things. Many test missions required ground tracks not compatible with others. In the end, he integrated all the sensor requirements with the rest of the flight program needs and produced a plan to derive the most for the fewest flying hours. Each flight had a profile and route packed with testing. After the flights, Don would contact engineers to ask if their objectives had been met. Yes? Then a square was checked off. No? That requirement was returned to the "to do" matrix and would appear at a later date.

To perform this operation efficiently we needed a system of notification of what, when, and where the next flight would go and what the profile would be. We also needed to know what tests had been allocated for that particular airframe. Don would sort all that out and provide each engineer with sufficient warning. This allowed the camera troops to load the correct film, the IR people to load the liquid helium in plenty of time, the radar techs to set up and so on. It also provided the navigation system handlers the opportunity to fit in all the characteristics of the flight path and put in commands for operating the sensors at the correct times.

Mission planning to prove we could do mission planning

With the master plan in place for the overall Cat II flight test program, we then began to whittle away at the mountain of chores to be done. Every mission, though not operational, was planned and conducted within a framework just as operational missions would be planned. We were not in a little bubble in southern California. The Blackbirds ranged all over the country and as a result had to have tanker support, radar tracking networks set up, portable photo resolution targets laid out, emergency landing fields identified and permission to over fly certain areas.

On every test flight, the aircraft had to climb through every flight level of the most heavily trafficked airline routes in the USA, and then had to return to Edwards by descending through this same high traffic area. This was done at speeds and climb rates airline pilots only dream about. FAA controllers did an outstanding job of keeping "incidents" out of the headlines while giving the SR–71 its needed flight priorities.

The mission planning guru was Lt.Col. Harold "Pete" Peterson, a crusty old SAC navigator who had planned enough U–2 missions to have seen it all. Pete had been there and done that in every sense of the word. The Edwards Blackbirds also had their own operations section managed by the pilots and RSOs themselves. They made the necessary arrangements for airspace clearances, arranged for tankers, calculated fuel profiles, and coordinated takeoff and landing times with the Edwards Flight Test Center.

Once the proposed mission skeleton had been sewn together it came time for the next layer of planning. Pete and Bruce Hartman worked on getting ground tracks laid out, way points and end points defined to assure flight paths stayed within radar–tracking corridors for the ground radar sites. Then they calculated the locations of resolution targets and inserted commands in the nav system so it would point and click the cameras at the right place at the right time. Tanker rendezvous were plotted from initial descent point, through the deceleration, to the hook up point. The planners laid out the acceleration path for the next hot leg to get the crew on their way again. When the mission requirements had been beaten to death, matched with the physical world and support services required, the plan was loaded into the ANS computer and run from end to end several times to be sure everything matched the plan. They programmed in the stars for the tracker to use for calculating fixes. Then it was back to Operations to arrange for fire truck support at start up and along the runway if it was a marginal mission. If there were some aspects of the takeoff or landing that needed photo coverage, camera crews were contacted. Mission planning, even in a test environment, was a big deal and we cut our teeth in a hurry.

Don't we get a map?

If a picture is worth a thousand words, then a map is worth tons more than that. From the beginning it was clear that the SR–71 would range over an extensive area of the western United States. The very nature of the SR made it impossible to conduct meaningful test missions while confined to the Edwards area. A 180 degree turn at cruise speed required a space 140 miles wide. An early out and back flight went from Edwards to Albuquerque, New Mexico, and return with an elapsed time of 53 minutes, ground to ground. Looking forward to longer and longer missions and toward the operational requirements to prepare a specific map for each mission, the planners began to explore how this requirement could be met. Enter the Pilot's Moving Map Display and the multiple migraines therefrom. First, lay out the flight paths on aeronautical charts, mark different comments and information along these paths, tape all the maps together in a long line, cut to size, and photograph. Next, process the color 35mm film in the MPC. Finally, load the film in the moving map display so it can be projected for the pilot to view. At the same time make another map, similar but still significantly different, for the RSO to view on his display. From the very outset this was not an easy task.

For starters, there was no camera in the Air Force inventory of suitable optical quality for this job. Who does piles of color 35mm photographs and makes animated movies? Who else but Walt Disney Studios. Who makes the animation cameras and stands for Walt? Some guy in the local LA area made these stands in his garage. Bruce and Col. Pete went to the person's "R&D facility," it really was in his garage. They did not buy the camera. They bought one camera stand and installed it in the mission–planning/conference/briefing/storage/document–assembly and safe–combination–drawer–repair room. Then a suitable camera was purchased from another Disney supplier. Nothing was standard and none of this was easy. If this had not been a semi–black operation at this point we would still be trying to get an animation stand and camera.

What should we put on the map?

The real end–user of the mission maps would be the SAC operational crews so Col. Pete, Bruce Hartman, and a newly assigned player, a SAC B–58 pilot named Dameron "Moose" Spruill were thrown into the briar patch along with every strap–hanger, horse–holder, and mission–planning weenie at SAC Headquarters. Here is where we made a mistake. The customer is always right, right? The staff at SAC Hq poured out their wishes for an endless variety of data to be added to information already printed on standard maps. When all that was overlaid on a sample map, nothing of the original ground features or annotations could be seen because of all the neat additional information. Even when someone suggested we make the added information smaller so there would be room between the facts to see the original map, the writing was so small it could not be read when the sample version was projected on the pilot's moving map display.

Pete and Moose and Bruce spent many hours at SAC Hq banging heads to get only the "right stuff" on the maps. After the final negotiated settlement, everyone discovered there were no aeronautical charts around with that data. So Bruce was dispatched to the Army Photo Mapping and Charting Service in St. Louis to negotiate (plead is a better word) for a whole new family of maps just for the SR–71. Air Force priorities don't cut much ice with the Army and DoD priorities from Washington don't move a lot of dirt in St. Louis, but Bruce was able to convince all involved that "it was the right thing to do." And it was done. But it was not all due to good looks and brain power. The test force agreed, and did supply the Army with complete and cohesive overlapping photographic coverage in a strip from Los Angeles, California to Florida. Life should not have to be this hard.

We visited many places to garner support

While the planning and flying were going on, there were people and organizations out there to be contacted and cajoled so they would support various test flights and ever–increasing requirements. At the tail end of one week–long trip, Lt.Col. Andre briefed the big wheels at White Sands asking for renewed tracking support, and maybe throwing in just a few of their captured emitters so the SR could listen to them as it went by. We flew on to Kirtland AFB in Albuquerque where he briefed recovery crews on possible emergency support should the Blackbirds ever land at Kirtland. With tanks full of fuel and our bags full of dirty clothes, we headed west toward home at Edwards AFB.

Out over the middle of nowhere in western New Mexico, Dan suddenly asked me, "Donn, does this airplane have a fire extinguisher?"

"Sure, it's right under your seat there."

He leaned forward and began to fumble around beneath the front of the co–pilot's seat. I was busy struggling to keep the airplane right side up in some strong turbulence and didn't pay much attention to what he was doing. It was a hot summer afternoon in the desert and we were doing the usual bouncing. The radio mike, having just leapt from its mounting hook, was dancing around in front of me at the end of its wire.

"I can't get the fire extinguisher loose, it's stuck."

"Well, kick it," I said without looking. Keeping the horizon somewhere within the confines of the front windscreen had my full attention at the moment. "Why all this sudden interest in the fire extinguisher?"

"Because we're on fire, dammit!"

This aircraft had no parachutes, we were over the boonies of New Mexico, and sure enough there was smoke curling up out of the map pocket on the passenger door.

Andre was a big cigar smoker and he always carried an ample supply of those terrible things tucked away inside his leather–billed uniform hat. He had been smoking one as we went along, knocking the ashes into the map pocket on the door. The map pocket was belching smoke. Now both of us were seriously interested in the availability of the fire extinguisher. That sucker was flat jammed in its mounting place. Tucked away under one of the bags strapped down on the back seat was a near–empty thermos of cold, day–old coffee.

"Use the coffee," I yelled. I watched as Dan, in one smooth motion, extracted the jug, wrenched out the stopper, and shot almost all of the remaining coffee directly onto the cabin ceiling as we reeled from the granddaddy of air bumps. Undistracted by the floating coffee globules and drips from the ceiling, he stuffed the open–mouthed thermos into the smoking map pocket. Problem solved.

We arrived at North Base about two hours later, funny looking, but safe. Our very understanding crew chief never complained. He was always glad we brought most of his machine back in one piece, even though it was the worse for wear.

Operational guys kept our feet to the fire

The bond between the RSOs and mission planners was a strong one. Perhaps it had to do with the responsibilities of the back seater. Throughout the course of mission planning activities and learning, the test force had the advantage of some of the best up–to–speed Reconnaissance Systems Operators in the business. Cecil Braden, Tom Smittou, Cosmo Malozzi, and "Butch" Sheffield all took their turns at planning and then flying the test mission to make sure it was done right. There was not an overabundance of qualified aircrews available at Edwards. Operational people carried a serious part of the load and added to our expertise supply where we were short. As the aircraft flying pace picked up and maintenance problems decreased, it was a welcome relief to have these guys onboard even if only for a little while.

A window into mission planning for real

Planning for operational missions was a tough and complex dance. Planners used some of the most sophisticated computer techniques of the time to make the best fit at matching the requirements. There was a large mission planning group at Beale with a computer to match. For remote locations there was the computer system installed in the MPC to perform the mix–and–match exercise for a final fit.

But there were questions facing operational mission planners. Where were the targets? Not just what country, or near some town, but exactly where were they located? Do you want radar, camera, IR, or ELINT coverage? Or all the above? What is the best sun angle? What is the best aspect angle to view the target? Where are the defenses? What and where are the search radars and what is their coverage? How do you turn to avoid the threats and still image the desired target in the desired way? Will there be jammer aircraft needed in the area or spoofing aircraft for distraction? Will you have other collection aircraft in other areas to view the enemy's response? Those were only a few of the questions directly associated with the immediate target area.

Where does the aircraft depart from and when? How much fuel is needed and where should the tankers be? What stars are needed for navigation by the astro–tracker? What are the best ways to get there and back? Is permission to over–fly another country required? Where are the alternate recovery bases and escape routes if things go wrong? Will there be orbiting search and rescue aircraft? No kicking tires and lighting fires here.

The test force took the first steps during Cat II testing and then the Beale pros took over and turned mission planning into a real science, especially when there was a hurry–up–and–get–it–done issue involved. Putting those planning puzzles together time after time took patience, skill, and long hours. Operational mission planning was a big damn deal and everyone involved deserves a huge pat on the back.

Epilogue

Epilogue

"It's a dumb idea to bomb and strafe a target surrounded by people and then parachute out right above them."
**Roger D. Ingvalson, Vietnam POW from
28 May 1968 to 14 March 1973**

Throughout the life of the Blackbirds, no matter which version, the A–12, the YF–12, or the SR–71, these aircraft brought a sense of pride to Americans. From designers to builders to the test crews to her handlers to the gutsy operational crews who flew her, all stood in awe of the capabilities and mystique of this grand machine. Everywhere she went she carried our flag with force and courage. From dumping fuel to show the Russian MiGs where she was so they could pant harder while they failed to intercept, to hauling the mail down the center of Hanoi, to setting international speed and altitude records anytime she felt like it, this was an aircraft like no other. The Blackbird went whenever and wherever she wanted. This lady never came home with her tail between her legs.

Collecting intelligence data was, of course, the primary purpose, but Blackbirds served at many other jobs. When we needed to rattle the Russians' cage, she would be sent out to set a world record. When the U.S. needed to show a national presence somewhere in the world without fear of being touched or shot down, we called on the SR. When we needed to put our best foot forward at the Paris Air Show or at Farnborough in England, the SR got the call. But these are all obvious missions.

Some missions took a different tack, like those she flew to tell our prisoners being held in North Vietnam that in spite of the plethora of political bedwetting going on in our nation's capitol and the total lack of national pride and dedication by a large minority of liberal hand–wringing wimps on our college campuses, our POWs were not forgotten.

Major Roger D. Ingvalson was an F–105 jock with a belief that one must be down there in among'em to do a workmanlike job of dive bombing and strafing. Roger, a career fighter pilot, like others of his kind, always took the fight to the enemy as fast and as hard as he could. Putting this philosophy into practice is not without risk. And all too frequently, as in any combat situation, there are dire consequences. That is where this story begins.

Roger, Gator Lead, and his wingman had just finished knocking out their assigned target with two air–to–ground missiles when they were contacted by a forward air controller "Misty." They still had a thousand rounds of 20mm ammunition each, so Misty suggested they proceed to another prime target near Dong Hoi, a convoy of several trucks. They found the trucks and began their attack. Roger would never leave his target unless it was destroyed or on fire. He was on his second strafing pass flying at 500 knots–plus and about 50 feet off the deck when he felt the explosion.

Gator Two called and said "You're on fire!"

I already knew that, Roger thought. He blew off the canopy to get rid of the smoke and pulled up about 600 feet where he lost control of that beautiful F–105D. There was no time or opportunity to make it out to sea for a rescue by U.S. forces. Reacting quickly, he pulled the ejection seat handle. He regained consciousness only a moment before hitting the ground.

No injuries! Clearly a miracle! At this moment and time, in the middle of a dried up rice paddy, Roger became a Christian. He peeled off his parachute harness and began to run. But it was no use, he was surrounded by the enemy and within five minutes he was a captive. As Roger observed many years later when he was finally released from the Hanoi Hilton, "It's a dumb idea to bomb and strafe a target surrounded by people and then parachute out right above them."

From 28 May 1968 until 14 March 1973 he was a prisoner of the North Vietnamese. He endured twenty straight months of solitary confinement. Major Ingvalson was starved, tortured, and disease–ridden during that time. Loneliness was his constant companion.

During this same period, the U.S. was overflowing with political indecision and the streets were filled with misguided fools who had no respect for the very Americans who were bleeding and dying just so these same self–centered crybabies could exercise their right to freedom of assembly and expression. The more divided this country appeared, the worse the treatment of our POWs became. The final insult occurred during the presidential campaign of 1972. The North Vietnamese told their prisoners that certain American politicians had contacted them and agreed that if they were successful in winning the election, the U.S. would accept any peace agreement the North Vietnamese might put forward. They also let it be known that if the U.S. got about half of the POWs back, that would be sufficient.

Roger's problems took an immediate and terrible turn for the worse.

Shortly after this revelation a column of seventeen canvas–covered North Vietnamese Army trucks rolled into the Hoa Ro, which is where Roger was being held. As near as he could calculate up to this point, he was one of four hundred and sixteen POWs being held. That night, 14 May 1972, Roger and fifteen other prisoners were forced into one of the trucks, along with a load of pigs and chickens. Exactly half of the American POWs, two hundred and eight in all, were loaded into the waiting vehicles. As they pulled out of the compound and headed north, Roger realized, as did the rest of the prisoners, they were in the wrong half. He and his group were dead meat. They would not be repatriated, they were going to be executed.

Thirty hours later they arrived at a location within spitting distance of the Chinese border, a camp the Americans named Dogpatch. The Vietnamese guards at the new camp confirmed the prisoners' worst fears. For seven months the American prisoners were kept inside, hidden from view. Obviously their captors did not want anyone to see them or know they were there.

On the second and fourth days of May 1972, two super–secret Blackbird missions were flown out of Kadena AB, Okinawa. On each mission there were two primary SRs and one airborne spare. The purpose of these missions was to lay down two sonic booms over Hanoi at a specific time. The two booms were to be exactly fifteen seconds apart. This was a signal to the high–level prisoners being held in Hanoi. Roger and his group did not hear these booms from their camp in the north. But there were other activities afoot.

On the morning of 15 October 1972, Roger's half, the wrong half near the China border, heard the unmistakable soft double sonic boom of a high–flier. A cheer filled the camp. Their hopes soared. They told their guards they had been found. The Blackbird had found them. Now the Air Force knew where they were. Each prisoner was convinced that somewhere photographs of their camp were being analyzed. Those pictures would provide leverage needed for U.S. military powers to act in their behalf. The POWs had no idea what would be done but they knew they had been spotted. There was more to come. For several noons thereafter the Blackbirds and their gallant crews returned again and again with sonic booms that said, "Hang in there, you will not be abandoned."

On 20 January 1973, seventeen canvas–covered army trucks rolled into the Dogpatch compound. The prisoners were loaded and driven south. Roger and his fellow POWs were elated. Not that going back to four of the several camps in Hanoi was a wonderful thing but it sure beat the hell out of being shot. On 30 January 1973, the POWs were informed that a peace agreement had been signed three days earlier. Within two weeks, the first of five groups were released to freedom in the greatest country on earth.

Once more Blackbirds and their crews had carried Old Glory over hostile territory, brought a message of hope to our POWs, and assured their return. It is just this kind of mission that gives every American a reason to walk taller.

This country does not currently have a replacement air–breathing reconnaissance aircraft with the legs, speed, and flexibility to do the intelligence collection job that the U.S. needs. Yet we let these unique and capable birds sit half–mothballed cooking in the sun at Palmdale,

California. With such a proud history and the unquestioned capability to successfully penetrate any airspace worldwide, the few remaining active SR airframes should not be relegated to an occasional NASA test flight. Others of their kind sit around the country on display like caged birds. Touched and admired for sure, but forever tied to the earth. What a waste.

Ken Hurley's Recollection

of People Involved

in the Early SR-71 Program

(includes RS-12 Period)

People are listed in alphabetic order except for the first two. These two men are singled out because of the magnitude of their contributions in leadership roles. Each brought special talents uniquely suited to SR–71 program management during their stay. This section was written by Ken Hurley (KDH) with added comments by Donn Byrnes (DAB).

Templeton, Horace A. (Temp), Colonel

Temp was the first person I met in an official capacity. He and Sid Brewer briefed me into the program in Building 14 at W–P. Temp, as we called him, was the Director of the YF–12 SPO, the U–2 SPO, the RS–12 SPO, the R–12 SPO, and later the SR–71 SPO. It is notable that these offices were not openly called SPOs until quite a bit later. Temp's office was called Advanced Plans and Programs for most of the time I was there. I consider Temp to be one of the real fathers of the SR–71. It was he who managed the RS–12 effort and managed the transition from that effort to the SR–71. He managed all the early weapon system tasks, ranging from configuring the airplane, to establishing the test program, to building the new gymnasium at Beale. This was a monumental effort with very few people, and very successful. (KDH)

Bellis, Benjamin N., Colonel

Ben Bellis came along just at the right time. He was the creator and father of the Air Force –375 series regulations This was arguably the greatest cookbook for creating and managing every aspect of a weapon system development program including transition to the using command. About the time that Temp retired, Bellis took the reins of the SR–71 SPO and guided that very difficult transition from invisible black get it done no matter what program to a major weapon system managed under both black and open program parameters. It was a significant coming of age for the Blackbird program. He was the right guy in the right place at the right time. Bellis later went on to manage the extremely successful F–15 development program. (DAB)

Andre, Daniel M., Lt. Colonel

Andre was one of the initial and permanent fixtures of the YF–12/SR–71 test force. He served as test FCO, and was one of the record setting YF–12 aircrews on 1 May 1965. Dan served as security expert and all around iron fist when that was needed. He created the persona spoken of in this book as part of a very tough shell. He was a tender and loving husband who cared deeply for his wife and took excellent care of her through many emotional traumas. In my view he was one of the real unsung heroes who slogged it out in the security and black program trenches of the Blackbird program. After a tour in personnel at the Pentagon where he saved me (DAB) from a fate worse than death by killing an assignment to the USAF Inspector General, Dan was assigned as Air Force Plant Representative at McDonnelll Douglas in St. Louis where the F–15 was designed and produced. They just don't make them any better than Daniel Andre. (DAB)

Bennett, "Frenchy," Colonel

Frenchy was assigned to the test force as Commander 4200th Operational Test and Evaluation Squadron. The 4200th was made up of all the SAC personnel that supported the SR–71 portion of the test program. As one of the few full colonels in the test force he carried a lot of weight. He managed the SAC assets assigned to the SR operation at Edwards and also represented SAC on–site interests in the FB–111 program ongoing at the time. (KDH)

Beezley, Jacques, Lt. Colonel

Jack was the other SAC pilot besides Frenchy. He never got the chance to fly one of our birds. He was killed in the back seat of a Test Pilot School airplane doing high L/Ds[1]. Jack broke his back when the aircraft hit and he died in the Edwards Hospital of a blood clot. (KDH)

Blanchard, William (Butch), Major General

We briefed Butch at SAC Hq. He was SAC Ops, I think. I remember the briefing but am having trouble putting in the right time. As I remember, we went to SAC to brief the CINC but couldn't get to him. This had to be after the RS–12 was well along. (KDH)

Bock, Charles, Major

Charlie was one of the most thorough and professional test pilots I have ever had the pleasure of knowing. I flew with him in the C–130 and other aircraft at Edwards. In addition to flying SR–71 test flights, he also flew frequently as aircraft commander in the B–52 mother ship for X–15 drops. After retirement from the Air Force he became one of the primary test pilots for North American on the B–1 program. Charlie was a test pilot's test pilot. Every time I flew with him I learned more about flying. I checked him out in our North Base Cessna 310. Talk about role reversal! What a humbling experience. (DAB)

Borio, Russell, Civilian

Temp brought Russ into the program when we started getting into high resolution radar. I had been involved in it before, but this time it was for real. It was a typical political move, I think. The WADC Commander encouraged Temp to consult with the technical laboratories at Wright Field as much as possible and within the security constraints. We briefed a few lab people, mainly to keep a lid on things and to get access to their programs when needed. One of the authors can personally attest to how this worked, as explained elsewhere in the book. Russ was an old timer in the business and our expert. Russ would not travel by air, so I did all the traveling when radar was involved. How to become an expert? Travel a lot, carry a big briefcase, and ask plenty of questions. (KDH)

---

[1]The term high L/D refers to a type of landing approach where the angle of descent is quite steep, the sink rate extremely high, and approach airspeed relatively low. More than one pilot at Edwards bent or broke his aircraft practicing this maneuver. It was a technique for teaching test pilots how to handle approaches such as the X-15 or the Space Shuttle might make.

Bowles, Ben, Captain

Ben was one of the younger test pilots who arrived in the middle of the program. He put on the suit, and flew the missions as dictated by the test card of the day. You couldn't ask for much more. Ben loved to ride his motorcycle and at one point traveled from Edwards to the School of Aviation Medicine at San Antonio, Texas. About El Paso, while cruising near seventy–five mph, he hit a big Texas June bug with his adam's apple. Ben said he just pulled off the road and cried because it hurt so much. After arriving in San Antonio his greatest anxiety was that he would have to ride that motorcycle all the way back to Southern California. Ben was a talented painter working in oils. His work had an almost photographic appearance. (DAB)

Brewer, Sidney, Lt. Colonel

Sid was the one who really brought me into the program. It was his recommendation that I be recruited for the RS–12 effort. Sid was the contracting officer for all of Temp's programs. He participated in my initial briefing. I had met Sid on a C–45 flight just before Christmas, 1960. (KDH)

Burchinal, David, Major General.

General Burchinal was DCS Ops at the Pentagon. I got to know him on both the RS–12 and RS–70. A fine gentleman. (KDH)

Burgenheim, "Burgey," Major

From the time the FY–12s initially arrived and throughout the SR–71 flight test program, Burgey was the Edwards Air Force Base Operations Officer and designated scapegoat for all the misbegotten things that happened to good people and their airplanes when trying to walk a fine line between the real and the black world. He lied, he cheated, he stonewalled, he waffled, he danced, and he covered our fannies. We never gave him anything in return except more problems. More than once he nearly bit the end off his ever present pipe. He made our lives easier. Dan Andre and I made his life a real pain. Burgey was the master of diversionary antics. And we joyfully hung him out to dry on a monthly basis. (DAB)

Chapman, Harold E., Major

Harold and I arrived at about the same time. He had been brought in primarily for his expertise as a fighter pilot and was originally aimed at the YF–12, I think. In any case, Harold was assigned to work the RS–12 and, later, the R–12 and SR–71 Programs. While at Edwards he made major contributions to the Category II Program. The knowledge and dedication he brought to the program were of incalculable value. (KDH)

Cooney, James P., Major

Jim was one of the record[2] Fire Control Officers (FCOs). He transitioned to the SR as an RSO. Cooney was with Frenchy the day Frenchy let the airplane overspeed to about 525 KEAS on climb. That was the time the turkey feathers banged together and broke themselves. Jim succeeded Dan Andre as security officer when Dan left the test force. Jim was there in the early early phases of the program when they were launching the YF–12 missiles from the B–58. (KDH)

Daniel, Walter, Lt. Colonel

Walt was one of the record pilots, of course. He flew many of the early SR–71 flights. He and I flew quite a few acceptance flights on the production birds at Palmdale. He was the first Test Force Operations Officer, before Charlie Bock took over. (KDH)

Doyle, Frank J., Lieutenant

Frank was a young engineer assigned to the performance section. This was his first Air Force as well as his first engineering assignment. He learned quickly. His knowledge of thermodynamics served him well in his stay with the test force. Frank has held several engineering positions since ending his active duty Air Force career. He currently lives in the Houston area. (KDH)

Drake, Norman S., Lt. Colonel

Norm and Fox Stephens had been together for many years. They were at Holloman together before Edwards. Norm was the Chief Engineer

---

[2]The term "record" means he was one of the aircrew that set the international records in the YF–12 on 1 May 1965.

when the test force was put together. I was Chief of Systems and Jim Scheuer was Chief of Performance and Propulsion, both under Norm. Scheuer left pretty early to go to Vietnam. Norm became Deputy Test Force Director and I became Chief Engineer. When Norm left I became Deputy and Harold Chapman became Chief Engineer. Drake, like Andre had been a Radar Observer (RO) during World War II. (KDH)

DuBois, Joe, Lt. Colonel

Joe was one of Leo Geary's guys. He primary job was to track the YF–12 and never really had anything to do with the later versions. (KDH)

Estes, Howell M., Lt. General

General Estes was deputy to Gen. Schriever at Systems Command. Everybody called him Mr. Clean, because he looked like the character in the commercials who sold soap. His son has now retired as a general. (KDH)

Evenson, Mervin, Major

Merv was the kind of guy who was always ready to go and get the job done. A skillful test pilot, he hung in there when we shuffled his activities on the flight card at the last minute and didn't bite our engineering heads off. (DAB)

Ferguson, James, Lt. General

Gen. Ferguson was DCS R&D at the Pentagon. I only briefed him once and only saw him once, but through that association I got to know Al Slay. Slay wasn't briefed on the RS–12, but was Ferguson's contact man for Dave Jones' *ad hoc* group. Ward and I worked with Slay quite a bit. Ferguson had polish, poise, and respect for all others, thus his nickname Gentleman Jim. (KDH)

Fox, Claire, Major

Claire was one of the very original members of the Edwards test organization. He was a maintenance man. His early work was with repair manuals and documentation. Because all the initial work on manuals was being done at the Skunk Works in Burbank, Claire bought a pickup camper and lived in the Skunk Works parking lot during the week and would drive home to Edwards for the weekends. Major Fox had a standing requirement to be flown up to The Area every Wednesday. That was the day they served steak in the mess hall. For all us visitors the food was free. We would return to Edwards as soon as the evening meal at The Area was over. Claire always carried a huge brief case on these weekly trips. I frequently accused him of lining his case with toast and bringing home as many steaks as he could fit in there. Because of security requirements I was never allowed a peek inside the case. (DAB)

Freas, L. Wayne, Lt. Colonel

Wayne worked for Temp long before I got there. He headed up a sub–office responsible for the U–2 Program. He had a few people, some of which we used from time to time, but the only one I remember for sure is Don Seehafer. Wayne was always there, but we had little interface with him and his group. Their office adjoined ours in Building 14. (KDH)

Geary, Leo, Colonel

Leo was a Project Officer for the Under Secretary of the Air Force for all kinds of clandestine programs. These included the U–2 and all Blackbird programs. His office was the first place we checked in when we went to the Pentagon. His was a small office, manned by a couple officers and a couple civilians. A major feature of Leo's office was a big vault room. Incidentally, Leo was at the Berlin Gate when the U.S. swapped Russian Colonel Abel for Francis Gary Powers. We all followed that exercise vicariously through Leo. When we visited he would brief us on progress of the negotiation. That was also very black, as you can imagine. (KDH)

Gill, Al, Lt. Colonel

Al was one of Frenchy's people. He was very helpful in developing the RSO operating techniques and mission planning. Al retired from the Edwards assignment and returned to Spokane. He died within a few years. (KDH)

Hess, Neil (Jug), Colonel

Jug Hess was the maintenance officer for the test force at the start. He was SAC. Jug did an excellent job. He left and went to Thailand. I don't think Frenchy ever forgave him for leaving so soon. In fact, I have a letter from Jug after he arrived in Thailand bemoaning the fact that Frenchy was mad at him. Jug retired after that assignment, went to school, and entered the Ministry. Jug and Dottie were living in Holland, Michigan, at the time of his death in about 1990. (KDH)

Hunnicutt, Bob, Lt. Colonel

Bob was one of Leo's guys. Bob retired and became a civilian doing the same job. He was a coordinator and had nothing to do with the SR–71 program in a technical way. He helped us negotiate the Pentagon maze. (KDH)

Keller, Richard, Major

Dick was the Propulsion Engineer from the start of the Test Force. There may have been someone outside of Lockheed who knew more about the total propulsion system than Dick, but I don't know who it was. Dick worked in one of the most sensitive areas of the testing. Both P&W and ADP held their performance cards very close to the chest. Dick Keller became the Air Force expert in performance and contributed greatly to the understanding of the SR–71 and in writing the handbook. Dick was one of those guys who had a sly smile all the time but would not always share his amusement. He patiently taught me to be a copilot in the C–118 and the art of smooth flying so the General's breakfast wouldn't jump around in the back of the plane. (DAB)

Lusby, Art, Major

Art started out working for Jim Scheuer on the performance side of the test force at Edwards. His area of expertise was aircraft performance and analysis. Art was a Naval Academy graduate. Art and Marcella came to visit us once in Bellevue after we went to Boeing. We had a pool table in the basement and thought we had become respectable pool players. Art proceeded to give us lessons in the art of shooting pool. He said it was one of the things he learned at the Academy. He could have made a living as a hustler, we think. (KDH)

Marscher, William, Major

Bill had been maintenance officer in the YF–12 Program and didn't have a job for a long time. He reported to Brad Urey, who didn't like him. When Jug left we needed a maintenance officer. I decided to make Bill Chief of Maintenance. Fox and I discussed it and Fox said, if I wanted him, it was up to me. Bill did an excellent job. After 1968, Bill was assigned to oversee aspects of the Logistics Command support activities for all Blackbirds at Norton AFB. (KDH)

Nye, Allen, Lt. Colonel

Allen headed up an office that supported Temp's YF–12 SPO. After we started the RS–12, his office supported that program, too. This office was really assigned to Temp, but, covered with a name and paper assignment totally separated from the other program offices under Temp. Allen had about twelve people assigned. Some of Allen's people worked full time for Temp, some on the YF–12, and some on the other programs. Allen carried one of those old fashioned brief cases that opened at the top like a suitcase with a foldover strap that went through the handles. When traveling, he would put a baggage tag on the handle of the case. The next time he traveled he put the tag inside the case and added another tag. The last time I saw that case the tags had built up to fill about a third of the total volume. Probably any of us could have built up a travel record like that, we traveled so much, but his was the only visible one I ever saw. (KDH)

Pahl, Phil, Major

Phil was one of Nye's group at first and came into the SR–71 SPO as part of Temp's effort to spread the work load. Phil worked extensively in the Side Looking Radar and IR area. When SPO management was transferred to Col. Benjamin N. Bellis, Pahl's responsibilities were expanded considerably. Phil was a Naval Academy graduate. (KDH)

Peterson, Harold L. (Pete), Lt. Colonel

Pete was Frenchy's primary RSO. He flew with Frenchy most of the time. Some of the other SAC RSOs flew with Frenchy, but none of the Systems Command RSOs did, except for Jim Cooney, as far as I can remember. At the time, Pete was the oldest man that had been to Mach 3 that we knew of. He was around 50 when he first flew, I think. Pete and Lou retired from Edwards and went to Florida. He died in about 1973. (KDH)

Protsman, Ward E., Lt. Colonel

Ward was assigned to Nye's office originally, but worked on the RS–12, R–12, and SR–71 from the beginning. Ward was a West Point graduate and World War II fighter pilot. He and I became *Gold Dust Twins* according to some. We worked the offensive system for the RS together. We configured the navigation system, the missile system, the operational concepts, etc. We were both assigned to David Jones' *ad hoc* group in the Pentagon. That group supported LeMay's efforts to save the B–70. Ward and I negotiated the transfer of GAM–87 assets for use in the Stellar INS for the RS–12 and later the SR–71 ANS. We did reviews resulting in moving the ANS computer from Hughes to Nortronics. Ward and I finally begged Leo to brief Jones, before Jones had us fired by LeMay. Ward retired after serving as Commander of Arnold Engineering and Development Center at Tullahoma, Tennessee. (KDH)

Quasney, William, Captain

Bill came to us from an operational assignment as a navigator serving in the Military Airlift Command (MAC}. I don't know who recruited him, but it was fortunate for us. Bill worked anything he was asked to, as far as I can remember. He was the Flight Test Engineer assigned to aircraft #954 and was deeply involved in engine testing both on the ground and in the air. I think he was really pleased to get out of MAC and all those long TDYs. Bill was an Annapolis graduate. (KDH)

Redmon, Larry, Captain

Temp brought Larry into the SPO when we were redirected to the R–12 to manage cameras. I don't remember where Larry came from, but I know he had been involved in BIG SAFARI for a long time. He was an older guy, and I always thought he had been a GI who earned his commission through excellent performance. He was still at Wright Field when I left for Edwards. Larry had one of the finest vocabularies of obscure English technical terminology. His teletypes to the test force not only required decryption but a dictionary at the ready as well. (KDH)

Rhude, Don, Major

As I remember, Don never came over to the SPO, at least while I was there. He worked the ELINT system from the beginning of its integration into the

SR–71. A quiet meticulous engineering wizard, he could think his way through almost anything. Never get in a contest of peeling away layers of technology with Don, he always beat you to the core answer. Don was a Naval Academy graduate. After leaving Edwards he returned to Wright Field to conduct a major threat analysis in support of the F–15 Electronic Warfare systems. (KDH)

Rifenbark, Edward, Civilian

Ed had been assigned to the SPO before I was briefed. His area of expertise was primarily propulsion but no one could ignore Ed's ability to operate in any area of engineering. He was a good head. (KDH)

Seehafer, Don, Major

Don helped us with the RS and SR occasionally, but he was primarily assigned to the U–2 under Freas. He was still in Dayton when we went to Edwards. Temp. called me one day and asked of I would like to have Don out at Edwards. He and Aleta wanted to come to Edwards. Of course I wanted someone with his experience. It turned out that he was an ideal guy to work with Frenchy Bennett, and that was what he did. He also put together the finest mix of test missions and objectives. A combining effort sorely needed to get all the tests done in the time and flight hours allotted. (KDH)

Shipley, Billy, Major

Billy, like many others, was already deeply involved in the Edwards operation before the major contingent of test force people arrived. He was a supply expert who knew where all the strings were that needed pulling. No matter what the request, he could find it and have the item delivered in short order. He worked very closely with a bunch of rough riding depot people at Norton AFB in San Bernardino. I'm sure the supply side of the house enjoyed the freedom and power brought on by the high priority the Blackbird program carried but it took more than just that to deliver the goods. All of us up on the desert benefited from Billy's ability to make the system produce. (KDH)

Simpson, Phil, Captain

Phil was one of Jug's assistants, also SAC. If we needed something done by the shops that didn't fit within the rigid SAC regulations, we went to see Phil. He was always there to help us pull Colonel Hess's chain when things were a little slow around the office. He joyfully helped one Sunday evening in anchoring a ten–foot submarine made of fifty–five gallon drums to the center of the Jug's personal reserved parking space. (DAB)

Skliar, William, Lt. Colonel

Bill came to us from Area 51 after the Edwards test program was under way. He was one of the CIA/Lockheed selectees taken out of the Air Force and employed by the CIA for the A–12 Program. Bill was the first non–Lockheed pilot to fly. He flew the A–12 trainer early on with the J–75 engines. When he requested return to the Air Force he was awarded the rank of Lt.Col. He always thought he should have been made a full colonel and, also, that he should have been designated Operations Officer when he arrived at the test force. He wasn't one of the good old boys at Edwards and had to earn his spurs from the bottom up. He and I flew together a lot. (KDH)

Spruill, Dameron R. (Moose), Major

Moose arrived at the test force shortly after things began to roll. He was a B–58 pilot. Assigned as part of the test force SAC contingent, he was extremely helpful in guiding us through the staffing hoops at SAC headquarters during frequent briefing trips there. Moose was also one of those lucky SAC assets time–shared by the FB–111 program at Edwards. Later in an F–111 runway accident he broke both ankles evacuating the aircraft to avoid the fire. He did not fly for a long time. He left Edwards and was assigned to the F–15 SPO in 1970. He was still on crutches at that time. (DAB)

Stephens, Robert L. (Fox), Colonel

The YF–12/SR–71 Test Force Director and king of the test pilots. Intuitive skill accompanied by excellent technical knowledge, and a masters touch when it came to aircraft control, they just don't come any better. On a return flight from Burbank, Fox was sitting in the back seat of the base U–3 and voiced his opinion that the wing on the aircraft was bent somehow from the way the aircraft was flying. Later in the maintenance hangar, using transits, it was verified. The wing was changed. (DAB)

Strother, Dean C., General

General Strother was the Vice Chief of Staff. I can't remember exactly when we briefed Gen. Strother, but it must have been pretty early. I don't think LeMay had come to the Pentagon, yet, because the next General was at Omaha and we briefed him instead of LeMay. This was in the RS–12 days. We never talked to LeMay in the RS–12 days, as I recall. With LeMay's feelings about B–70 competitors, that shouldn't be hard to understand. Gen. Strother was not far from retirement, as I remember but he was still around on 1 January 1965. (KDH)

Sudderth, Robert, Civilian

We got Bob from The Flight Test Center. He is a stability and control expert. Bob was instrumental in analyzing the 952 incident. He had been involved in the B–58 program that developed the ejection seats for that program. Stanley Aviation of Denver, Colorado, made those seats and part of the flight test program involved ejecting live bears who then had to be recovered, sedated again, and examined before being returned to their cages. No volunteers for that job! [Both authors knew the Air Force veterinarian on that job, his name was Neville Clark. (DAB)] I brought Bob to Boeing after I got here. He is now retired from Boeing. (KDH)

Townsend, Guy M., Colonel

Colonel Townsend's first association with the Blackbird, I think, was as head of SAC Requirements in Omaha. Later he became Chief of the Test Organization at Edwards. Guy was very involved during the setup phase of the SR–71 flight test program and in structuring early test force leadership. He not only figured in the Blackbird program, but was a key player in several other major Air Force Programs of the time. He was one of the very few officers to serve as SPO Director for two major Weapon Systems, the B–1 and the C–5. Another was Benjamin Bellis, as noted elsewhere in this list. Col. Townsend left Edwards upon being promoted to B.G. (KDH)

Trost, Fred, Major

Fred came into the office just before we left Dayton. Fred was a Naval Academy graduate assigned to Nye's shop and then transferred to the

SR–71 office. He was responsible for test coordination at the program level and came to Edwards often. Fred's responsibilities included endless coordination with many government and civilian agencies. The SR–71 test program involved every U.S. organization that had anything to do with control and monitoring of aircraft in our airspace. Fred kept a lid on undesired publicity while permitting the test program to continue flying nationwide. He was the master organizer for the ELINT testing conducted at Eglin AFB. Not an easy job. (KDH)

Urey, Brad, Lt. Colonel

Brad was one of the original officers assigned to the YF–12 portion of the Blackbird test program at Edwards. He remained as the senior officer for the YF–12 throughout his assignment. He never worked on the SR–71 program. Brad was able to piece together parts, people, and program funding to keep the YF–12 program moving along. (KDH)

Wachter, Robert, Captain

Bob came into the SPO at Wright Field after the flight test program at Edwards was in full swing. He was deeply involved in the 952 accident investigation. He supported simulation efforts to duplicate the exact aerodynamic conditions surrounding this crash. His area of responsibility was airframe and systems. Bob was a huge hulk of a guy and he loved to sing barbershop. He was also quite direct at times. One evening two rather short encyclopedia salesmen came to his home and offered the usual free set of books. As they talked through the screen door he said, "OK, I'll let you in but if you even so much as hint that this set will cost me even one penny, I will throw you both out of this house and I won't open the door first." The salesman who had been doing all the talking said, "Thank you Mr. Wachter, I believe we will be moving on to our next customer." (DAB)

Warner, Noel T. Major

Noel was one of the record Fire Control Officers (FCOs). He transitioned to the SR–71 as an RSO. After we left Edwards, Noel and Bill Skliar survived destruction of one of the test airplanes on the runway at Edwards. That incident is described elsewhere in the book. (KDH)

Weaver, Ralph W. (Wally), Captain

Wally was a C–124 line pilot transferred from MAC. Technically meticulous, and determined to a fault, Wally was handed test engineering duties associated with the wheels, tires, brakes, drag chute, and other equally non–glamorous areas. A SAC resource assigned to Frenchy Bennett, Wally divided his time between the SR–71 program and FB–111 test activities at Edwards. He also flew the U–3 in support of the base as well as the test force. When I was first checking him out in the U–3 he had trouble getting close enough to the ground to land. His C–124 experiences told his brain that you never came closer than about sixty–five feet before your tires hit the dirt. It was a tough habit to break. Wally's real forte was bombs and explosives. He served in that area of expertise after a Vietnam tour when he was assigned to the armament engineering section of the F–15 SPO. Wally was and still is a very accomplished artist in oils and acrylics. Those of us fortunate enough to have one of his paintings treasure our original Weavers. (DAB)

Wheeler, Earl, General

General Wheeler was the Army Chief of Staff. Leo thought briefing him would be good politics. I remember reading about his retirement later. The reporter asked him what he intended to do in retirement. His reply was, "My wife and I own a farm in the mountains and we are going to take up bird watching." As far as I know, that's exactly what he did. Never heard of him again. (KDH)

White, Denny Civilian

As the configuration of the RS–12 developed, Temp started bringing in other experts to spread the work load. Denny was brought in just after we made the decision to move the ANS computer to Nortronics and he became the SR–71 SPO manager for the ANS. Denny stayed with the program throughout Cat II and was a frequent visitor to Edwards. (KDH)

Acronyms and Definitions
of terms used in this book

AAA   Anti–aircraft Artillery.

ACIC   Aeronautical Chart and Information Center. Located in St.
          Louis, Missouri.

ADC   Air Defense Command.

ADP   Advanced Development Projects. A pseudonym used to refer to
          the Lockheed Skunk Works.

AFB   Air Force Base.

AFEWS   Air Force Electronic Warfare Simulator. An Air Force contracted
          facility operated at the General Dynamics, Fort Worth plant.

AFFTC   Air Force Flight Test Center. The organization resident at
          Edwards AFB that manages and conducts the majority of Air
          Force flight test programs. AFFTC also operates the Air Force
          Test Pilot School.

AFSC   Air Force Systems Command. This was the parent organization
          for ASD, RADC, Edwards AFB, and Eglin AFB, to name only
          a few. AFSC headquarters was located at Andrews AFB, Maryland.

Afterburner In modern jet engines it is possible to achieve higher thrust by
          injecting additional fuel into the exhaust. This mixture is then
          burned providing additional thrust. The J–58 engine was one
          of the few ever designed to cruise in afterburner. The term "reheat"
          is also used to describe this method of thrust augmentation.

AGE   Aerospace Ground Equipment. Flightline equipment used to
          support the care and feeding of aircraft, missiles or other Air
          Force operational equipment.

AIL   Airborne Instrument Laboratories.

Air Start (Engine)	After experiencing a flameout (literally the fire goes out in the engine) the process used to restart the engine in flight is called an airstart. Defining the flight conditions under which an airstart may be accomplished is of critical importance and one very important element of any jet aircraft flight test program.
Air Start (Navigation System)	When an inertial navigation system has experienced some form of in–flight failure requiring a restart or starting over, it is called an airstart. Airstarts of inertial based navigation systems are complex and in a fast moving aircraft such as the SR–71, were seldom successful in returning the ANS to proper operating conditions and accuracy.
Alpha	A flight test term used to describe angle of attack
Altitude	In this book we have used the word altitude for the most part as altitude above sea level unless otherwise stated.
AOA	Angle of Attack. The angle between the longitudinal axis of an object and the relative wind.
ANS	Astroinertial Navigation System. The type of inertial navigation system coupled with a star tracking system. This combination allows updating of geographic position through star fixes and does not require any external electromagnetic radiating sensors (like Doppler radar).
Antenna Loading	The term applies to the method in which the real antenna length is adjusted electronically to compensate for the wave length of the signal being transmitted.
ARC–50	A UHF radio with the capability for secure voice communications and some ranging capability. These radios were used on the SR–71s as well as the tankers.
ARCP	Air Refueling Control Point. A defined location used to facilitate the rendezvous of a refueling tanker and the receiver.
ARCT	Air Refueling Control Time. A defined time associated with activities of the approach and rendezvous of the refueling tanker and the receiver.

ASD Aeronautical Systems Division. An Air Force research and development organization located at Wright–Patterson Air Force Base, near Dayton, Ohio. The primary focus of this group was aircraft and aircraft systems.

Astro Tracker A telescopic device mounted within an aircraft and electronically connected to the navigation system. The astro tracker, at the nav computer's direction, tracks known navigational stars. The computer reduces the data and computes a navigational fix based upon the selected star's observed azimuth and elevation.

Bar Targets Photographic test patterns used to determine the resolving power of a particular lens, camera, film combination. The bar sets (three bars oriented parallel to the flight path paired with three bars at 90 degrees to the flight path) are laid out progressing from largest to smallest. There are standards for contrast and bar length–to–width ratios.

Barrage Jammer A powerful transmitter that emits multiple frequencies within the general frequency band of the systems to be jammed.

Beam Steering A technique and process in which the SLR or SAR beam is maintained at exactly the desired angle to the zero Doppler line.

Beta A flight test term used to describe angle of yaw

BIT or BITE Built in Test or Built in Test Equipment. An electronic system imbedded in another that functions to identify failures or degraded performance in the mother system.

Blowdown Turbine A device used to convert hot air from a jet engine compressor bleed, to extremely cold air used to cool aircraft components, equipment, and air crew.

Boundary Layer An aerodynamic term used to describe the airflow immediately next to the surface of the wing, the inlet duct, or any solid object affecting the local airflow.

BTL Shutter Between the Lens Shutter. A series of interleaved metal petals that open and close for a fixed time to allow light to enter the camera body and expose the film. This type of shutter is mounted, as suggested, between some of the elements of the lens.

BTU	British Thermal Unit. A measure of thermal content or unit of thermal energy transfer.
Bypass Engine	A jet engine that allows some of the air compressed by the forward segment of the compressor to pass around the burner section of the engine and be reintroduced into the exhaust stream aft of the turbine section.
Bypass Ratio	The ratio of air bypassed to the amount of air entering the engine.
Camera Head Slewing	Long focal length cameras cannot be moved around easily and are usually mounted horizontally within the aircraft. The camera views the ground or desired target through a movable mirror. The camera can be pointed by rotating the mirror so the camera looks out at different angles.
Camera Stabilization	A suite of small jacks used to maintain the camera in a fixed spatial orientation while the aircraft may be moving with respect to the camera.
Camera Window	Optically ground glass mounted on the airframe to allow the camera to see out. The SR–71 camera windows were composed of two layers of different kinds of glass with a space between the layers. Each of the four surfaces had a specific coating.
CEP	Circular Error Probable. A term used to define the size of the area into which fifty percent of the bombs or rockets or whatever will hit. With respect to a navigation system it refers to the geographic accuracy of the aircraft's location.
CG	Center of Gravity.
Chemical Imbedding in Emulsion	This was a technique patented by Charlie Dotson of Goodyear Aerospace wherein all but a single chemical of the film developer are pre–imbedded in the film's emulsion. When instant development is required after exposure, the final chemical is added and the image is read through a liquid gate. This process was used in the 665A ICP and the SR–71 RCD.
CIA	Central Intelligence Agency or as some would say, simply the "Agency."

CIT   Compressor Inlet Temperature. Refers to the temperature of the air reaching the face of the engine compressor. The actual speed limit of the SR–71 was a function of CIT. The limiting temperature for the J–58 engine was 427° Centigrade.

CL   Center of Lift. The point on an aerodynamic body where the overall lifting forces due to airflow seem to be concentrated.

Class 1   A ground survey of great precision accomplished with physical
Survey   measurements of the ground and features in the area within the survey boundaries. Provides accuracy to less than one foot over great distances.

Clutterlock A technique whereby the SLR or SAR system could track the zero doppler line and using that information, keep the antenna pointed at exactly the correct angle–off from the aircraft's flight path.

Coherent   Coherent as used in this book applies to the manner in which certain side looking radars process their signals. A coherent system remembers the characteristics of its out bound pulse and compares it to the echo of that individual pulse when received. Noncoherent do not perform this function.

Collimated   A light source producing parallel rays of light.
Light Source

COMINT   Communications Intelligence. The practice of collecting information by listening to communications between people, units, and governmental agencies.

Compartmented A practice where the overall make up of a program is
Program   seldom disclosed to anyone but the highest level clearance
Clearance   holders, "the ones with all the tickets." Each person or group
Structure   has just enough knowledge of the program to accomplish their part without gaining too much information of the overall objectives or overall content.

Compressor   A process of measuring and recording the pattern of pressures
Face   across the face of the compressor. A practice used to determine
Mapping   how well the inlet is providing well distributed and relatively undistorted air to the face of the engine.

Cooling System Balancing | The process of matching the flows and speeds of airflow within any ducted air delivery system. When there is no black box to receive the air then a place holder orifice is attached to the ductwork to simulate the resistance to flow of that particular box. In high performance aircraft this is an art.

Corner Reflectors | Radar reflectors looking like little three–sided pyramids. These reflectors are cut to the precise dimensions to give the best reflection for a particular radar wavelength. Corner reflector arrays for radar are the equivalent of bar targets for cameras.

Correlation | The process used to convert the phase histories collected on the SLR radar data film to a map film presenting a radar image of the ground that can be interpreted by humans.

CP | Center of Pressure. The precise location where all the forces of pressure over a surface seem to be concentrated.

CRT | Cathode Ray Tube.

Deception Jammer | A jamming technique where the transmitted pulse of the threat radar is received, modified by the system and returned. This causes the threat radar to believe its target is in a different location than it actually is.

Detector Temperature | In Infrared systems the inherent sensitivity, the wavelength, and the thermal discrimination of the system are all a function of the detector's chemical composition, and the temperature to which it is cooled.

Diffraction Grating | The process of correlation to reduce the SLR data film to the SLR map film depends upon the phase histories collected on the data film acting like a diffraction grating. In the case of the SLR phase histories they were not only a diffraction grating but were FM–ed . That is, they changed frequency (physical spacing on the film) as the phase history was recorded. This made the diffraction grating not only bend light rays like a lens but also caused it to focus the light to a point.

DoD | Department of Defense

Doppler History | As each little reflector passed through the radar beam it caused a shift in the frequency of the pulse being returned to the radar.

This shift as a function of time is recorded on the SLR data film and makes a unique signature of that reflection source.

DOUSER   Doppler unbeamed search radar. A concept first conceived by Carl Wiley of Goodyear Aerospace, Akron, Ohio. This concept was the first step in side looking radar development. DOUSER technology was not used in the SR, but was basic to the SR, SLR concepts.

ECM   Electronic Counter Measures.

ECS   Environmental Control System. An air conditioning system which supplies cooling air to both aircraft equipment and cockpit crews.

ELINT   Electronic Intelligence information. This class of information usually refers to the science of discovering electomagnetic radiators, their location, and their purpose, through analysis of the signals transmitted.

Emissivity   A term used to describe a figure of merit associated with the ability of a particular material or surface to radiate or reradiate in a particular spectrum and frequency.

EO   Electro–Optical. A term used to describe imagery generated through a set of optics forming an image in the visual spectrum and acquired through a video receiver and projected on a television–like display.

EW   Electronic Warfare. An all inclusive term used to describe the world of electronic intelligence gathering, jamming, deception, decoying, and spoofing.

FBI   Federal Bureau of Investigation.

FCO   Fire Control Officer. A term identifying the radar observer or back seater in a two–man interceptor crew. Another term for the same man is WCO or weapons control officer. The YF–12 carried an FCO/WCO. The SR–71 second crew member was an RSO, Reconnaissance Systems Officer.

FM   Frequency Modulation. An electronic technique where the carrier frequency is varied about a center frequency rather than in amplitude (AM) to incorporate the signal desired. FM–ed used as a verb refers to the act of creating an FM signal.

Focal Plane Shutter/ Curtain
In many long lens reconnaissance cameras, the shutter function is performed by a curtain at the focal plane of the lens system. The curtain is located just in front of the film to be exposed. These curtains can be fitted with various width slits and the curtain pulled at different speeds. Using various combinations of curtain speed and slit width, a wide range of exposure times can be provided.

FPS
Full Pressure Suit. A system of garments and valve systems which completely encloses the aircrew member and protects him from a surrounding low pressure atmosphere.

FPS–16
A type of tracking radar having very precise antenna elevation and azimuth readouts available. These radars were used nationwide as test instrumentation in most aircraft and missile test programs for generating time–space–position–information (TSPI) data.

FTTA
Office symbol of the organization used to park incoming Blackbird personnel when the Air Force test force was first being assembled at Edwards AFB, prior to the announcement of a formal test force organization.

GD
General Dynamics The part of the company referred to in this book was their facility at Carswell AFB, Fort Worth, Texas. The F–111 was being produced and long wing B–57 mods were being accomplished during the time period of the book. The B–58 QUICK CHECK program was supported and flown out of this facility as well.

Geometric Fidelity
A term used to describe the ability of a camera to reproduce exactly what was photographed while retaining the true geometric relationships between objects within the exposed image.

GPS
Global Positioning System. A satellite based navigation system allowing receivers of the signals to very accurately establish their geographic coordinates and altitude.

HF
High Frequency. The SR–71 carried a 1,000 watt HF receiver/ transmitter made by Collins Radio. The antenna was the aircraft

pitot tube. This system required some very creative antenna impedance matching (loading) to make it work effectively.

HRB   Haller, Raymond, and Brown. An electronics company started in State College, Pennsylvania, by three Pennsylvania State University people. Their specialties were IR and ELINT.

HYCON   The camera company that designed and produced the Technical Objective Camera (TEOC).

ICBM   International Continental Ballistic Missile.

ICP   In–flight Correlator Processor. The term applied to the in–flight display producing unit flown as part of the 665A program.

IMC   Image Motion Compensation. Adjustments made within the camera to compensate for motion of the image during exposure of the film.

Inlet Pumping   In the Blackbirds this referred to the interrelationship between the two inlet systems and aircraft cyclic yaw. As the aircraft yawed from side to side the inlets tried to accommodate the changes in airflow and airflow direction. This was done through translation of the spikes and usually adversely affected the aircraft's yaw stability.

INS   Inertial Navigation System.

Instant Processing   A technique for rapid film processing where almost all developing chemicals are already imbedded in the film's emulsion but do not react because the P_h is not at the right level. The film is instantly developed when it is passed through a P_h–changing chemical.

IR   Short for infrared. IR radiation is electomagnetic radiation in a frequency band just below the visible spectrum.

IR Signature   A particular set of infrared characteristics always commonly present for a particular class or type of target. (Operating or recently operated motor vehicles always show extensive heat radiation for the engine area.)

IR System Window   A piece of infrared transparent material used to allow the infrared system to look out but at the same time be protected from the outside environment.

IRTRAN   Infrared transparent. A trade name for a series of compounds developed by Eastman Kodak that were transparent to infrared radiation. Various compounds were used to accommodate various IR frequencies. The SR–71 IR window was made from IRTRAN IV.

IRBM   Intermediate Range Ballistic Missile.

Iron Paint   A rubbery type of paint applied to U–2s and also tested on SRs. The paint contains iron or other metallic particles which absorb/diffuse radar radiation thus reducing the detectability of the aircraft. Also Iron Ball paint.

ITEK   The camera company that designed and produced the Operational Objective Camera (OOC).

ITT   International Telephone and Telegraph.

JP–7   Blackbird fuel. Formerly called SK–1.

KC–135Q   The designation of an aerial tanker specifically equipped to carry and dispense SK–1 later called JP–7.

KEAS   Knots Equivalent Air Speed

Liquid Gate   A sealed area which allows recently processed film to pass through. This gate has a glass on the top and bottom. A light can be passed through so a video camera can record what has been exposed on the film.

LH   Liquid Helium. The cryogenic used to cool the detectors on the Blackbird and other infrared detection systems. The temperature of liquid helium is −269°C, only about four degrees above absolute zero.

LN_2 An abbreviation for liquid nitrogen

LOX   An abbreviation for liquid oxygen

LRU   Line Replaceable Unit. This term refers to individual "black box" components of aircraft systems that can be removed and replaced on the flight line.

Mach Number | This is the velocity of something expressed in terms of the speed of sound. Named after the German aerodynamicist Ernst Mach.

Mann Comparator | A photographic light table with a precisely controlled traveling microscope mounted above the table. This allows very exact measurements of distances between features on a photographic negative affixed to the top of the light table.

MIT | Massachusetts Institute of Technology.

MPC | Mobile Processing Center. A group of trailers varying in numbers up to more than fifty.

MRS | Mission Recorder System. An internally mounted recording system carried in the SR–71 to record internal conditions and signals within the aircraft and its subsystems. Important during the test program because security regulations prohibited any engineering telemetry from being transmitted during test flights. Important operationally because of the troubleshooting information recorded on the two tapes. A–deck recorded aircraft and sensor systems. B–deck recorded ANS parameters and information.

NCD | Navigation Control and Display. A panel in the rear cockpit of the SR–71 used to control the ANS and to read out information relative to various ANS functions.

NVN | North Vietnam.

OOC | Operational Objective Camera. Used a thirteen–inch focal length lens and 70mm wide film. The SR carried two, one on either side of the centerline.

OOB | Order of Battle. As used in this book this is refers to the electronic and communications actions taken by a country's defense system when an aircraft penetrates or threatens to penetrate their airspace. What emitters come on, what commands are sent, what command and control links are activated and what messages they carry.

OSI | Office of Special Investigation.

PFRT | Preliminary Flight Rating Test. An extremely rigorous ground test program to establish an engine's readiness for an initial flight test program. A mandatory requirement for engines for new airframes as well as new engines for existing (currently flying) airframes.

Phase History	A Doppler record of a single reflective point as it passes through the SLR or SAR beam.

Pitot Tube — An open tube at the front of an aircraft used to measure the pressure of the oncoming air. This pressure information is translated via instrument or computer into airspeed. High performance aircraft have additional components at the pitot tube that measure differential pressures to provide both angle of attack and angle of yaw information.

Place Holder Orifice — See Cooling System Balancing

Platen — A flat or slightly contoured surface at the focal plane of a camera. This device holds the film in place and in the proper shape during the brief period the film is being exposed.

PMR — Pacific Missile Range.

POW — Prisoner of war.

PPS — Partial Pressure Suit. An altitude protection suit worn by aviators to compensate for extreme altitudes. The primary mechanism of this type of pressure suit is to compress the body tissues and thus create an apparent lower altitude within the body itself.

Processing Head — In this book the term refers to a compartmented, multi–bath photo processing device. Exposed film enters one end of the head and very shortly thereafter fully developed film leaves the other end of the device.

Radar Cross Section — A relative measure of how much radar energy is reflected from an object. This is based on comparison with a standard and usually expressed in square meters.

Radar Data Film — During the time frame of this book the first information from side looking radar returns (Doppler phase histories) was recorded on data film.

Radar Map Film	The final radar image of the ground or target. The real usable product of the SLR is the radar map. The map film in generated through the process of optical correlation applied to the data film. It took 10 feet of data film to create 1 foot of radar map film.
Radar Signature	Reflected characteristics uniquely identifying a particular class of target or object. Includes radar cross section, phase shift, polarization shift, and pulse–to–pulse idiosyncrasies.
RADC	Rome Air Development Center. Located at Griffiss AFB, near Rome, New York, this organization was one of the Air Force facilities involved primarily with ground based radar and other electromagnetic radiating equipment.
RB–47	Reconnaissance version of the Boeing B–47 Stratojet. The letter "R" designated these aircraft as reconnaissance versions of the original bomber configuration.
RB–57	Reconnaissance version of the Martin B–57 Canberra based on the English Electrric bomber design for Britain's Royal Air Force.
RCD	Radar Correlator Display. A device used to do in–flight processing and rear seat display of SLR data collected by the SR–71.
Reseau Dots	Very small donut shaped images exposed on TROC film at the same time the image of the ground was exposed on the film. The pattern of these dots allowed the exact shape of the negative at the time of exposure to be reconstructed.
RPM	Revolutions per minute of a shaft or engine or any rotating body.
RS	Reconnaissance/Strike. A designation applied to aircraft capable of searching out a target and attacking that same target once found. RS–70 and RS–12 are the two aircraft of that type referred to in this book.
RSO	Reconnaissance Systems Officer. The title carried by the SR–71 crewmember who rides in the rear cockpit.
RTO	Refused Takeoff. A term to describe an aborted takeoff roll once the aircraft has begun to accelerate down the runway.
SAC	Strategic Air Command

SAM   Surface–to–Air Missile. The Russian SA–2 was the SAM that brought down Francis Gary Powers' U–2 in 1960.

SAMOS   The name of an early photographic reconnaissance satellite using film. After the photo passes were completed, the film magazine was returned from orbit and snagged in midair over the Pacific.

SAR   Synthetic Aperture Radar. See SLR below for comparison of the two and definition.

SAS   Stability Augmentation System. A triply–redundant electronic system used to augment the stability of an aircraft by sensing aircraft motions and flight conditions, then if necessary, applying corrective control movements.

Schuler Period   An oscillation that appears in inertial systems. A cyclic error due to the natural laws of disturbed pendulums.

Shock Wave Angle   In supersonic flow around a moving object the angle that the shock wave makes with respect to the object's path. At Mach 1 that angle is 90 degrees and at Mach 3 the angle is roughly 60 degrees.

SK–1   Special Kerosene #1. This was the original designation of Blackbird fuel. Later the name was changed to JP–7.

SLR   Side Looking Radar. There are two main categories of this type of radar, coherent and noncoherent. Coherent SLR is called SAR for synthetic aperture radar. In both systems the antenna is mounted to look out at about 90 degrees to the flight path. The antenna is not scanned as in other radars but covers the ground due to the progress of the aircraft along the flight path.

Spatial Positioning   This term refers to the act of defining the geographic coordinates and altitude of an object in space. The answer is a precise location with respect to a common datum.

SPO   System Program Office. A term used to refer to an Air Force management office for a contracted weapon system design, development, and production program. These offices can be populated by as few as ten people or have as many as 400 assigned or attached personnel.

Spread Spectrum
A technique of spreading the information transmitted from a single device over a variety of different frequencies. A technique used in the ARC–50 Radio to provide secure conversations between aircraft and the ground or other aircraft.

Squint
A term applied to SLR when the antenna is deliberately pointed significantly ahead of the aircraft beam. A squinted SLR would let the carrying aircraft view the target before coming abreast of that target.

SR
Strategic Reconnaissance

Stagnation Temperature
The temperature at a point on a fast moving object where the air molecules hit and stop abruptly. On the SR at speed the heat created by this type of collision on some parts of the aircraft was above 800 degrees Fahrenheit.

Strut Walk
A structural dynamic of landing gear struts where they move fore and aft as the brakes are applied and released. This is a particular problem when the cyclic rate of the brake anti–skid system is set to a resonate frequency of the strut / wing structure combination.

TACAN
Usually a ground based navigational radio system which can provide aircraft with their azimuth and range from the TACAN station. In the Blackbird program the KC–135Q tankers carried an airborne version of TACAN so the approaching aircraft could find the tanker more easily.

TDI
Triple Display Indicator. An instrument present in both front and rear cockpits of the SR–71. This instrument displayed, knots equivalent airspeed (KEAS), Mach number, and altitude in the front cockpit. In the rear cockpit the TDI displayed true airspeed, Mach number, and altitude.

TEB
Tri–Ethylene Borate. A chemical compound that ignites when exposed to air. This chemical was injected into the J–58 engine on start up to ignite the fuel. SK–1/ JP–7 fuel has such low vapor pressure at normal temperatures it could not be ignited by a spark plug like most jet fuels. A shot of TEB was also used to ignite the J–58 afterburner each time it was lit on the ground or in flight.

TEOC   Technical Objective Camera. It had a 48–inch focal length lens and used nine–inch wide film. The SR carried two, one on each side of the centerline.

TEWS   Tactical Electronic Warfare System. The term used to identify the electronic warfare system as installed on the initial F–15s. A frequently used comment around the F–15 SPO was, "Every day is TEWS day."

TROC   Terrain Objective Camera. Six–inch focal length lens, nine–inch wide film. The SR carried one on the centerline.

TSPI   Time Space Position Information. Refers to the definition of an object's precise geographic location and altitude above a common reference.

Turkey Feathers   Turkey feathers were part of the ejector nozzle for the engine's jet exhaust and were free–floating panels located at the rear of the engine nacelle. ADP added little pads to the edges of the feathers to prevent them from slipping over each other and tearing themselves up. Those pads can be seen on all the airplanes today. They were free–floating afterburner nozzle panels at the rear of the engine nacelle.

TWT   Traveling Wave Tube. A type of high power amplifier used in radar and jamming systems during the time discussed in this book.

UHF   Ultra High Frequency. The standard communication radio type used in most aircraft for air–to–air and air–to–ground voice communication.

USGS   United States Geodetic Survey

V/H   The ratio of velocity over height usually expressed in milliradians per second. This value is used to derive the amount of image motion compensation (IMC) needed by an aerial camera. IMC holds the image still on the film during exposure.

VHF   Very High Frequency. Aircraft and ground communication systems operate in this frequency band. It is below the UHF band and was in common use before the latter came along. Some aircraft are still equipped with VHF radios.

View Sight An optical periscope used to view the ground and make some measurements and observations such as V/H, drift angle, and other visual information.

WADC Wright Air Development Center, at W–PAFB, later became ASD, the Aeronautical Sysems Division.

Water Separator A mechanical, sometimes cloth device, used to separate entrained moisture from cooling air generated by the environmental control system (ECS).

WCO Weapons Control Officer. A term identifying the radar observer or back seater in a two–man interceptor crew. Another term for the same man is FCO or fire control officer.

Wet Runway Tests A serious and dangerous set of tests to determine the stopping distance and controlability of an aircraft traveling along a wet runway. SR–71 aircraft 950 was destroyed during a wet runway test. She wasn't the first, and she won't be the last.

Wheel Cans Insulated cans used to enclose the SR–71 landing gear wheels once the gear was retracted into the wheel wells. These cans would insulate the tire and brake assembly from the heating associated with high Mach cruise speeds. On the down side, if the wheels were hot when retracted it also held that heat in and did not permit efficient cooling of the heated wheels, tires, and brakes as the vehicle climbed out at lower speeds and cooler ambient temperatures.

W–PAFB Wright–Patterson Air Force Base located near Dayton, Ohio.

References

The following reference materials and sources were used to verify certain dates and situations described in the text of this book.

The E.J. Baldes I Knew, The Harry Schroeder I Knew, The Development of the Partial Pressure Suit, Autobiographical book by David M. Clark, published by the David M. Clark Company in cooperation with the USAF Armstrong Laboratory, 1992

Numerous internal records and documentation provided by the David M. Clark Company

Lockheed SR–71: The Secret Missions Exposed, Paul F. Crickmore, Osprey Aerospace

SR–71 Revealed: The Inside Story, Richard Graham, Motorbooks International

Skunk Works, Ben R. Rich & Leo Janos, Little, Brown and Company

SR–71 Blackbird in Action, Lou Drendel, Squadron/Signal Publications

North American XB–70 Valkyrie, John M. Campbell with Garry R. Page, Schiffer Publishing

Congressional Record: Military Posture and Authorizing Appropriations for Aircraft, Missles, and Naval Vessels, Volume 4, Jan 30 – Feb 25, 1963

The CIA and the U–2 Program, 1954–1974, Center for the Study of Intelligence

Me and U–2: My Affair With Dragon Lady, Glenn Chapman, Spectrum Printing, Tucson, Arizona

Additional materials were provided by Freida Johnson of the Edwards AFB History Office. We are sincerely grateful for her extra effort.

SR–71 Final Report, Category II Flight Test Program, 1 July 65 – 30 June 67 Volume I

SR–71 Final Report, Category II Flight Test Program, 1 July 65 – 30 June 67 Volume II

SR–71 Category II Performance Tests, Abrams, Evanson, Lusby, and Skliar, March 1970

SR–71 Category II Stability and Control Tests, Suddereth, Allender, Evanson, Pyne, and Skliar, July 1970

The Flight Crews of the Blackbird, Buddy L. Brown. Current as of July 1993

SR–71 Milestones, author or authors unknown, no date

Internet sources and web pages were a great help to us in putting some of the individual historical elements into proper perspective. Check them out and get more Blackbird history.

David Allison, The Online Blackbird Museum, www.habu.org

John Stone, Jr. http://www.thepoint.net/~jstone/blackbird.html and www.Blackbirds.net

Troy Adams, http://www.bitcorp.net/~habubuff/sr71c/index.html

Leland Haynes, www.wvi.com/%7eleland/sr–71%7e1.html

To purchase additional copies of *Blackbird Rising: Birth of an Aviation Legend*, visit our web site, www.sagemesa.com or e–mail us directly at sagemesa@swcp.com. The fax number is 505–866–0038. You may contact the authors by e–mail at dbyrnes@swcp.com.